TOO FAST TO LIVE,
TOO YOUNG TO DIE

TOO FAST TO LIVE, TOO YOUNG TO DIE

JAMES DEAN'S FINAL HOURS

Keith Elliot Greenberg

APPLAUSE
THEATRE & CINEMA BOOKS

An Imprint of Hal Leonard Corporation

Published in 2015 by Applause Theatre & Cinema Books
An Imprint of Hal Leonard Corporation
7777 West Bluemound Road
Milwaukee, WI 53213

Trade Book Division Editorial Offices
33 Plymouth St., Montclair, NJ 07042

Printed in the United States of America

Book design by Michael Kellner

Library of Congress Cataloging-in-Publication Data is available upon request.

ISBN 978-1-4803-6030-3

www.applausebooks.com

To George Dennis Planding, 1960–2013

"It is such a mysterious place, the land of tears."

—James Dean's favorite book,
The Little Prince by Antoine de Saint-Exupéry

Contents

Acknowledgments

This book would not have come about were it not for Bernadette Malavarca, the editor at Hal Leonard Performing Arts Publishing Group who had previously worked with me when I wrote *December 8, 1980: The Day John Lennon Died*. It was Bernadette who first suggested I examine not only the tragic circumstances of James Dean's death, but also the effect it continues to have on so many people.

It was an intimidating project. Because Jimmy made only three movies, it's difficult to articulate why he still fascinates. When I discussed the challenge with my wife, Jennifer Berton Greenberg, she encouraged my instinct to find the people who love him. Once I understood them, she emphasized, I'd have my story.

Still, I was uncertain as I drove alone from Indianapolis to Fairmount. Would there really be that much of James Dean left, so many years after his death? But like the fans quoted in this book, I discovered that the answer was apparent the moment I stepped into the sunlight on East Washington Street and peeked through the glass into the Fairmount Historical Museum. Personally, I didn't believe I'd arrived home, the way Jimmy's fans do when they come to his hometown. But at least I knew how they felt.

So, as I have at the conclusion of so many other projects, I once again thank Jennifer—along with my kids, Dylan and Summer, who seem alternately amused and proud that this is the way their father has chosen to support his family.

I'm also grateful to Hal Leonard Group Publisher John Cerullo for assigning the illustrious Mike Edison to edit this book. Mike and I enjoy a shared history and have been friends since a chance meeting at Manitoba's on Avenue B in the East Village. As in the past, Mike delicately trimmed and shaped my manuscript, maintaining my voice and building the story. Given Mike's own credentials as an author, I feel like I'm getting away with something by having him as my editor.

In addition to the people quoted on these pages, I relied on the resources of the Los Angeles Public Library and, in particular, the Fairmount Public Library, which has a pretty impressive archive of material devoted to the town's favorite son. Unexpectedly, my childhood friend, Howie Pyro—best known as a founding member and bass player of the Blessed and D Generation—had an imposing collection of vintage publications featuring both authentic and fallacious tales about James Dean, along with an assortment of monster magazines, rock rags, and *Mad* rip-offs. I appreciate him making his annals available to me during my Tinseltown sojourns.

In the course of every project, I become fixated on a peripheral character in the story. When I was writing the John Lennon book, it was Rory Storm, lead singer of Ringo Starr's previous band, the Hurricanes. In this case, it was Rolf Wütherich, Dean's German-bred co-passenger. As I sifted through information about Wütherich in his native language, my friend Mara Wollong assisted me with the munificence for which she is known, translating as well as using her storytelling skills to highlight the more absorbing points of his saga.

Special thanks also goes to Dave Engleman, media relations manager for Porsche Cars N.A., copyeditor Gary Sunshine, and transcriber Justina Chong.

When I first began researching this book, I discussed the project with my friend George Planding. He became animated, describing the reasons why Dean endures as an icon and his multifaceted performance in *Giant*.

A few days later, he came to my door with a copy of Robert LaGuardia's Montgomery Clift biography, *Monty*, suggesting that I read it to create the right mindset for the James Dean book. Unfortunately, by the time I started writing, George had passed away. But I was reminded of him every time I saw the Clift biography amongst my James Dean material and am honored to dedicate this book to my generous and colorful friend.

SOMETHING THE OTHER BOYS DIDN'T HAVE

T here wasn't anything that stood out about the town, but if you grew up there, it never left you. At night, you'd smell the clover and alfalfa in your sleep and hear the sheep bleating, even if you moved to a big city and resided over a Chinese restaurant or a parking lot. Everyone from Fairmount, Indiana, felt this way, including the ones who'd gone on to live in Indianapolis or Chicago or—in one case, at least—Hollywood.

Marcus Winslow Jr., or Markie, as his friends called him, was eleven years old on Friday, September 30, 1955. On a normal day, he'd wake up in his family's fifteen-room farmhouse, then come home from school to romp around the 178-acre lot, studying the cattle, the sheep and the hogs, and the tractors going up and down the driveway. Behind the barn his grandparents built next to the house in 1904, there were the two large chicken coops. Markie liked to inspect them with fascination, even though he knew to keep a distance.

"The chickens were always Mom's," he remembers. And she didn't want her son setting them loose.

But, on this day, his mom, Ortense Winslow, and her husband, Marcus Sr., weren't around to keep an eye on Markie. For the last few weeks, they'd been in California visiting family, and Markie was staying just down Indiana 26 in the spare bedroom of the home of his older sister, Joan Peacock. It had felt like a vacation, particularly when Markie was with Joan's son, Reece. Although they were uncle and nephew, Markie and Reece were just four years apart and more like brothers. As the only boy, Markie was quick to become friends with the other males in his family. Before Reece, there was a much older cousin who'd grown up in Markie's home and took him for motorcycle rides to buy ice cream.

Sometimes, Markie would watch that cousin, Jimmy Dean, lie down on his bike, a 1947 Czech Whizzer, and fly past the corn and soybean fields, hitting speeds of fifty miles per hour. It wasn't that Jimmy was reckless. He was just adventurous.

After performing in plays at Fairmount High School, Jimmy left Indiana, determined to become a professional actor.

While Markie's parents were in Los Angeles, they'd visited Jimmy and realized that Hollywood was as much his element as Fairmount. But they already knew this—everyone did. Just a few months earlier, Markie and his family went to a special event at a movie theater in Marion, the county seat for Grant County. There, they saw James Dean up on the screen, kissing actress Julie Harris on the Ferris wheel in *East of Eden*—not as an extra or supporting actor, but a genuine movie star.

"He told my dad that when I got a little bit older, he'd like to take me to California and try to get me involved in some things," Markie says, staring out the window of the farmhouse, nearly sixty years later. "You just never know what the future could have been. You wonder what roles he would have played, what movies he would have starred in, and so forth. You can speculate all day, but that doesn't really solve anything."

The farm where Markie grew up—the place where Jimmy Dean had baled hay, shot hoops, and raced his motorcycle as a teenager—had been in the family since 1830. In fact, Joseph Winslow—the man who cleared the land of brush and trees—was Fairmount's first official settler. The actor's antecedents had first arrived in Grant County, Indiana, about fifteen years earlier from the area around Lexington, Kentucky. Over the course of the next century, the clan would marry into other pioneer families—the Woolens and Wilsons, among them—and take advantage of the region's good water and rich soil to carve out homesteads on land once populated exclusively by the Miami Indians.

When Fairmount's population hit three hundred, in the 1850s, David Stanfield, a major landowner, proposed naming the settlement Kingston. In England, the name meant "from the king's village," so Stanfield may have been attempting to convey something regal. But his son-in-law, Joseph Baldwin, lobbied for Fairmount, claiming he'd heard of Fairmount Park in Philadelphia and thought it gave the Indiana landscape a certain cosmopolitan air.

Despite the understated nature of the Hoosiers, Fairmount people viewed themselves as a little more special—and innovative—than their neighbors. Bishop Milton Wright, founder of Fairmount's first telephone company, was also the father of Orville and Wilbur Wright, who are credited with inventing the first successful airplane. In 1903, the same year as the Wright Brothers' celebrated flights in Kitty Hawk, North Carolina, Fairmount resident Cyrus Pemberton is said to have created the first ice cream cone. And, despite at least a half dozen contradictory claims, Fairmount citizens insist that Bill Dolman—who operated a lunch wagon in town from 1885 to 1907—sold the first American hamburger. Years later, when *Rebel Without a Cause* was released, Jim Davis was a ten-year-old boy growing up on a farm near Fairmount that he shared with the regular menagerie of animals, as well as twenty-five cats. The feline encounters eventually inspired his most famous creation: in 1977, the editor of the *Pendleton Times* in Madison County, Indiana—a fellow Fairmount High graduate named Jerry Brewer—took a chance and debuted Davis's comic strip, *Garfield*. A year later, it was syndicated in forty-one newspapers. In time, it would reach 263 million readers each day.

• • • •

In 1955, Fairmount's population was 2,600, mainly Quakers and Baptists. There was a railroad depot, a few factories, a volunteer fire department, and a two-block-long, brick-paved business district on Main Street.

Then, as now, most residents read the *Fairmount News*, a weekly newspaper published on Wednesdays. In 1955, its advertisers included Hasty & Son, a grain elevator firm still operating in Fairmount more than a half century later, and Everett E. Corn, an auctioneer and Realtor whose smiling countenance, below a wide-brimmed hat, appeared on the classifieds page. An Indiana & Michigan Electric Company notice described a clothes dryer as a "wife saver," while Hills Supermarkets offered fifty pounds of Wisconsin Russet potatoes for $1.89. At the Fairmount Implement Company, a local John Deere dealership, farmers could purchase Purina Pig Startena. "Purina Pig Startena is built to grow pigs fast and at low cost," the copy read. "Pigs love it, eat lots of it, and Pig Startena is loaded with 'growth boosters' pigs are known to need. That's why Pig Startena–fed pigs are such 'whoppers' at weaning." The ad featured a cartoon of a farmer in overalls shaking hands with a checkered bag of feed possessing a nose, eyes, and feet.

The newspaper covered events like a gathering of the United Society of Women at the Dean family's spiritual home, the Back Creek Friends Church, one of three Quaker sanctuaries in town. During a Thursday meeting at the parsonage, the *Fairmount News* reported, the participants "enjoyed a pot luck dinner. Mrs. Russell Gaddis had charge of the devotional period in the afternoon." Another story highlighted two local students attending the forty-eighth annual meeting of the National Future Farmers of America in Kansas City.

Although Jimmy was never part of the organization, he did join the 4H Club in high school, caring for baby chicks and cattle and tending a garden. Eventually, his Guernsey bull won the grand prize at the Grant County Fair. Yet, once the task was accomplished, he apparently grew disinterested and focused the bulk of his extracurricular time on basketball—and acting.

Jimmy's paternal grandparents, Charles and Emma Woolen Dean, lived on Washington Street in downtown Fairmount. Charles had worked as a stock buyer and car salesman, managed a livery stable, and ran horses. But he always farmed, as well.

"We're not rich, but we're not poor, either," Emma was quoted in *Photoplay* magazine. "So as long as I live, I'll always have a porch to sit on, a rocking chair to rock in, and a clock that strikes."

Charles Dean's father, Cal, was an auctioneer with a flair for the dramatic. "They're all showmen," Bing Traster, the owner of a Fairmount nursery, said of the Dean family in the 1957 documentary *The James Dean Story*. "Old Cal Dean, the great-grandfather of Jimmy, he was quite a showman himself." He also mentioned Cal Dean's cousin, a sales crier and celebrated storyteller. A few of the cousin's tales were off-color, Traster noted with a sly touch of modesty, but "they could get the crowd laughing."

Their public flamboyance, though, was tempered by the Midwestern reserve the Deans exhibited in private. Emma said that the family rarely displayed outward signs of affection, "lallygagging around, kissing and hugging each other." Yet, when someone was leaving for an extended period of time, everyone cried—so long as people outside the family were not around to observe them.

Although farming came naturally to the family, even young Markie was aware of the hardship related to the vocation. "It was tough back then," he recalls. "Farming is such an expensive operation. It costs so much money to have equipment. And to put out a crop, you're pretty much dependent on the weather to determine whether it will be a success or not. There's a lot more than most people realize."

During the period when Jimmy lived with the Winslows—after a family crisis he endured at age nine—he did his share of the chores, showing a propensity for fixing machinery and caring for livestock.

From the big, square main house, the land sloped down to a farmyard with a white barn and sheds. There was a pond in the rear pasture, where Marcus strung a series of electric lights so Jimmy and his friends could ice-skate in winter. A collection of timber was piled by the creek that ran along the property.

"It's a beautiful place," Emma said of the spread. She noted that a number of farm magazines had done cover stories on the property, while camera clubs regularly traveled to the Winslow spread for assignments. For generations, she mentioned, every Winslow had done something to enhance the farm.

Yet, as much as Dean loved the land and felt an affinity for the people in Fairmount, Marcus Sr. and Ortense knew that he wasn't going to stay. There was just too much innate talent that couldn't be contained in the rural setting. In 1957, when Marcus was asked what made Jimmy so special, he answered with a farming analogy.

"Well, I couldn't say about that. That's just like two sows, one having seven pigs, one having fifteen. Why, how does that happen?"

Ever since his toddler years, Jimmy had a keen talent for both observing the world and interpreting it for what was primarily a small but receptive audience. If his grandfather Charles crossed his legs, Jimmy imitated the gesture. If Charles then stretched his legs, Jimmy did it too. "It was more than just mocking Charlie's gestures," Emma said. "Even then, Jimmy seemed able to *be* another person."

And people wanted to watch Jimmy perform. "From the time I can remember him, he was cute, and he was always the center of attention, wherever he went," Joan Peacock told CNN.

There was also a depth that separated Jimmy from his contemporaries. "Jimmy had a little something up here that the other boys don't have," Traster said, motioning at his temple. The nursery owner remembered Jimmy as a teen, becoming sullen and taking off on his motorcycle—Traster pronounced it "motor-*sicle*"—to the family property, where he'd "medidate" in private.

By Traster's estimation, the young man "derived a certain amount of comfort" from being on the land that defined his ancestors. "He had the spirituality the average kid didn't seem to have."

In February 1955, Jimmy had returned to the farm with Dennis Stock, a photographer for *Life* magazine, working on a photo essay that would be entitled "Moody New Star." *East of Eden* was already generating excitement, and—while he wasn't yet a household name—the comparisons to Brando had begun. It was the public's opportunity to see Dean not only in the place that shaped him, but also with the people who loved him in a way that his fans never could. The depth of the relationship between Markie and the actor he considered a brother was particularly evident. In one photo, Jimmy is waiting for the school bus with his younger cousin. In another, Markie looks over Jimmy's shoulder as he reads. In a third, the two pay a solemn visit to Cal Dean's grave.

Markie never forgot any of it. "That was kind of a special visit," he says. "When Jimmy would go to town or something, he'd want to know if I wanted to go along. That's why I'm in so many of the pictures. And, of course, even when I look at those pictures now, it brings back all those memories."

Because of Dean's death on the highway, people would later focus on the picture of Dean pushing his little cousin in a miniature race car, as well as the image of the pair playing with toy racers on the floor.

Jimmy's grandfather Charles Dean also loved fast cars, purchasing his first vehicle in 1911 and disrupting the order of Fairmount by rocketing down the road at a then-blistering thirty-five miles per hour. Jimmy was a child when he began driving a tractor but quickly graduated to motorized bikes. Recounted Emma, "His motorcycles got larger and larger."

Over the years, Jimmy owned an Italian Lancia scooter, English cycle, Harley, 500cc Norton, Indian 500, and British Triumph T-110—with "Dean's Dilemma" painted on the side—in addition to a number of cars. But recently, he'd made his fastest and most expensive purchase: a Porsche 550 Spyder, a two-seat race car, possessing neither a windshield nor a roof, and capable of going as fast as 150 miles per hour. Costing in the neighborhood of $7,000, it would have been an extravagant choice, had Dean's agent not just arranged a new deal securing the actor $100,000 for every future film.

Not since the Czech Whizzer had Dean been so exhilarated over a ride. Jimmy had been driving the 550 Spyder—one of only ninety the manufacturer produced—all over Hollywood, regularly stopping at his favorite restaurant, the Villa Capri, so friends could gawk at it. It was particularly thrilling to have his relatives, Marcus Sr. and Ortense, and another aunt and uncle, Charles Nolan and Mildred Dean, in town to view this material symbol of their nephew's success. On Saturday, Jimmy was scheduled to race the Porsche about three hours north, in Salinas, and he asked his relatives to watch him from the stands. Marcus and Ortense couldn't make it; they'd been away long enough and were driving home to see Markie, Joan, and the rest of the family. Charles Nolan and his wife expressed interest in attending the race, and Jimmy had their tickets in his pocket as he made his way up the winding highway to the track. But, at the last moment, the couple decided to drive to Mexico instead.

Even so, Jimmy was overjoyed to be steering the Porsche around the curves of Route 466. Observers would later theorize that the twenty-four-year-old star was simply infatuated with the race car's power. He'd named it the "Little Bastard," a proclamation, some thought, about the way Jimmy perceived himself. But, below his snarling facade, Dean's sensitivity allowed him to appreciate the Spyder as a work of automotive brilliance, renowned for its aerodynamic design, lightweight aluminum chassis, and air-cooled engine that could expand and contract as the temperature changed.

Two years earlier—in a merger of the two worlds Jimmy adored—it had been featured in an exhibit at the Museum of Modern Art. And in 1954, Porsche officially entered the realm of American car culture, when a model appeared at the New York Auto Show. As Americans began to measure their status by the vehicles they drove, a German brand was about to become engrained into the fabric of southern California, less than ten years after the end of the war, representing not only speed, but freedom and glamour.

The excitement was heightened by the knowledge that the Porsche— along with its primary competitors, Aston Martin, Ferrari, Jaguar, and Mercedes-Benz—was a dangerous machine that could terrorize, as well as titillate. On June 11, 1955, forty-nine-year-old Frenchman Pierre Levegh was rounding Lap 35 in the 24 Heures du Le Mans—the twenty-four-hour endurance race in Le Mans, France—in his Mercedes-Benz 300 SLR, when Britain's Mike Hawthorn suddenly braked his Jaguar. The Jaguar was equipped with a new type of disc brake, and other drivers—accustomed to the slower drum brakes—did not have time to react. In the confusion that followed, Levegh—his vision obscured by a cloud of dust—slammed into another vehicle, sending the Mercedes into a somersault and igniting its magnesium body. Levegh was ejected from his car, his skull was crushed, and he died instantly.

Even worse, the fire, combined with the flying car parts, killed eighty-three and injured one hundred and twenty in the packed audience. Even today, the accident is considered the worst disaster in motor-sport history.

With this and other, less spectacular accidents in mind, some of Dean's friends worried that he lacked the experience and judgment to race the 550 Spyder, whose high pivot angles could lead to over-steering a turn and spinning out of control.

George Stevens, the director of Jimmy's most recent film, *Giant*, had been so concerned over the way that the young actor drove that Dean was prohibited from racing on his days off. But now, the movie was wrapped, and Dean could ignore the warnings of Stevens and the other squares.

• • • •

It was just before six o'clock in the evening, Pacific Standard Time, or nine o'clock in Indiana, September 30, 1955, when a Cal Poly San Luis Obispo student named Donald Gene Turnupseed attempted to make a turn at the intersection of California 41 and 466 and failed to notice that Jimmy Dean was sailing toward him in his low-slung Porsche.

It would be several hours before Dean's relatives in Fairmount heard about the tragedy. Marcus Sr. and Ortense—the couple Jimmy called "Mom" and "Pop"—were on the highway themselves, coming home from California and listening to the radio. Aside from music—Bill Haley's "Rock Around the Clock" was the biggest record that year, and Pat Boone was on the charts with his watered-down version of Fats Domino's "Ain't That a Shame" (Elvis was still a year away from his first hit)—news came on with regularity. President Dwight D. Eisenhower was recovering from a heart attack, and there was speculation that he'd step down before the end of his term, ceding the commander-in-chief role to his vice president, Richard Nixon, before the 1956 election. The United Nations was discussing the unification of North and South Korea. Argentine President Juan Peron had been deposed in a coup d'état and fled to Paraguay, leaving his underage paramour, Nélida "Nelly" Rivas, behind. And, after beginning a relationship with playwright Arthur Miller, and classes at New York's Actors Studio, Marilyn Monroe was telling interviewers that she was interested in more "literary" pursuits than her previous work.

As the Winslows' vehicle rolled through the Midwest, they heard nothing about James Dean.

It was up to Joan Peacock to tell Jimmy's grandparents, and she did it by visiting Charles and Emma Dean in person. When Markie woke up the next morning, Joan had already left, and her mother-in-law, Lucille Peacock, was waiting for him.

"I don't remember the exact words," he says. "Just that Jimmy had been in a bad accident in California. And we're over here in Indiana, of course, and didn't really know how it happened or anything." After absorbing the information, Markie thought about his parents, still on the road, and wondered if they knew. He assumed that they didn't, and dreaded reuniting with them and having to watch their faces when they learned. It had been hard to fill the space that Jimmy left when he moved out to become an actor. Now, the void was permanent.

In a few days, the first wave of James Dean fans would arrive in town to pay homage to the actor and to his family.

THE APPLE JUST OUT OF REACH

The Quaker Classics auto showroom draws its inspiration from two elements of James Dean's persona: his Quaker heritage and the classic cars associated with James Dean nostalgia. On the day I pass the building on the way to the actor's grave, the selection of cars includes a 1962 Bel Air station wagon and 1969 El Camino SS.

My companion for the day, Jack Nusan Porter, a research associate in the Russian Studies department of Harvard University, visits Fairmount at least once a year. Porter, a child of Holocaust survivors from Ukraine, is charmed by the sense of Americana he finds in the town and considers several members of the Dean family his friends. "I think everybody sees something of themselves in Dean because he was a little bit of everything," he says, as he drives me toward the cemetery. "He was a radical, but he was conservative in a way, too, rooted in this Quaker town. You can focus on the sides that you like and ignore the other parts. He really was for everyone."

Staring at the passing fields, I feel like I'm getting to know Dean the Hoosier; every fan comes away with the same feeling after a day in Fairmount. It's easy to imagine him scanning through a religious newspaper and cutting out the clipping he kept in his wallet:

The need for love and security,

The need for creative expression,
The need for recognition and self-esteem

For all the bohemian implications of Dean's artistic pursuits, he was raised to be a solid citizen of Fairmount, augmented by the honest values of the Winslow household. "Being a good actor isn't easy," he once said. "Being a man is even harder. I want to be both before I'm done."

I have an image of Dean and his uncle Marcus, seated at the kitchen table, deliberating the responsibilities of adulthood, with the dishes washed and in the drying rack, and the sun sinking behind the silo outside.

Across the road from a well-maintained trailer park, we pull into Park Cemetery. The tombstones are austere, the setting pastoral. There are no opulent monuments that stand out, so the only way to find Jimmy's grave is to look from tombstone to tombstone. That can be confusing, since so many of the monuments are labeled DEAN.

We drive for a while, cautious about inadvertently knocking over a grave. Then, we park and begin walking.

"We're close now," Jack theorizes, spotting the name Winslow. "I know he has to be buried around here somewhere."

We talk about Dean's onscreen performances, the state of agitation that made it awkward to watch him but nearly impossible to look away. "You don't really know where he's coming from, unless you know something about him," Jack opines. "He never got over the death of his mother. It traumatized him, and you see it in his acting. He has these long silences that come out of the blue. He shocks you. And it's all internalized."

Eventually, Jack and I realize that we're passing the same graves we saw earlier and get back in the car. The cemetery is larger than I realize, and as we move toward the side of the graveyard close to the Winslow family farm, I spot a sign considerately posted to guide visitors to their destination.

"James Dean," it says in script. "Second drive on right. Top of hill."

We turn onto a pathway labeled DEAN ROAD, and there it is. The simple headstone looks out over a cornfield. The beige-colored marble is polished and adorned with the basic details: JAMES B. DEAN, 1931–1955.

There are fresh flowers everywhere, and hand-written signs:

"You will forever be the perfect apple hanging from a tree branch, just out of reach."

"For my beloved Jimmy. I love you more than words can say."

Out of deference to their idol, fans also bring flowers to the neighboring headstone, a dual monument for Marcus and Ortense Winslow. The visitor learns that the couple married on June 15, 1924. Marcus passed away in 1976. Ortense lived on until 1991.

Jack and I are not alone. As we approach the memorials, a group of bikers are already there. One laughs and introduces himself to me as Beev. He tells me that his real name is Ryan, but he'd prefer not having his last name in print. His girlfriend, Heather, sits on his 2003 Harley-Davidson Sportster.

The two have driven about forty minutes from Wabash, Indiana. They're not fanatical Dean admirers but like him well enough. "I had a James Dean T-shirt when I was a kid," Beev explains, "but I didn't get into him too much."

Still, they're drawn by the sense of fraternity the Dean mystique has engendered in Fairmount. "Good people," Beev says, then motions toward the town. "And good food down the road."

Heather gets off the bike to study the grave. Watching a number of cars pull up behind us, she smiles.

"Just an experience," she says.

For fifty-five-year-old Mari van den Anker, the visit to the headstone carries far greater meaning. Once, the Dutch factory worker—he works at the Mars chocolate plant in the town of Veghel, in the Noord-Brabant region—used to journey to Fairmount with his girlfriend, Louise Angelique Donk. The pair made friends with other fans, who came to visit them in Holland. Then, on January 15, 2005, Louise was riding in a car when someone hurled a brick from an overpass onto the A4 motorway near Rijswijk. She was hit in the face and died at the hospital a short time later.

The story received coverage around the country, with Dutch citizens decrying the random act of violence. Mari was left with a sense of powerlessness, as well as happy memories of his girlfriend's admiration for the late actor.

It wasn't until he met Louise, he says, that he realized how much James Dean was embedded into the universe.

When she first mentioned the actor, early in their relationship, Mari claimed to be unaware of the screen idol. "She tells me, 'You know James Dean,'" he says. "And she goes into my closet."

He asserts that Louise found the actor's image on three separate articles of clothing. "Yeah, it was James Dean," Mari says. "But I didn't know that was him. Everybody knows his face and that is fascinating to me."

Mari has been to Fairmount a total of fifteen times. Always, he remembers his girlfriend placing flowers on Dean's grave. Today, he continues the tradition at Park Cemetery. "When I put the flowers there, I do it for two people. I feel my girlfriend very close. It helps me. I'm calm. And then, the feeling comes. Because she loved James Dean so much, she's there. I feel it."

Almost every week, Markie dispatches someone to the cemetery to clean the area and wipe down the tombstone. "I certainly don't encourage people to put their lipstick on the headstone," he told the *Chronicle-Tribune* of Marion, Indiana, in 2005. "But, on the other hand, it could be so much worse."

He knows this because, over the years, fans have attempted to walk away with graveyard souvenirs. In 1956, a bronze bust of Dean was installed on a brick pillar at the entrance of the cemetery. It disappeared a short time later.

In April 1983, the four-hundred-pound tombstone vanished. It was found in May—high up in the branches of a tree in another part of the county. It was reinstalled but stolen a second time in August.

Four years later, a stranger dropped it off on the Winslow farm.

Since then, the tombstone has been bolted into the ground. But in

1998, the grave was pilfered again. Days later, a deputy sheriff in Tippeca-noe County destroyed his transmission by running over the monument.

Interestingly, the tombstone had only sustained a scratch. It was brought back to the graveyard, buffed, and secured with longer, more robust metal rods.

"It'd about take a wrecker to get it off there now," Markie told the newspaper.

THE LIFE YOU SAVE

A pproximately two weeks before his fatal accident, on September 17, 1955, Dean was called back to the Warner Brothers lot to reshoot some scenes for the movie *Giant*. While he was there, he agreed to leave the set and film a public service commercial for the National Safety Council with actor Gig Young.

Young, the host of the *Warner Brothers Presents* television series on ABC, greeted Dean in a dark suit. Jimmy was dressed as his Jett Rink character in *Giant,* in a Stetson, jeans, a denim shirt, and boots. A cigarette dangled from his lips, while he twirled a lasso.

"We asked Jimmy over today because he's a racing man himself," Young addressed the camera, as the two sat across from each other in office chairs, "a real one, not a crazy one. Incidentally, I think I should explain that Jimmy just stepped over from the set of *Giant*. Need I add, he plays a Texan."

Dean smirked and took a drag on his cigarette.

"Speaking of racing," Young continued, "have you ever been in a drag race?"

Dean exhaled and leaned back on his seat. "What are you—kidding me?"

"I just thought I'd ask." Young looked at the camera and spoke to the audience. "No, Jim races in the tradition, you might say. Real racing cars, real tracks." He turned back to Dean. "How fast will your car go?"

Jimmy slouched and seemed to digest the words. A mouthful of smoke exited his lips. "Oh, in honest miles an hour, clocked one-oh-six-seven."

"You've won a few races, haven't you?"

"Oh, one or two." Dean looked down, seemingly embarrassed about listing his accomplishments.

"Where?"

Dean rubbed his eyes. "I showed pretty good at Palm Springs. I ran at Bakersfield."

"Jimmy?" Young began with an air of sincerity. He hesitated. "We probably have a great many young people watching our show tonight. And, for their benefit, I'd like your opinion about fast driving on the highway. Do you think it's a good idea?"

"Good point," Dean answered, raising a finger. "I used to fly around quite a bit. I took a lot of unnecessary chances on the highways. And I started racing and now"—he grinned and looked at Young—"I drive on the highways and I'm, uh, extra cautious. 'Cause no one knows what they're doing half the time. You don't know what this guy's going to do or that one. On the track, there are a lot of men who spend a lot of time in developing rules." He shrugged slightly. "Ways of safety. And, uh"— he stared down at the cigarette in his hand—"I find myself being very cautious on the highway. I don't have the urge to speed on the highway."

There was a cutaway of Young listening.

"People say racing is dangerous," Dean emphasized, tinkering with the knots of his rope. "But I'll take my chances on the track any day than on the highway."

He rose, swinging a section of rope back and forth on his lap. "Okay, Gig. I better take off."

No one is sure if the section was scripted. Either way, Dean, the method actor, appeared legitimately ready to leave. Young followed Jimmy, as the younger man began moving toward the office door.

"One more question. Do you have any special advice for the young people who drive?"

Dean paused in the doorway and turned back to Young. Then, he gazed into the camera and waved his hands from side to side. "Take it easy driving." He motioned at himself with his thumb and smiled. "The life you save might be mine."

THAT MOMENT OF YOUTH

In March 2014, with his singing career on the verge of becoming a footnote to his bad choices—following arrests for drunken driving and drag racing—Justin Bieber attempted to remind the public that he was some sort of icon.

He did this by posing for a black-and-white photo, dressed as James Dean.

With his hair swept back, twenty-year-old Bieber sported a white T-shirt and looked dreamily off-camera, a cigarette protruding from his upper lip.

"This is James Dean inspired," he wrote on Instagram. "Don't ask me if I smoke ciggys cuz I don't."

For the short-term, the Dean impersonation garnered J-Beebs the profuse attention he apparently coveted. Referring to Bieber's on-again-off-again romance with Selena Gomez, *US Weekly* asked its readers, "Will Justin be Selena's James Dean? Tell us your thoughts!"

The online responses were less than approving:

"LMAO! Bieber is a rebel without a CLUE. Please go away."

"He's more of a Jimmy Dean sausage. Total Weenie."

Other replies compared Bieber's alleged street racing to the circumstances of Dean's death, confusing the racing scene in *Rebel Without a Cause* with the real-life traffic accident that ended the actor's life.

But, on the issue of character, the readers were resolute in their belief that the "Baby" singer and movie legend were in separate leagues.

"What an absolute INSULT to James Dean who was one of a kind . . . and hardly a douche bag."

"James Dean is rolling in his grave as we speak."

"Exactly! Punk Bieber wishes he could be that cool."

Lost in the dialogue were questions about Dean's continuing appeal. Why was it that, fifty-nine years after his death, a onetime teen heartthrob needed to channel James Dean to ingratiate himself to the public? And why did the mere mention of the film star's name still induce this type of emotion?

Joel Dinerstein, co-curator at the 2014 "American Cool" exhibit at the National Portrait Gallery in Washington, DC—a collection that included Dean, along with Jimi Hendrix, Billie Holiday, and Frank Sinatra—saw a timelessness in the black-and-white photos of the handsome actor. "'What is cool' is synonymous with what's fashionable in the moment," he explained to the *New York Post*. "But when you talk about 'who is cool,' then you're talking about impact."

The moment one met Dean, colleagues remembered, that ability to make an impact was instantly recognizable. "He was not just a normal person," Mark Rydell, a director and producer who befriended Dean when they were both starting out as television actors, told CNN in 2004. "This kid was special. You knew it the minute you set eyes on him. . . . You knew you were in the presence of something very unusual. . . . His acting was impeccable. His sensitivity was overwhelming. Those guys come along once every ten, fifteen years."

Dean's father, Winton, who sent Jimmy to live with the Winslows after the death of his mother, never seemed to comprehend his son's magnetism—or his ambitions. In an interview with *Modern Screen* magazine in 1955, Winton conceded that he viewed his only child as a paradox: "My Jim is a tough boy to understand. At least, he is for me. But maybe that's because I don't understand actors, and he's always wanted to become one. Another reason is that we were separated for a long period of time, from when he was nine until he was eighteen. Those are important, formative years when a boy and his father usually become close friends. Jim and I—well, we've never had that closeness. It's nobody's fault, really. Just circumstances."

Although Jim and his dad resided in the same city, Winton conceded that they might as well have been on separate continents. "The actor's world," Winton said, was a culture he'd never grasp, and, as a result, the two rarely saw each other. Nonetheless, he described his only child as "a good boy" and expressed pride in his achievements. "Not easy to understand, no sir. . . . But he's all man, and he'll make his mark. Mind you, my boy will make his mark."

To this day, the interview—the only known time Winton Dean made himself available to the print media—is examined by Dean devotees hoping to gain insight into their hero's motivations. It is safe to assume that Winton's disapproval of acting as a viable profession fueled the alienation Jimmy projected onscreen. And those long silences don't seem unusual when you consider the fact that Dean not only lost his beloved mother, but also mourned the separation—both physical and emotional—from his father. Then, there was the line about Jimmy being "all man," which sounds a lot like an intractable father reassuring himself that his suspicions about his son's sexuality are probably unfounded.

Nonetheless, Winton's overall confusion about Dean is understandable, since, even in Hollywood, the actor stood out as an oddity. LA might have been a city of eccentrics, but they often fit into neat categories. Because Jimmy was adverse to labels, it was difficult to make sense of his quirks.

And those quirks were plentiful—even if he was the only one in on the joke. Once, Jimmy turned up for a party dressed as his bad-boy peer Marlon Brando. When Brando arrived in a suit and tie, he was bewildered by the young Indiana transplant, then relatively unknown, adorned in leather, mixing fine wine with 7 Up.

In many ways, the actor was the embodiment of the slogans woven throughout his favorite book, *The Little Prince* by Antoine de Saint-Exupéry—a French aristocrat whose disappearance over the Mediterranean while on a mission for the Free French Air Force in 1944 inspired almost as much intrigue as Jimmy's tragic end would eleven years later:

"I am who I am and I have the need to be."

Those who were allowed to get close to Dean believe that there was nothing deliberate about his idiosyncrasies. Rather, he was preoccupied with the need to expand himself as an artist, while questioning the conformity of the 1950s.

"When it came to his craft, there was no ceiling," recalls close friend Lew Bracker. "He just thought he could continue to improve and learn, and he would take any class that he thought might help him in that direction."

While in New York, he took dance lessons with Eartha Kitt, the cabaret star, actress, and social activist—she was later involved with an inner-city youth group called Rebels with a Cause—whom Orson Welles called the "most exciting woman in the world." Kitt—who spent the end of her life advocating for LGBT causes, and once insulted Lady Bird Johnson at a White House luncheon by accusing the government of sending "the best of this country off to be shot and maimed" in Vietnam—regarded Dean as a kindred soul. "Jamie and I were like brother and sister," she said. "He told me in fact he thought of me as a sister. Our relationship was strictly platonic and spiritual."

Certainly, Dean had his swagger. But it was balanced by his attitude that "only the gentle are ever really strong."

"Jimmy Dean contributed a lot in the twenty-four short years he lived," the *Fairmount News* editorialized days after his death.

A great many people who didn't understand him called Jimmy eccentric. Perhaps he was. But then again, when a person becomes so wrapped up in something, he forgets everything else but that one thing.

When he lets off steam, it is apt to be outside the regular bounds of activity, according to the measure of society.

His homefolks understood him, though.

And they'll miss him.

Interestingly, the fascination with Dean seems disproportionate to his body of work; David Bowie, Joan Jett, Madonna, the Goo Goo Dolls, John Cougar Mellencamp, Lou Reed, Kid Rock, Nickelback, Morrissey, Jay Z, and Lady Gaga are among the entertainers who have referenced James Dean in their songs. In David Essex's hypnotic "Rock On," the English singer-songwriter climaxes with a recitation of the actor's name:

Jimmy Dean
Jimmy Dean
Rock on
Rock on

Yet, Dean's entire film career spanned two years, during which he starred in three motion pictures: *East of Eden*, *Rebel Without a Cause*, and *Giant*. But the movies, along with Dean's performances, remain timeless.

"He lived with such burning intensity that, in retrospect, it almost seems that he knew he wouldn't be with us long," noted *Giant* producer Henry Ginsberg less than a year after the actor's death. "His work was truly remarkable."

Dennis Hopper appeared in both *Rebel* and *Giant* and attributed the legacy of Dean to his ingenuity on set. "I've never seen an actor as dedicated, with the extreme concentration and exceptional imagination, as James Dean. He could take the written imaginary circumstance and make it his own by improvising . . . giggling while being searched in the police station because it tickled, standing up in a drunken daze, making the sound of sirens with his arms outstretched . . . things that were not written on the page, things that were invented by the actor."

Sal Mineo, who appeared in the same two Dean films as Hopper, described Jimmy as "the first rebel. He really was the first young guy who played a young guy in a film who rebelled against the establishment and gave the teenager an identity."

But Natalie Wood, the female lead in *Rebel*, found the insurgent characterization of Jimmy simplistic. "Really, he was not a rebel," she said in the 1974 ABC special *James Dean Remembered*. "He was really saying, 'Listen to me. Hear me. Love me.' . . . He was trying to get the connection."

Even so, Dean spoke to a generation that might have felt overlooked by previous leading men. Said Hopper, "He seemed to capture that moment of youth, that moment when we're all desperately seeking to find ourselves."

Lois Smith, Jimmy's costar in *East of Eden*, was one year older than the actor and empathized with the struggles he attempted to express onscreen. To her, Dean was "suspicious, filled with need, filled with longing. With tenderness, as well. And an insufficient hopefulness. A reluctance to pass through those gates on the brink of adulthood."

To be certain, Dean was a young man who wanted to live, not flame out in a car wreck on a sleepy highway surrounded by grain and hay fields. Still, one night, he suggested that he was nervous about aging, asking Martin Landau—a friend from his New York theater days—about "what happens to actors when they become old boys, as opposed to men."

What Dean never anticipated was that he'd serve as a role model to every young actor who exuded a certain type of angst—from Mickey Rourke to Johnny Depp to Colin Farrell. At some stage of their respective careers, each would be labeled "the next James Dean."

It's a goal to which thousands, if not millions, of thespians continue to aspire.

Nicolas Cage claimed that he first felt motivated to act while watching the scene in *East of Eden* in which Dean's onscreen father, Raymond Massey, rejects his son's birthday gift. "His father says it's not good enough, and he (Dean) has this breakdown," Cage told *MTV.com*. "That was so painful to watch, and it was so real to me that I knew that acting was what I wanted to do. It affected me more than any song or painting or TV show."

Al Pacino was a teenager in the Bronx—nicknamed The Actor by the kids in his neighborhood—when he noticed other young men acquiring red jackets like the one Dean wore in *Rebel Without a Cause*. But as much as Jimmy encouraged Pacino's wayward impulses, the older generation could sense that, at his core, Dean was the kid who loved and honored his aunt and uncle.

"It was kind of a phenomenon when you think about it," Pacino said. "And I remember at that time my mother loved him. He reached every-body."

In Liverpool, England, Stewart Sutcliffe, John Lennon's close friend and, at one time, the fifth member of the Beatles, patterned his style after Dean—while Lennon fed off the signals he received from his confidant.

"Stewart died young before we made the big time," Lennon reflected. "But I suppose you could say that without James Dean, the Beatles would have never existed."

"It's pretty amazing," says Markie Winslow. "If people like John Lennon were influenced that much, it makes you think about the influence he had on everybody."

When actor Martin Sheen was in acting school, his fellow students adhered to a slogan: "If Marlon Brando changed the way people acted, James Dean changed the way people lived."

Said Sheen, "He was simply a genius."

While many fans confuse James Dean the human being with the tor-mented characters he played, a more precise perception of the actor might come from a clay sculpture he left behind. Dean titled the small, faceless work "Self."

In some ways, the nondescript molding symbolizes the way fans proj-ect their own feelings onto the actor, convinced that a young man they know from a T-shirt or a poster represents them—and every generation since the auto accident that claimed his life.

5

"I LOVE HIS LIFE"

On the night before his accident, Jimmy appeared at his friend Jeanette Mills's home and dropped off his Siamese cat, a gift from Elizabeth Taylor. Despite his rising position in Hollywood, Dean was sentimental enough about his family in Indiana that he named the feline Marcus. He left Jeanette a note that included complicated feeding instructions and the name of a veterinarian.

Later, fans would fixate on this incident and wonder if Jimmy was giving away his possessions. He wasn't. The same night, he attended a party in Malibu and appeared to have a great deal of living left inside of him. Dean simply knew that he'd be away for a few days, racing in Salinas, and wanted to ensure that his pet was in capable hands. Nonetheless, adherents of the cult of James Dean's death cling to any suggestion that he had a premonition of his early demise.

One of their favorite quotes was delivered to interviewer Jack Shafer on a New York radio station. Dean acknowledged the basic truth that, in the scheme of the universe, human life was short. As a result, he stated, he tried to appreciate his interactions on earth:

"I think I'm like the Aztecs in that sense, too. With their sense of doom, they tried to get the most out of life while life was good. And I go along with them on that philosophy. I don't mean that 'eat, drink, and be merry for tomorrow we die' idea, but something a lot deeper and more valuable.

I want to live as intensely as I can. Be as useful and helpful to others as possible, for one thing. But I want to live for myself, as well. I want to feel things and experiences down to their roots."

He articulated those feelings more succinctly in another quote popular with present-day fans: "Dream as if you'll live forever. Live as if you'll die today."

. . . .

When I meet Kevin Juliat in Fairmount, he shows me his DREAM AS IF YOU'LL LIVE FOREVER tattoo. Although Kevin lives in Paris, he wanted the slogan to be etched onto his wrist in English and inked before he turned twenty-four, Dean's age at the time of his death.

"It is very different here than in France," he says. "In France, when a famous person dies, the fans go to the cemetery. That's all. Here, we can see James Dean's jacket"—that and other items are in a museum devoted to the star—"see his house, see his cousin, Marcus Winslow, still living there. It's very emotional to walk on the streets and think seventy years ago, he was here, too."

He's particularly impressed by the way the town welcomes Dean fans, and the fact that the largely agricultural setting resembles the Fairmount where Dean grew up: "It's very special to know James Dean and understand his life."

To arrive in Fairmount, Kevin flew from Paris to Charlotte, then transferred to a flight to Indianapolis, fifty or so miles away. It was a journey he'd been planning for years, since discovering Dean at age fifteen while watching a televised version of *Rebel Without a Cause*, dubbed into French. "He was a teenager in the movie. I was a teenager. So—I don't know—I recognized myself in him. And just after that, I read a book, a biography, about James Dean. I love his life. And after, I buy another book and another book, and I see all three movies. And I love them. So I searched the Internet for information about James Dean, and, then, I wanted to see Fairmount.

"For me, he was just a cool boy born in a little town."

Yet, Kevin also sees something very French in James Dean: "If he didn't die, I know he'd come to Paris. He loved art. He loved to read. I want to think James Dean is like a Parisian. His thinking was like someone who is French—that art is a religion."

But to fans making the pilgrimage to Fairmount, the religion is centered around Dean himself. Even to the more pious members of the Fairmount community, the actor's name is uttered with as much, if not more, reverence, as that of George Fox, the seventeenth-century visionary whose declarations about trembling at the word of the Lord aroused observers to coin the term *Quaker*. From a painting on the town's water tower, the movie star, in his red *Rebel* jacket and pompadour, looks down at James Dean Boulevard, the road leading to the elementary school.

Somewhere, I hear Johnny Cash's version of "One Piece at a Time" blaring over a set of speakers. It was recorded in 1976, but the tale it tells—about a Kentuckian who leaves home in 1949 to work at the General Motors plant in Detroit, then defies the corporation by stealing spare parts and building a Cadillac—and country tone fit into the Dean dogma.

Over the years, the Fairmount Historical Museum has turned into a cathedral to James Dean. The building was constructed in 1888, and the institution it houses acknowledges the early settlers, along with natives like *Garfield* cartoonist Jim Davis and CBS television news correspondent Phil Jones. However, it takes work to find any artifact that isn't tied directly to Fairmount's most visible commodity.

Fans can view the knives used in the famous duel at LA's Griffith Observatory in *Rebel Without a Cause*—after Jimmy's death, Warner Brothers had the movie's name and the year it was filmed painted on the handles and presented to Winton Dean—the sink from Dean's New York apartment, his monogrammed shaving kit, a book on Mexican Revolutionary general Pancho Villa, gold pocket watch, motorcycle jacket—replete with Triumph pins—and the Triumph motorcycle itself.

In a separate case, the Ceska Zbrojovka—Czech Whizzer purchased

by Uncle Marcus in 1947 for Jimmy's sixteenth birthday—rests, alongside a photo of the young man riding the motorbike through downtown
Fairmount.

Cases are devoted to specific periods in the actor's life. In one, there's
the pair of chaps he wore while filming *Giant* in Marfa, Texas, along with
his cowboy hat and the rope he twirled during his public address announcement cautioning young people to drive carefully. There are also
samples of items he wore when he wasn't in front of the camera: a set of
oil derrick cufflinks he purchased in Texas, a white pullover—with red
stripes covering the upper chest area—he'd put on while going over his
lines on the Warner Brothers lot, a big cowboy belt with his name en-
graved in the buckle. The accessory is positioned alongside a Marlin .22
rifle used to shoot jackrabbits in the scrublands near Marfa.

On a crowded Friday afternoon, a visitor from New England contem-
plates a locket containing two photos of Dean's onetime girlfriend, Pier
Angeli. According to numerous accounts, Jimmy was in love with the actress and grieved over their breakup—and subsequent marriage to singer
Vic Damone. When the guest questions whether the actor was gay, an
elderly man cuts him off.

"That's bull."

A section includes the personal effects of Dean's friend and sometime
mentor, the Rev. James DeWeerd, whose worldly tastes intrigued the
budding thespian. Although Dean was a Quaker, the Wesleyan Methodist minister took great interest in the teen, cultivating a relationship that
would be considered less than appropriate today. There is the silver cup
from which Dean drank soda pop during their nights together in the cler-
ic's home, as well as a sculpture of a matador and bull; DeWeerd is said to
have introduced the teen to the allure of the sport. A painting Jimmy did
of a bullfight is also in the museum.

During his last visit home, in February 1955, Dean purchased his aunt
and uncle a telephone stand. It can now be found in the museum, close to
a rocking chair that had been in the Winslow family since the 1880s. Even

more interesting is a small reel-to-reel tape recorder Jimmy snuck onto the Winslow home during his final trip.

Sitting at the dining room table, the actor secretly recorded his grandparents and other family members. "Grandpa Dean told Jimmy about the Dean family history," says the explanation posted alongside the object, "and spoke about Jimmy's great-grandfather, Cal Dean, and how excited they were that Jimmy's character in *East of Eden* was also named Cal. Jimmy wanted to know if there were other actors and artists in his family, and where his acting talent originated."

Newspaper headlines begin in Jimmy's youth. A 1949 *Fairmount News* banner screams "FHS Students Win State Meets" above the subhead "James Dean First Place Winner in Dramatic Speaking." Below is a photo of Dean looking not like a movie star, but a shy Midwestern high school boy in a tie and jacket, stunned by the camera flash, his ears jutting from nearly combed hair.

Photos span the course of Jimmy's life: early childhood; a high school trip to Washington, DC; graduation. On a poster of his high school basketball team, a caption reads, "James Dean, brilliant senior guard, was one of the main cogs in the Quaker lineup this season." On the set of *Giant*, a bespectacled Dean smokes and grimaces for the camera, his look resembling that of FDR with a cigarette holder in his mouth.

Eventually, visitors are led to a photo of Dean's body being loaded into an ambulance at the intersection of California 41 and 466. The snapshot has been reproduced often and generally induces the same general comment from the public:

"What a waste. He was so young and talented."

6

LITTLE BASTARD

James Dean had a lot of plans.

"If I live to be a hundred," he said, "there will be time to do everything I want."

There was the house he wanted to buy, a two-story stucco structure with a red tile roof, beamed, vaulted ceiling, and pegged wood floors. It was situated in the Hollywood Hills, just below Mulholland Drive. Before smog shrouded the view, the large windows looked over west Los Angeles, all the way to the ocean. Jimmy envisioned hanging speakers from the rafters for parties. The price was $50,000, but Jimmy knew he'd be able to afford it, as soon as his new contract was signed, after the Salinas race.

In the immediate future, there were two television shows scheduled, including a version of the play *The Corn Is Green*. Jimmy was to portray an illiterate Welsh miner whose well-bred British teacher—Bette Davis had starred in the cinematic version in 1945—takes him on as her personal project, as opposition to her quest to persuade him to receive a university education.

In *The Battler*, an Ernest Hemingway adaptation, Dean was supposed to play a man thrown off a train only to encounter a depressed former boxing champion living in the woods. In addition, he'd already done wardrobe fittings for the movie *Somebody Up There Likes Me,* about a real-life pugilist, ex-middleweight titlist Rocky Graziano. He also hoped to act in *Hamlet*, as well as a screen version of *The Little Prince*.

He'd purchased his Porsche 550 Spyder after blowing the engine in his previous race car, a Porsche 356 Super Speedster, while competing on the track in Santa Monica. Jimmy knew that he stood out among the drivers and wanted his car to project an image consistent with his public persona. So he hired George Barris, the self-professed King of Kustomizers, to paint the number 130 on the front, back, and sides of the vehicle—he actually wanted the number thirteen, to flout his disregard for superstition, but both the California Sports Club and the Sports Car Club of America refused to allow this—along with the slogan "Little Bastard." As sleek and stylish as the racer looked, it was far from Barris's finest achievement. A decade later, he'd design the Batmobile.

The upcoming race in Salinas, Dean predicted, would silence the cynics dubious of an actor dabbling in the dangerous sport. Even if he didn't come in first, he intended to make an impressive showing, and the contest would prove that Jimmy deserved to command a machine as lustrous and rare as the 550.

He'd spent the past several days visualizing the race and the reception he'd receive afterward. According to his friend Lew Bracker, the actor hadn't been so happy since his mother was alive.

The log cabin–style abode where Dean was living—off Ventura Boulevard, at 14611 Sutton Street in the San Fernando Valley town of Sherman Oaks—no longer exists. After burning down, the house was replaced, rebuilt in a modern, Tuscan style in a neighborhood of comfortable brick dwellings behind fences and shrubbery, minutes from Ultrazone Laser Tag, Black Dog Yoga, and the modeling studios of Porn Valley. In 1955, Jimmy paid $250 per month, plus utilities. What he liked most about the place was its landlord, Nicco Romanos, the Greek-born maître d' at the actor's favorite restaurant, the Villa Capri.

To a degree, Nicco reminded the actor of the friendly neighbors he'd known in Indiana. It was particularly reassuring to know that Nicco and his wife lived in a larger house on the same lot.

Given his life circumstances—despite his instinct to deny it, he was becoming a celebrity, and it was often easier to blend with industry people than civilians—the Villa Capri, located on McCadden Street, near Highland Avenue and Hollywood Boulevard, offered Jimmy the right mix of glamour and authenticity. He knew the staff on a personal level and enjoyed them as individuals. Generally, Jimmy entered the restaurant from the parking lot, through the kitchen, picking food from the antipasto bin and joking with Carmine the chef. He was particularly fond of a developmentally disabled busboy named Eddie, who circulated the eatery, telling loud stories and laughing at his own witticisms. Eddie didn't care if a patron was an electrician, police officer, or movie star. If he felt compelled to tell a story, he'd come over to the table. Owner Patsy D'Amore—who counted Frank Sinatra and Dean Martin among his friends—only wanted a clientele that appreciated his loveable employee.

Besides restaurant work, Nicco was a movie double who had a unique side job, working on Groucho Marx's quiz show, *You Bet Your Life*. When a contestant mentioned the "magic word" of the night, a paper duck fell from the ceiling, dangling a cash bonus. Nicco would make duck sounds for the audience then joke with both the guest and the host.

The Villa Capri was a constant for Jimmy on a circuit that included Musso & Frank, Don the Beachcomber, and the Brown Derby. Although Dean was partial to the jazz clubs around Hollywood and Sunset Boulevards, the Hollywood elite—long-established stars like Clark Gable and Lana Turner—could regularly be sighted in Scandia, the Marquis, Cock 'n Bull, and similar restaurants, along with such nightclubs as Ciro's, Mocambo, and Trocadero.

Although Jimmy regularly stopped in Schwab's drug store at 8024 Hollywood Boulevard, for ice cream and snacks—the joke was that the working actors went to Schwab's, while the aspiring ones hung out at Googie's coffee shop in West Hollywood—he loved the original Hamburger Hamlet, located on the border of Beverly Hills, where he could eat cheesecake and sit with Lew Bracker on the terrace, making observations about the cars and people on Sunset Boulevard.

Like Nicco, Lew was comfortable around show business people—some were in his own family—but he wasn't one of them. He lived at home and, during the day, went to an office and sold insurance. Although he was impressed by certain aspects of the movie industry, he was never starstruck. In fact, even without Jimmy, he'd been in social situations with actors and actresses. Yet, he was a regular guy—years later, he'd visit Fairmount and become friends with several of Jimmy's high school classmates—and Dean enjoyed having his companionship, as they drove from place to place.

"Hamburger Hamlet and the Villa Capri were his basic haunts," Lew recalls. "We could go to those places late at night and know that no one was going to bother him. Not yet. He was *going* to be bothered. He just hadn't achieved that level of fame yet. But it was coming."

Still, Bracker describes the Hollywood of that era as a community that hadn't fully lost its innocence. "My parents' front door was never locked, and we weren't the only house like that. We weren't guarding anything. When I was in high school, and even junior high school, we could hitchhike all over LA without a care. We'd even get picked up by women— young mothers and whatnot, who looked after us. You could also get on the trolley for five cents and go all the way to Long Beach.

"The Long Beach Pike was still a big deal, with carnival rides and booze and all that stuff. When Jimmy wasn't working, we'd go swimming, then hop into one of our Porsches in our bathing suits, shoot down to the hot dog shop, and bring the food back up to the house. There was a small-town feeling to the city that I know Jimmy liked a lot."

From the street, Jimmy's home resembled a chalet, with a sliding glass door leading inside. In addition to a basement den, there was also an enclosed front yard that Dean showed off to friends like Elizabeth Taylor and Natalie Wood. There was no bedroom inside the residence, just a second-story alcove. Yet, Jimmy liked what the Romanos provided: mounted horns, a white bearskin rug, seven-foot stone fireplace, bronze sculpture of a shrieking eagle, and wheel lamp suspended from the beams. Nicco's gun collection contributed to the eccentric flavor. When Jimmy was alone,

he played his music loudly, exhibiting a preference for Hungarian composer and pianist Béla Bartók. Sometimes he played the bongos—for crowds
at parties and for himself, alone in bed. "When I can't sleep at night," he
said, "I like to get up and beat the skins. It drives away the blues."

Once in a while, Nicco stopped by to clean the apartment and make
coffee. On the morning of September thirtieth, the maître d' put a pot
on the stove and called Jimmy down from the alcove. Groggily, the actor
raised his head from the pillow and said he'd be right down. Instead of
using the ladder leading up to the bedroom space, he swung a leg over the
wooden balcony railing, and, despite the height, jumped to the ground.

Nicco handed him a cup of coffee. Jimmy appeared grateful but too
tired to even thank his landlord. Instead, Dean—clad only in pajama
bottoms—sat down, infused himself with caffeine, then shot Nicco the
crooked smile audiences would ponder for decades. Nicco speculated
over the thoughts swirling in the actor's head, deliberating about where
his character ended and the real Jimmy Dean began.

Banging on the bongos, Jimmy chatted briefly with Nicco and lit his
first Chesterfield of the day. He inhaled, set the cigarette on the table, and
hit the bongos another time.

Once Nicco left, Dean pulled on a white T-shirt and a pair of faded
jeans. Looking around the apartment, he found a windbreaker and a pair
of sunglasses. Then, grabbing his overnight bag, he stepped outside and
saw his 550 Spyder sitting on a trailer connected by a ball hitch to his
other recent purchase, a Ford station wagon.

He'd gained a feel for the Spyder the evening before, when he and a
friend, stunt driver Bill Hickman, drove it up the coast highway toward
Santa Barbara. When a fog rolled in, they decided to turn around and play
it safe. But Jimmy felt that he still needed to break in the car and hoped to
do so on the long ride to Salinas.

It was Bracker who'd first informed Dean about the availability of the
Spyder at Competition Motors, a North Hollywood dealership for sports
car enthusiasts who enjoyed testing their purchases along the scenic

turns of Mulholland Drive. During a meal at the Villa Capri, Dean had be-seeched his buddy to join his small entourage at the race. Had it been an-other weekend, Lew would have agreed. But on Saturday night, the USC Trojans were opening the football season against the Texas Longhorns at the LA Coliseum. "I thought it was going to be a great game," Bracker says, "and that's where I was going."

Jimmy drove over to Competition Motors, where Rolf Wütherich, the twenty-eight-year-old German-born Porsche mechanic who planned to accompany the actor to Salinas, was waiting to work on the engine. Because of his accent, Rolf could be difficult to understand, but he and Dean were able to communicate in the universal language of motor sports. Despite being officially known as a 550, Wütherich would refer to the motor as a 547—or a Fuhrmann engine—with its dual overhead camshafts, driven by bevel gears, for each of the two cylinder banks. To Dean, Rolf was as much of an artist as anyone the actor had met on a soundstage. When Jimmy pondered the mechanic's handiwork in the garage, he loved everything he saw.

Eventually, the pair were joined by Hickman and Jimmy's other travel-ing companion, photographer Sanford Roth, who'd been trailing the star for weeks on assignment for *Collier's*, a weekly magazine known for its cartoons, fiction, and investigative journalism. Roth—who, with his wife, Beulah, regularly invited Jimmy over to their home, photographing him as he played with their pet cat—was planning to attend the race, then ride with Dean to San Francisco and take more pictures there.

Dean's visits with his father were irregular. But with his uncle, Charles Nolan Dean, in town, Jimmy was in the mood to display the race car to his family. At around ten o'clock in the morning, Winton Dean and his brother also turned up at the garage.

Jimmy looked at Wütherich and grinned. Rolf put the hood down.

"How'd you like to take a ride?" Dean asked his relatives.

Charles motioned at Jimmy's father. "Take Winton."

Winton shook his head from side to side, keeping up his reserve.

"What about you?" Jimmy was staring at his uncle with the same look he charmed audiences with from the big screen.

"Well, I . . ."

Jimmy continued to smile. Charles looked over at Winton, then at the car.

"Go ahead," Winton said.

The actor's gaze remained fixed. Even Wütherich, who was generally all business in the garage, appeared amused by the uncle's mixture of curiosity and apprehension.

Charles shrugged. "Okay."

Jimmy was elated. With Winton awkwardly standing near the mechanic, Dean helped Charles wedge himself into the passenger seat, then ran around to the driver's side, turned the ignition, and circled the block a few times before inviting his father and uncle to join him for an early lunch. The three headed over to the Los Angeles Farmers Market, where he led Winton and Charles to Patsy's Pizza. The actor was clearly showing off. Patsy's was owned by Villa Capri owner Patsy D'Amore—who graced the pizzeria with photos of celebrity friends like Frank Sinatra and Dean Martin—and Jimmy knew that his family would be treated regally there.

Jimmy took it for granted that he couldn't get Winton to come up to Salinas for the race. But when Dean invited his uncle, Charles Nolan promised to consider the offer. Feeling animated, as well as anxious about starting the long ride north toward the racetrack, Jimmy drove his relatives back to Competition Motors.

Outside the building, Dean asked Roth to take a souvenir photo of the race preparation. He and Wütherich posed in the Spyder, with the actor playfully hoisting up the mechanic's arm in victory.

Everything was feeling so good that Dean made another attempt to convince his buddy Bracker to come to Salinas.

Lew had been at lunch and was just getting back to his desk at the insurance office when the phone rang. Jimmy's voice on the other end sounded nothing like the sullen characters he played in the movies.

"Come on," he began with lively aggression. "You know you're going."

"I told you I'm going to the game."

"What's another football game, when this is my first go with a Spyder?"

Patiently, Lew reiterated his stance that he just couldn't allow himself to miss the opening game of the season.

Dean tried another tactic: "My dad's here."

Lew was surprised. Jimmy had spoken to him about the tension he often felt around Winton. Bracker and Winton had never met, but Lew had the impression that Jimmy believed that his father would approve of this particular friendship—with a kid who had a regular job, was close to his family, and wasn't drawn to the bohemian lifestyle. It would be interesting to observe the two and gauge how they were getting along. But that could all be discussed later in the week.

"I thought that when I saw him again, I'd kind of bring it up," Lew remembers. "Maybe I'd say, 'You're seeing your father again?' Something nonconfrontational. Just let him talk about it if he wanted to talk about it. Maybe I'd meet Winton another time. But right now, all I cared about was going to that game."

Still, Dean continued to argue. When Lew mentioned that Dean would have plenty of company on the ride to Salinas, Jimmy said that the others would be riding to the race in the station wagon. This unnerved Bracker a little bit, who imagined Jimmy opening up the Porsche on the highway.

"You're towing the car, right?"

He didn't think that driving the low-slung race car up and down those unfamiliar, winding roads was a safe idea.

"Yeah, yeah. But I want you to go so we can talk about everything as it's going on."

"Don't worry. We'll have a lot of race weekends coming up." He urged Dean to handle the car wisely. On Monday, Lew emphasized, the two could go over all the details of the race.

Disappointed about not having his way, Jimmy responded with a popular phrase that would ring in Bracker's ears for the next sixty years.

"It's your funeral."

HOMECOMING KING

On Sand Pike, Markie watches the cars slow in front of his farmhouse, faces gawking at the property where James Dean once played with his younger cousin. A few vehicles pull over to the side of the road so passengers can take photos. When folks venture onto the farm, Markie is polite, listening to their tales about journeying to Fairmount from New Zealand or South Africa or the Philippines, smiling as a camera is raised, shaking hands, and returning to his day-to-day life.

Because he regards himself as Jimmy's younger brother, he appreciates the good will most visitors show and believes that whatever piece of James Dean is left in Fairmount belongs to those who refuse to forget him.

He's built the farm up nicely and could easily sell it and relocate to a place where no one would realize that the Winslows and Deans are related. But he's never found the will to do so.

Marcus Sr. was sixty-one when his son graduated high school, and Markie felt that his father needed him to assist with the physical labor on the farm. "He wanted me to stay here, if I could," he recounts. "So that's what I did."

He had other jobs, too. At one time, he owned a Laundromat in Fairmount and was a township trustee assessor. For seventeen years, he worked as a parts manager at a farm implements store. But the goal was always subsidizing the family business. James Dean aside, Markie could never abide by the thought of someone other than a member of the Winslow clan operating the farm.

Over time, the James Dean brand has become part of the enterprise. So when fans arrive, Markie understands that they want to meet him. He's enjoyed many of the exchanges and received heartfelt invitations to visit parts of the globe so remote Markie had to look them up in an encyclopedia or on the Internet. Likewise, he wants the town's guests to go home with an enhanced appreciation for James Dean.

During the last weekend in September each year, twenty thousand people flood the town of three thousand to commemorate the anniversary of Dean's final day. Like Mexico's Dia de Muertos and Brazil's Dia de Finados, the gathering memorializes the departure of a loved one, as opposed to celebrating his entry into the world. Yet, there's nothing grim about the mood in Fairmount, and the visitors include people who remember attending Dean's films at the time of their release, well-mannered teens, and small children in strollers.

As a young man, Markie would be astounded by the sheer volume of people descending on Fairmount. Now, he takes it as a given:

"I'm not really surprised anymore. I've seen how Jimmy really affected people's lives, and people from all walks of life admire him through his work. I guess it's very complimentary that they still look at him that way."

He also takes pride in the fact that, so many years after his passing, Jimmy has managed to give back to the place where he grew up, as tourists cram into local restaurants, souvenir stops, and convenience stores.

"I think everyone here is grateful to Jimmy for more or less putting Fairmount on the map," his cousin says. "I don't think they'd want it to be this way all year long. But for one weekend out of the year, they're proud to show the town off and enjoy the company of a lot of nice people."

On the Thursday afternoon leading into the James Dean Festival, the downtown streets are still open to traffic—the police erect barricades on Friday—and classic cars and motorcycles begin rolling down Washington Street, past well-maintained shops whose window displays include cardboard cutouts and posters of Fairmount's favorite son. The Giant Bar & Grill, named after the star's final movie, is crowded. On one corner, a group gathers to inspect a restored Schwinn bicycle from another time, positioned on the rear of a 1951 Studebaker truck.

Music plays everywhere—not all of it from Dean's era, but nothing too modern. Like a Civil War reenactment, the idea appears to be journeying back to another period of history, not exactly 1955, but the age James Dean represents.

The Hi-Fi Stereo Shop, at 111 South Main Street, bills itself as the state's oldest record store. Shelves are filled with 45s, 78s, cassette tapes, and eight-tracks. One wall is devoted exclusively to Dean.

Down South Main Street is Dragon X Tattoos where twenty-six-year-old artist Brittany Pile is laying out stencils in anticipation of a deluge of James Dean fans, requesting etchings and silhouettes of the actor, as well as his notable quotes:

"Only the gentle are ever really strong."

"Dream as if you'll live forever. Live as if you'll die today."

"Fist in the air in that land of hypocrisy."

"I'd rather have people hiss than yawn."

"We actually have the same people that come in year after year," Brittany notes. "It's the only time of the year we see them. It's like a tradition for these people."

Brittany first became aware of James Dean when she was in kindergarten at Park Elementary School in Fairmount, looking out the window at the classic cars lined up for the James Dean Festival. "I just didn't know who the man was and why he had a festival all to himself," she says. "But, as I got older, in school, they made it a point to talk about him. Every year, we'd do a report about him around the anniversary of his death. In art class, we'd do drawings of him and enter it in a contest. It was part of the curriculum."

It was one aspect of her education that she appreciated in adulthood. "He was a go-getter, for sure. He just lived the way he wanted to live, and that's the way everybody should be, man. Live life to its fullest."

After hearing so much about James Dean, Brittany feels as if she knows him and imagines the actor as the type of person who'd be her friend, slipping her books and texting her links to new music, or social media posts about nitwits who'd never have a clue.

"He was so ahead of his time. And we're still in the Bible Belt, man. Very Christian-oriented. People are very judgmental, very old-school. The whole town knows your business. For example, people who are gay and lesbian, even to this day, they have to be hush-hush behind closed doors. Like, why would you even care about something like that? I guess some people can't help but judge because it's the only mentality they know.

"I get stared at a lot because I'm female and I have a tattooed head and face. My attitude is, 'If you don't like it, don't look.' But there are people here like James Dean, too. For every person that doesn't like it, there are ten who are like, 'Oh, that's awesome.'"

And perhaps, Brittany theorizes, those were the types of people who inspired Dean to keep returning to Fairmount, the relatives and neighbors who knew him his entire life and loved him without condition.

"Families don't usually move away from here," she claims. "They stay. They're close-knit. They keep each other grounded. And I know he must have appreciated that. And we appreciate him for coming back here and always remembering what this town meant to him."

At times, Brittany and her friends have speculated about what would have occurred in Dean's life after September 30, 1955. "I think he'd even be more hardcore than he was. I think he'd have quite a few tattoos actually. I hope he wouldn't travel down the drug path like other celebrities. He had a lot of self-confidence, so I'm pretty sure he wouldn't."

As we speak, a couple enters the shop to survey the designs up on the wall. Brittany walks over to assist, exchanging small talk about the rush of fans expected the next day. Asked if she finds it morbid that Dean's death still inspires such interest, she takes a philosophical approach. Jimmy's popularity has been good for Fairmount, and good for her, not only because it draws people to the tattoo parlor, but because Brittany is able to stay in her small town and meet visitors with a multitude of interests from an exotic menagerie of places.

Yet, she never loses sight of the fact that none of this would have occurred without the tragedy that took a talented artist at age twenty-four.

"It's sad, but sometimes the ones who die young get more attention."

THE FEEL OF THE SOIL

The story of James Dean began on a chilly Sunday, February 8, 1931, twenty minutes away from Fairmount, in the city of Marion, home to Indiana Wesleyan University, the largest evangelical college in the Midwest.

Winton and Mildred Dean summoned a doctor to their home at the Seven Gables Apartments, a sprawling house that had been subdivided into rental units, across from what was then the New York Central railroad depot. Dr. James Emmick arrived promptly and delivered the baby.

Jimmy was a big kid—eight pounds, ten ounces.

Winton paid the doctor his fifteen-dollar fee in cash. The couple also honored the man who made the house call by naming their son after him.

Winton and Mildred had been hastily married on July 26, 1930, by Methodist clergyman Zeno Doan—who'd briefly gain national attention by being one of the ministers officiating at James Dean's funeral. Although Winton's clan were proud, active Quakers, the former Mildred Marie Wilson, the daughter of a former barber who now ran a farm in nearby Gas City, prescribed to the Methodist faith.

It was early in their relationship when Mildred discovered that she was pregnant—two months after meeting Winton at a dance. Soon after that, the pair paid an unannounced visit to their friends Dave and Hazel Turner. "There came a knock on the door, and it was Mildred and Winton, who said they'd been around the corner and had been married and didn't have a place to stay," the Turners' son, Jerry Payne, told the Marion *Chronicle-Tribune*. "They wanted to know if they could stay at my parents, and, of course, they could."

James Dean's most devout followers might draw a parallel to the "no room at the inn" tale in the New Testament. As with the Christ child, life on earth would be short but divine, with disciples experiencing both pain and glory when it ended.

At first, the two appeared exuberant about their circumstances. Said Payne, "It was like a big party that lasted a couple of weeks," until the Deans found their own apartment.

There was a reason why Jimmy was an only child. Winton, a slim, practical dental technician at a local Veterans Administration hospital, believed that parents should consider their financial circumstances before reproducing. The Deans were young and, by Winton's estimation, couldn't afford siblings for their son.

Dark-haired and vivacious, Mildred was more of a free spirit. Like her son, she had a penchant for sports—both played basketball in high school—and viewed herself as a creative person, reciting poetry in church. While Winton worked, mother and son would draw with crayons and make up plays, using dolls as performers to act out the stories in a cardboard theater they built. At night, before bedtime, Jimmy would tell his mother a wish, and she'd write it on a piece of paper and help him tuck it under his pillow. The next day, she tried making that wish come true.

The family moved around the general area, at one point living near the Winslow farm in a small rented cottage within sight of the Back Creek Friends Church.

Despite Winton's preoccupation with budgetary matters, when Jimmy was five, Mildred arranged for the boy to receive violin lessons and attend dance classes at the Marion College of Dance and Theatre Arts.

A short time later, the family was faced with a daunting challenge. Winton was offered a promotion to director of the dental laboratory at Sawtelle Veterans Hospital in the beachfront city of Santa Monica, California. Neither had ever been to California—or seen the ocean, for that matter—or wished to uproot the family from its Hoosier support network. But the opportunity was too good to pass up. And so the Deans took a risk and dislodged themselves.

Had Jimmy remained on the West Coast, it's uncertain if the Indiana traditions that so defined him would have played a factor in his life. Immediately, he appeared to blend well into the city where he'd later find fame, living first in a duplex off Wilshire Boulevard, then a ranch house near the Pacific Coast Highway. On the wooden planks of the Santa Monica Pier, Jimmy spent his free time observing the fortune tellers, fishing boat captains, and Muscle Beach bodybuilders. He finished the first through third grades at McKinley Elementary School.

But he always looked forward to his trips to the place that he truly considered home. In a high school essay, he'd recount his "luck" at having the opportunity to journey between California and Indiana, "going and coming a different route each time. I have been in almost every state west of Indiana. I remember them all."

When Jimmy was eight, twenty-nine-year-old Mildred started complaining of chest pains. Eventually, she went to a doctor who told her that she was dying of cancer. Never comfortable discussing his feelings, Winton struggled as he told his child about the development.

"Jimmy said nothing, just looked at me," Winton told *Modern Screen* magazine. "Even as a child, he wasn't much to talk about his hurts."

Back in Fairmount, the family learned the sad news from a letter Winton sent to his mother, Emma. Good jobs were scarce, and he couldn't take the time away from work to care for his ailing wife and their child. So he asked Emma to travel to California to help. Before leaving Indiana, Emma went to a local doctor and described her daughter-in-law's condition. The medical professional estimated that Emma would be in Los Angeles between six and eight weeks.

She was there for seven. On April 14, 1940, Mildred died.

Her body was transported back to Indiana for the funeral; Jimmy was on the same train. "Jimmy's dad had missed an awful lot of work because of his wife's illness and was on the verge of losing his job," Markie says. "So he wasn't able to come back here for the funeral."

Surrounded by extended family, Jimmy did not feel alone. Nonetheless, the ceremony left him traumatized. He'd never been to a funeral before. While Mildred's coffin was still open, he broke away from his family to adjust his mother's hair, then snipped off a lock to take part of her with him.

The question that now possessed the family was what they were going to do with Jimmy.

Before the trip back east, Emma had discussed her grandson's future with Winton. "Now, Winton, I want you to think about this carefully," Emma said—according to a 1956 article attributed to her in *Photoplay*. "If you see fit to let Jimmy come back to Fairmount, Ortense and Marcus would . . . raise him for you." She argued that a boyhood around loving relatives on a farm was preferable to being a latch-key child in the house where his mother died, in a far-off section of the country.

"Well, poor Winton just sat there and stared," Emma said. "At last he said, 'It never occurred to me I might be separated from Jimmy.'"

Ultimately, Winton concluded that it was better to have family raise Jimmy than a housekeeper. "I had no choice but to send him to Fairmount," Winton explained. "I was deep in debt with doctors' bills from Mildred's illness, and I was alone without anyone to look after the boy while I was at work. I had to get my feet under me again."

When he did, Winton rationalized, he might even be in a position to reunite with the child.

"When we learned that his mother would not recover, we asked for him," Ortense remembered in the documentary *The James Dean Story*. "We had read where he was sort of pushed off onto us, but that is not true. We wanted him. We were happy to have him."

Winton realized that his sister was sincere, and—despite outside perceptions that Jimmy was abandoned—the close relatives understood the circumstances. "Hard as it was," Emma said, "I've always felt Winton made the right choice, particularly since it turned out that he was drafted about eighteen months later" after World War II began.

Sympathetic over the boy's loss, the Winslows gave Jimmy their own bedroom and moved to another one across the hall. "He liked our bedroom set better," Ortense told *Photoplay*. "It was maple and that seemed right for a boy."

For the first two weeks, Jimmy slept with his mother's hair under his pillow. Gradually, though, Ortense and Marcus became "Ma" and "Pa" to him. On Sundays, he accompanied them to church, feeling proud when Ortense played piano. Even when Marcus was tired, he made time to toss a football or shoot baskets with his nephew. "Theirs is what a Quaker home should be," Emma said. "You never hear a harsh word. Best of all, they are happy as well as good—and that's what Jimmy needed most after the shock of losing his mother."

However, there was one member of the clan who harbored reservations about the arrangement. Markie's older sister was deep into her adolescence when her cousin moved into her house and less than enthusiastic about sharing it.

"He was kind of a pain to me," seventy-nine-year-old Joan Peacock told the *Chronicle-Tribune* in 2005. "I was fourteen, so I was beginning to get interested in boys. So my girlfriends would come over and we'd go upstairs to my room to talk about these boys. Well, in a little bit, you'd hear the stairway creak, and Jimmy would come sneaking up there. Oh, that'd just make me so mad.

"So I'd call Mom, and she'd make him come back down. Then, in a little bit, here he'd come again. Just annoying things like that."

Markie had yet to be born and, like Jimmy, Joan was accustomed to being an only child. "We had a lot of adjusting to do," she told CNN.

Nonetheless, even Joan could be taken by her cousin's magnetism: "When my folks' relatives would come, he was always entertaining them. He just had a charisma that drew people to him. Oh, he could really charm, especially when he was wanting something. He knew how to work it so that he'd get what he wanted."

At North Ward Elementary School, Dean slipped back into the life-style his family left behind when they moved west. Classmates called him "Jim," "Jimmy," "Deaner," and "Rack"—a nickname friends used for Uncle Marcus, based on his youthful fondness for tennis—but never "James."

Trailed by the Winslows' border collie, Tuck, Jimmy and his friends built intricate tunnels out of hay in the barn. He'd later claim that he became a better actor by studying the cows, pigs, and chickens: "There are a lot of things I learned from animals. One was that they couldn't hiss or boo me. I also became close to nature and am now able to appreciate the beauty with which this world is endowed."

Adeline Nall, his high school drama coach, recalled her celebrated student loving "the feel of Indiana soil under his feet, and I think that was the source of much of his strength."

Still, his sensitivity distinguished Dean from other kids in the area. Harold "Whitey" Rust lived near the Winslow farm, and was one of Jimmy's regular playmates. One day, the two went hunting and Rust discovered a rabbit hiding in a pipe. Whitey lifted the object to shake out the creature, and Dean fired his rifle.

He missed numerous times, and Rust wondered whether his friend was deliberately avoiding the kill. After dozens of tries, though, Jimmy's bullet hit its target, and the rabbit collapsed on the ground. Rust was happy. "That was food," he told *Chronicle-Tribune* reporter Sean F. Driscoll. "We were poor."

Dean's reaction was different: "He started crying. That really, really upset him."

But Jimmy's world wasn't limited to Fairmount. Several times a year, he traveled to Los Angeles to visit his father, an exotic vacation for a farm boy from Grant County, Indiana. Upon his return, he'd invariably stand up in front of the class and describe the sights of Hollywood. Everyone was impressed. To his classmates, Los Angeles was as distant as Hong Kong or Antarctica.

9

THE DEANERS' DEVOTIONAL

The Back Creek Friends Church is positioned just north of Park Cemetery, the site of Jimmy's tombstone, and just south of the Winslow Farm. Each week, fifty members enter the austere worship hall, where the minister stands in front of a painting of Jesus the Shepherd instead of a cross, and the glass in the missile-shaped windows is frosted rather than stained. There, they slide into the long wooden pews, below stark white ceiling fans, the way their ancestors have since the structure was built in 1899. When he lived with his aunt and uncle, Jimmy counted himself among the faithful, attending services and appearing in church skits and plays. Behind the building, there's a prayer garden donated in 2001 by a Dean fan, James DeCaro, in honor of his father, David.

"We're known as the James Dean Church," Pastor Linda Cabe told the Marion *Chronicle-Tribune* in 2005. "That can't be helped."

On the Monday following the James Dean Festival, about one hundred of the actor's most loyal followers—the stragglers who need to stay that extra day—file into the sanctuary for a memorial service. When I enter, the woman at the piano is playing not a hymn, but "Love Me Tender." At one time, I'm repeatedly told, the church pianist was Jimmy's beloved aunt, Ortense Winslow.

Over the years, the Deaners—as Jimmy's fervent admirers call themselves—have become the equivalent of a fraternal organization. Their full-color publication, *The Deanzine*, can be purchased in Fairmount. There's a section called "Dean Art by Dean Fans"—the March 2013 issue features a two-page spread with four illustrations by Mel Dormer, a fan from Aurora, Illinois. Columnist Kip Brown reports on an eBay auction in which one of Dean's New York library cards was sold for $511. Seventy-two-year-old David Brown from Glen, New Hampshire, writes about a high school yearbook he's acquired, apparently signed by the icon. He adds, "I also have a swath of cloth, 3x4 [inches], from the sports jacket, which he wore in *Rebel*."

It's not the celebrated red jacket that everyone remembers. But anything that rubbed against Jimmy Dean's skin is pretty impressive.

In the same edition, to the left of the table of contents, is an editorial by Pam Crawford, the president of the James Dean Remembered fan club. It mentions the recent passing of eighty-one-year-old Bob Pulley, the last surviving pallbearer at the actor's funeral and the first president of the Fairmount Historical Museum. Writes Pam, "All our beautiful friends and family who have left us behind recently greeted our cherished friend, Bob Pulley, in heaven with open arms. And his old pal, Jim Dean, jostled his way to the front of the line to be the first to shake his hand."

Pam then mentions a more personal trial: "I'm sure you noticed that this issue of *The Deanzine* is late. Unfortunately, the reason for my tardiness is a sad one. Our little Molly Maila, the Deanerweiner, had a disc blow in her spine, resulting in paralysis of her hind legs. She had neurosurgery on her spine over a month ago. Shortly after the surgery, she had a blod clot go to that area of the spine. Since then, she has required round the clock care. . . . Please keep our precious little Deanerweiner in your prayers."

In the church, fans approach Pam and ask about the welfare of her dog. She's touched by their concern, but has a larger mission today—articulating the sentiments of the Deaners who've come to the worship hall to meld the secular world of the celebrity with the religiosity they attach to their idol.

"We are not here to mourn James Dean's death," she says from the podium. "We are here to celebrate his life and the talent that God gave him to entertain us. Don't ever forget that."

She reads from a poem she wrote about the screen legend in 1984, describing him as a comet whose glow beguiles the young, as well as the old.

Tom Berghuis, one of the organizers of the service, is equally poetic. "In the fall, Indiana distills its juices," he tells attendees in the soothing tones of his native Michigan. "The community of Fairmount, Indiana, begins to slow its pace and prepare for the long winter nights ahead. But the crisp atmosphere and feasts and fires was absent in Fairmount in October of 1955 as the town prepared to bury James Dean."

Berghuis reverently talks about specific Deaners who've died in the past year and invokes the name of Jimmy's speech and drama teacher, Adeline Nall, who was invariably quoted every time a reporter stopped in Fairmount to do a James Dean Festival story. "She shared a lot of her experiences with me, as well as anyone else who would listen at the time," he says. "She has not been with us since 1996 and, yet, she is with us every day."

To underscore the Deaners' sentiments for Nall, an empty seat is left for her at the memorial.

Phil Ziegler, who graduated from Fairmount High School with Dean in 1949, then takes the podium, asking how many guests have journeyed to Indiana from "across the pond." One by one, fans stand and announce their home countries: France, England, Australia.

Ziegler shares a sentiment from another classmate, Jim Curran: "Sending greetings and love from Massachusetts. I wish I could be with you today, but nursing homes do not issue visas."

There's mild laughter in the church. Far away as Curran might be, he's very much a part of the scene.

In the Quaker tradition, participants stand and testify about the factors that drew them to this event. Tom McCord, a stylish Canadian with a goatee and ruffled hair, expresses "gratitude" to the actor and describes the "transformative experience" of seeing a story about James Dean on *Entertainment Tonight* some twenty years earlier: "My parents were splitting up for the second time, and I felt this immediate connection." Anxious to learn more, he rented *Rebel Without a Cause* from a Toronto video store and went to the public library to peruse a book of Dennis Stock's *Life* magazine photographs of the movie star.

It was Dean, McCord says, who allowed him to understand "what an artist really was," and inspired him to become an actor himself. "He was actually all these amazing things, this powerful creative force."

Phil Timos from Australia—he lives in a suburb of Melbourne, approximately 9,700 miles from the Hoosier State—praises the citizenry of Fairmount: "Thank you for opening your hearts to me . . . I have traveled a long way, and I know because I traveled it. The thing is, the journey doesn't stop. And, as the days go on, it gets better and it gets better and it gets better. Jimmy, James, you brought me here. But what's keeping me around is you guys . . . You've shown me around. I've eaten hamburgers. I've drunken buckets of Coke."

Like McCord, Timos was a teen when he discovered James Dean— from an African exchange student who tended to sit alone but was willing to share her interests. A few days later, he watched *East of Eden* on television. "It touched my heart. It really brought home to me what I was going through at that stage. And I thought, the actor, well, he's good-looking, of course, as you know. But it was . . . the substance and what was underneath." At that point, he began compiling James Dean materials. "And I haven't stopped," Phil concludes. "And I won't stop."

Elaine Chambers replaces Phil at the podium, telling a similar story. Elaine's from England, and she first watched *East of Eden* on September 30, 1975, the twentieth anniversary of James Dean's death—at her mother's behest. "She stopped me from watching *Top of the Pops*," Elaine says.

> You know the story. I was fuming. And by the end of *East of Eden*, I was hooked
> . . . What's astounded me all these years later is I'm still learning things about

him and finding new pictures of him, which I still find stunning to this day when I see an image I've never seen before. But there's something much deeper. Through Facebook, the Internet, coming here . . . talking to people, realizing that all of us find something in Jimmy that resonates and makes our lives worth living. Because we aspire to live in the moment and be mindful and make every day as good as it can possibly be. Because you have someone who died at twenty-four and . . . he's still inspiring people now. And I just find that stunning. . . . And I love the fact that people from all over the world, regardless of their backgrounds . . . their religion, their color, their age, their gender find something in Jimmy that inspires them, and it brings us all together. . . . We all have this commonality.

It was Dean's fascination with *The Little Prince*, Elaine continues, that awakened her interest in French authors and the French language. Around the room, several Deaners nod. "I'm a total Francophile," Elaine says, then quotes the book: "What is essential is invisible to the eye. It's only from the heart that we see rightly."

The ceremony ends as it does every year, with Nicky Bazooka, a mysterious, leather-clad figure in sunglasses and a motorcycle hat, entering the church and leading the Deaners outside. There, he mounts his 1969 Kawasaki-made replica of a British BSA, the closest bike Nicky can find to Jimmy Dean's Triumph, and heads the procession to Dean's grave.

Back in the day, Adeline Nall would drape a scarf around his neck every year.

The graveside ceremony is reverent but festive. People smile, enjoying the companionship of those who not only understand their fixation but live it. Flowers are placed on the headstone, along with small American flags and messages scrawled on pieces of paper. Soon, everyone will leave, driving to their hometowns in other parts of the country, and the international airport in Indianapolis for the long trek home. By nightfall, Pam Crawford will be back in Little Rock, tending to her Deanerweiner.

But she'll know the Deaners are thinking about her. After so many years, this group of fans considers itself a loving, extended family. Just as importantly, Pam reminds the followers, they accomplished something that transcends the passage of time:

"You brought Jimmy back to Indiana today."

A REGULAR JOHN BARRYMORE

When the war ended in 1945, Winton Dean remarried and returned to California to work for the Veterans Administration. His wife, Ethel Case, was willing to have Jimmy move in with them. But after spending the past five years with the Winslows, the boy appeared to be in no hurry to leave Indiana.

On the surface, it looked like he might remain on the farm forever. When one of the pigs gave birth, Dean decided to care for the runt of the litter, bottle feeding his new pet and running across the field with his dog—as the squealing piglet raced behind them. Inside the farm house, Ortense tried passing on her piano-playing skills to her nephew and encouraged him to study the bass horn and drums—all with varying degrees of success. Having already taken dance lessons as a small child, he accompanied his older cousin, Joan, to her classes. It was not a choice men in the Dean and Winslow families generally made. But his aunt and uncle were tuned into Jimmy's sensibilities and embraced them.

Although he often withdrew and retreated into his own thoughts, the boy could be gregarious and sociable, and Marcus and Ortense provided a welcoming environment for local kids to play basketball at the farm or swim in the pond.

"People talk about him being a loner," classmate Wilma Smith Brookshire said as an adult. "I don't think he was. I think he was in the group. He was a very talented child. He acted, even when he wasn't acting."

Bob Middleton did odd jobs for the Winslows, occasionally helping them plow their fields at night. Sometimes, Jimmy also visited the Middleton family farm, about a mile away. One day, Bob's father, Cecil, showed the boys a .45-caliber revolver and allowed them to fire at cans on the property. Jimmy hit every one.

Bob felt a surge of jealousy. "At dinner that evening, Dad commented, 'Man, why can't you do that?'" Bob said in 2005. "Well, that's great. I'm not a famous actor, either."

Early in their teen years, Bob's sister, Barbara Jane, was offered a ride from another family's home on Jimmy's bicycle. She was seated on the handlebars when they skidded on a patch of gravel. Barbara Jane tumbled forward and over a barbed wire fence, ending up with an X-shaped scar on her right arm.

Jimmy viewed the accident as a bonding experience. Whenever they saw each other, he'd jokingly point at his arm and shout, "X marks the spot." Remembering the episode in 2005, she told Marion *Chronicle-Tribune* reporter Sean F. Driscoll, "Anytime anyone is talking about Jimmy or finds out I went to school with him, I always have to show them our scar."

The mishap did nothing to discourage Jimmy's taste for going fast. He subsequently had Marvin Carter, the owner of an Indian Motorcycles shop on Grant County Road 150 East, install a small motor on his bicycle. It was Carter who also sold Marcus the Czech Whizzer for Jimmy's sixteenth birthday.

Bob Pulley, who'd later serve as a pallbearer at his friend's funeral, remembered Jimmy's excitement as the motorcycle accelerated. Once, Pulley was sitting behind the future actor, holding on to Dean as he revved the bike and set it on its hind wheel on Main Street. "I slid off the back," Bob said. "Jim crossed the street, turned around, and came back and just sat there and laughed at me."

For Bob Middleton, only one ride on the Whizzer was enough: "He got me on that thing and I thought, 'Boy, if I get off this, it will be my last ride.'"

In fact, Jimmy's penchant for speed inspired a nickname: One Speed Dean. The one speed, his friends said, was "wide open."

"If he'd only fallen once, things might have been different," Marcus Sr. told *Redbook* in 1956. Instead, he said, Jimmy continued to challenge himself with new stunts, walking away from each one with an inflated view of his ability to survive anything. In the aftermath of Jimmy's death, Marcus wished his nephew had learned to think twice before driving at high velocities, instead of growing into young adulthood with a sense of fearlessness.

While attending Fairmount High School, Dean became paranoid about leaving his Czech Whizzer in public after some fellow students tinkered with it while Jimmy was in class. As a result, he asked the owner of a Shell station at Washington and Main Streets for permission to park at the garage. Jimmy not only kept his bike there when he was at school, but whenever he needed to walk around downtown.

During school breaks, Jimmy worked part-time in a canning factory, returning to the farm with boxes of ketchup and other condiments. "Of course, he used to help Dad on the farm," Markie recalls. "If Dad was baling hay or something, he'd ask Jimmy to get some kids he knew in town to come out and help. Jimmy would get three or four of his friends, and they'd bale hay or bale straw or whatever needed to be done."

There were exactly forty-nine seniors in Fairmount High's Class of '49. They were a spirited bunch. Those still living instantly remember the class colors—white and gold, in contrast to the black and gold of the school's sports teams—and their official flower, a yellow rose. It's unclear, though, how seriously Jimmy took their motto, "Look before you leap."

In the classroom, Dean was an inquisitive student. "He knew something about everything," said teacher Myrtle Gilbreath. "He had a keen mind." Even so, his grades revealed that he was selective about where he applied himself: A in art—Jimmy molded clay, painted trees, streams, and chipmunks and made Adeline Nall an orchid—B-plus in psychology, C-minus in United States history, and D in both algebra and spelling.

Basketball intrigued him more. This was his mother's sport, and she would have been proud to watch him from the stands. During a game against Gas City in his senior year, he scored the winning field goal at the buzzer, as the Quakers triumphed 39–37. During the sectional tournament the same year, he accumulated forty points in three games.

"Jimmy broke fifteen pairs of glasses, just trying to be an athlete," Marcus Sr. would recount in the *James Dean Story* documentary. "He'd break them as fast as I could get them."

Dean also lettered in track. When others told him that, at five-foot-eight, he was too short to pole-vault, he competed in a tournament, breaking a county record. As the story goes, Jimmy—satisfied that he'd decisively silenced his critics—never pole-vaulted again.

The one interest that never seemed to wane was acting. His high school roles were memorable, particularly his darker depictions as Frankenstein's monster and the tormented, frightening Herbert White in *The Monkey's Paw*. Even as a teen, he understood the source of his angst: the sudden separation from his mother at age nine. "I never knew the reason for Mom's death," he said in a 1948 letter (later published in the *Chronicle* in 2005) to his principal, Roland Dubois. "In fact, it still preys on my mind."

Later, he'd say that his love of drama was the healthiest way to deal with anguish and loss: "To me, acting is the most logical way for people's neuroses to manifest themselves, in this great need we all have to express ourselves. To my way of thinking, an actor's course is set even before he's out of the cradle."

Still, some of Dean's peers resented the way he drew attention to himself and teased him about it. While Jimmy was doing a dramatic reading in class one day, a student named Paul Smart taunted him, "What are you trying to do, Dean? We know you're a great talent, a regular John Barrymore."

As the other pupils chuckled, Jimmy responded like Cal Trask in *East of Eden* or Jim Stark in *Rebel Without a Cause*—slugging his antagonist and earning an expulsion from school.

When he returned home that night, Marcus Sr. is said to have told his nephew to take his gun and go hunting the next day. Jimmy was a good kid, Marcus reasoned, and disciplining him would be pointless.

In Marcus, Jimmy received the support that Winton was unable to provide. But despite their genuine compassion for their complicated nephew, the Winslows could not guide the aspiring actor any further than where their own experiences had taken them. In order to get closer to his dreams, Jimmy turned to Rev. James DeWeerd, pastor of a local Wesleyan Methodist church.

According to the *Redbook* article, the minister was the most sophisticated man Jimmy had ever met: "Dr. DeWeerd was openly critical of Fairmount and its limited way of life." The magazine described Dean dining with the reverend on a table adorned with white linen, sparkling silverware and multi-colored light bulbs, while Tchaikovsky's music played on the phonograph. The conversation apparently included dissertations on poetry and philosophy. Afterward, the pair would watch films of bullfights the minister had taken himself while visiting Mexico.

As the projector clattered and cast shadows, the minister is said to have reminded the student never to limit his imagination or experiences.

DeWeerd educated Dean not only about culture, the article stated, but the passion that would claim the actor's life, instructing Jimmy on how to drive a car, bringing him to a race in Indianapolis, and introducing him to legendary driver Cannon Ball Baker. As they rode back to Fairmount, the pastor and the young thespian discussed the dangers of racing and the possibility of dying on the track.

Yet, Jimmy was unafraid, DeWeerd told *Redbook*, since he shared the reverend's belief in "personal immortality." Death was not something to fear, DeWeerd emphasized, and could be controlled by exercising "control of mind over matter."

Jimmy wasn't the only young male in whom the confirmed bachelor invested. Allegedly, DeWeerd had a habit of bringing boys to the YMCA in the town of Anderson, some thirty miles away, and watching them skinny-dip in the pool.

Elizabeth Taylor, Jimmy's costar in *Giant,* claimed that Dean had confided to her that DeWeerd molested him, an experience that "haunted him the rest of his life. . . . We talked about it a lot. During *Giant,* we'd stay up nights and talk and talk, and that was one of the things he confessed to me."

The actress had allegedly specified that she didn't want this story revealed until after her death. But the rumors about Dean and the pastor were rife even in the 1950s. Hollywood columnist Joe Hyams, author of the 1992 biography *James Dean: Little Boy Lost,* claimed to have tracked down DeWeerd and asked about the allegations. The minister apparently contended that the sex was always consensual.

"Jimmy never mentioned our relationship, nor did I," DeWeerd was quoted as saying. "It would not have helped either of us."

Few of Jimmy's classmates would have been aware of either his sexuality or inner struggles, as he returned to school after his three-day suspension and continued to thrive on the high school stage. In the senior class play, *You Can't Take It with You,* he portrayed Grandpa Vanderhof, the eccentric family patriarch. "I think my life will be devoted to art and dramatics," he wrote. "And there are so many different fields of art, it would be hard to foul up. . . . A fellow must have confidence."

He also won first place in the National Forensic League's state contest in Peru, Indiana, reciting "A Madman's Manuscript" by Charles Dickens. Perhaps self-conscious over the attention he'd been receiving, he kept his preparation quiet, not even telling Marcus and Ortense that he was entering the competition, as he memorized his passage by flashlight in his room. Rev. DeWeerd is said to have coached him, as well.

Although the subject of the story is a killer, there were elements of the character to which Jimmy could relate:

I remember days when I was *afraid* of being mad . . . when I rushed from the sight of merriment or happiness to hide myself in some lonely place, and spend the weary hours in watching the progress of the fever that was to consume my brain. I knew that madness was mixed up with my very blood, and the marrow of my bones . . . and when I cowered in some obscure corner of a crowded room, and saw men whisper and point and turn their eyes towards me, I knew they were telling each other of the doomed madman; and I slunk away to mope in solitude.

He delivered his oration in a strong, convincing voice. But Adeline Nall believed that his eyes made the greatest impression at the meet.

About three weeks later, the pair traveled to Longmont, Colorado, for the United States finals. Jimmy came in sixth place, but it almost didn't matter. James Dean was good enough to receive national attention.

"There should be a goal in this crazy world for all of us," he said. "I know where mine is, anyway."

HEY GRAMPS, I'LL HAVE A CHOC MALT

During his high school years, Jimmy appeared in a church play called *To Them That Sleep in Darkness*, and if his loved ones in Indiana hadn't yet understood his need to live an actor's life, this play confirmed it. "Jimmy played the blind boy," his grandmother, Emma Woolen Dean, told *Photoplay* magazine. "Well, I'll tell you. I wished he wasn't quite as good at it. I cried all the way through."

When Jimmy considered colleges, he was partial to Earlham, the Quaker school that his uncle Marcus attended in Richmond, Indiana. Earlham was so progressive that administrators deliberately registered a number of Japanese students during World War II to prevent their internment. But Marcus realized that Dean needed to reach beyond Indiana. "You've already got a father in Los Angeles," Marcus advised. If Jimmy wanted to act, that was where he needed to go.

There was already a long-standing offer for Dean to relocate in California. Accepting his uncle's logic, Jimmy moved in with Winton and his wife, Ethel, and enrolled at Santa Monica City College.

Unlike the Winslows, Winton could not comprehend why Jimmy was so dedicated to acting. It was financially unstable, and professional performers appeared to be an odd lot. Since Jimmy was a good athlete, he was encouraged to become a physical education teacher. Teachers might not have been highly paid, but the job was dependable, and Jimmy could pick up some extra money coaching basketball. A career in law, Winton counseled, would be even more lucrative. With Jimmy's public speaking skills, he'd make a superb litigator.

On the surface, Dean appeared to acquiesce. He was living in strange surroundings and wanted to build his relationship with Winton. For his part, the elder Dean purchased his son a 1939 Chevrolet to get around. But before the semester even started, Jimmy joined the Miller Playhouse Theatre Guild in Los Angeles, and—reversing his first and middle names—appeared in a production as Byron James. Although he registered for a selection of prelaw classes, his schedule included courses in theater history and acting. And in addition to playing on the Santa Monica City College basketball team, Jimmy made it a point to join the drama club.

Winton sensed that he was being undermined, while Jimmy tried to balance his own passions with the demands of his father. After becoming familiar with the range of acting prospects in Los Angeles, he began lobbying for a transfer to UCLA, where he knew that there'd be greater choices for someone who needed to be onstage. When Winton resisted, Jimmy transferred anyway.

As a concession to his father, Dean actually enrolled in a prelaw curriculum at his new school. But Winton was angry that Jimmy hadn't heeded his advice. Although each had hoped to make up for all the years apart, the arrangement wasn't working. When Winton and Ethel decided to move out of their home to purchase a house in Reseda, Jimmy announced that he was going to live on the UCLA campus instead, joining the Epsilon Pi chapter of the Sigma Nu fraternity and auditioning for the role of Malcolm in a school production of *Macbeth*.

It was a challenging task. Los Angeles wasn't Fairmount, and Jimmy had a great deal of competition. About 1,600 actors and actresses tried out for the play. But Jimmy won the role of the defiant young man who overthrows the king and rises to the throne.

In a letter to Ortense and Marcus, he called the opportunity "the biggest thrill of my life."

While Jimmy and his father now resided in the same city, to the young actor, his aunt and uncle were still "Ma" and "Pa." Before leaving Indiana, Marcus had made it clear that if Jimmy was ever short on funds, he could turn to the people who raised him.

At the time, though, Dean's concerns were bigger than money. In LA, he'd have to prove himself over and over. "Being an actor is the loneliest thing in the world," he said. "You are alone with concentration and imagination, and that's all you have."

Looking beyond the college campus, Dean began to envision himself as part of the Hollywood fabric. Like every other actor, he'd have to learn to process rejection and find encouragement when confronted with pessimism. Aware that his height could be an impediment to success, Jimmy convinced himself of a retort that he'd use repeatedly: "How can you measure acting in inches?"

Dean's instinct about UCLA and the possibilities he'd encounter there were proven correct when another student told him about a Pepsi commercial being filmed in Griffith Park—the future site of the iconic knife fight in *Rebel Without a Cause*. Extras were needed, but when Jimmy showed up, he managed to catch the director's attention. Soon, Jimmy was the star of the commercial, handing out sodas to a group of kids on a merry-go-round—including future *Rebel* cast mate Nick Adams—and appearing onscreen for the entire time.

He was overjoyed just to be in front of the camera. "The gratification comes in the doing," he'd say of acting, "not the results."

His take-home pay: twenty-five dollars. But the experience confirmed to Dean that Winton was wrong, and the decision to move to LA and pursue acting was right.

Even so, the reaction to Dean from peers destined for workaday lives was no different than it had been in Fairmount: while the majority of Jimmy's associates admired his drive and talents, some were annoyed by the fact that the handsome youth received a lopsided amount of attention. When a fraternity brother jokingly implied that actors tended to veer toward homosexuality, Dean knew what he had to do to save face, punching out the student the way he had his heckler at Fairmount High School.

As in Indiana, there was a price to pay—Dean was expelled from Sigma Nu.

He didn't seem to mind. Although he initially enjoyed the camaraderie of the fraternity, he found the conformist nature of the Greek life restricting. In fact, college seemed like too much of a make-believe world. He hadn't uprooted himself to theorize about what it would be like to be an actor. He needed to start acting now. Several weeks into the spring semester of 1951, he stopped attending his classes entirely.

At the time, the Korean War was waging, but Jimmy managed to avoid the draft. He may have invoked the Quaker canon of nonviolence. Or it might have been the fact that he had poor eyesight. Later, a wholly unsubstantiated rumor had Dean "coming out" to the draft board, confessing that he couldn't serve in the military because he felt attracted to men.

When questioned about his sexual leanings, Dean—like most public figures of his time—denied that he was gay. But, according to folklore, he was known to follow up with the assertion that he didn't intend to "go through life with one hand tied behind my back."

This was an era when every aspiring performer took the casting couch as a given in Hollywood. By numerous accounts—including the books *Surviving James Dean* by the actor's friend William Bast, and *James Dean: Little Boy Lost* by Joe Hyams—Jimmy was willing to have sex with men who could influence his career. At one point, he moved in with Rogers Brackett, a well-connected, older advertising executive who is said to have facilitated meetings with friends in the entertainment industry. Some contend that Jimmy was engaging in sex "for trade." But, with so much natural talent, he knew that he didn't need to take this route and apparently felt bad about acting like a male hustler.

Either way, his looks and skills were attracting attention. When he played the role of John the Apostle in Father Patrick Peyton's *Family Theatre* television program, a group of Catholic schoolgirls formed a James Dean Appreciation Society.

He also began to receive bit parts in movies. In *Has Anybody Seen My Gal?* in 1952, Dean has an uncredited role as a kid in a malt shop, wearing a sweater vest and proclaiming, "Hey Gramps, I'll have a choc malt, heavy on the choc, plenty of milk, four spoons of malt, two spoons of vanilla ice cream, one mixed, and one floating."

It was the first line he ever spoke in a movie.

"I seem to be getting a very cheap theater education," he wrote in a letter, later printed in *The Deanzine*, to his aunt, uncle, and younger cousin. "The work I am doing here is easy and advancement is unlimited, as to talent. We get very little pay, if any, but . . . I choose to sacrifice the money for the education I am getting in television and movie production."

Yet, he wasn't sure that he wanted to remain in Hollywood. His fellow actors were the most "criticizing narcissistic bunch you ever saw, always at each other's throat," he said in his letter home. "But let an outsider try to interfere, and they flock together like a bunch of long lost buddys [*sic*]." On the advice of his drama coach, James Whitmore—who'd later receive an Academy Award nomination for portraying President Truman in *Give 'em Hell, Harry!*—he relocated to New York to study theater.

Martin Landau became friends with Jimmy when they were both searching for work—Landau had already been an artist of sorts, working as a cartoonist for the New York *Daily News* starting at age seventeen, but he quit to pursue dramatics—spending much of their time walking around the breezy streets of the city, discussing books they'd read and films and plays they'd seen. With the Winslows far away, Dean looked forward to the invitations he received to the Landau family's house in Queens, particularly on holidays, when he'd chat amiably with the older members of the family and play with Martin's younger nephews.

It was also in New York that Jimmy met Liz Sheridan, the actress who'd later play Jerry Seinfeld's mother on *Seinfeld*. Jimmy was instantly flirtatious and tried charming her in his own distinct way. Displaying a bloody cape that he said had belonged to Brooklyn-born bullfighter Sidney Franklin, he invited Sheridan to re-create an exhibition with him in Central Park.

"I always got to be the bull and I never got to be the matador," she told CNN.

The two dated, and Sheridan was drawn into the enigma that was James Dean. "He was playful," she said. "He was serious. He was sad." At one point, she maintained, Dean asked her to marry him. "I said, 'I don't know.' We were very young and having a good time, and just something inside said, 'Sure, but I don't know.'"

Despite his interest in Sheridan, Dean continued to travel in gay circles. Nearly two decades before the Stonewall Riots helped ignite the gay rights movement, discretion was the rule on this circuit. But Jimmy's presence there was so well known that it was even mentioned in *Redbook* shortly after his death.

According to the article, because of Jimmy's good looks, he was "sought by homosexuals," who offered him presents, as well as acting jobs. Their obsessive behavior, the story continued, appeared to worry Jimmy. Although he regarded himself as "a man," he was quoted as complaining to a friend, he feared that he might begin to "doubt" himself if the attention continued.

Said Sheridan, "One night, he was very upset and said that he had met this guy in Los Angeles who picked him up in a parking lot. He was a big producer. They had met. They had gotten on a train together to Chicago . . . and the word he used was 'succumbed.'"

Others have described Dean as less of a victim in these encounters. "In New York, Jimmy would be more sexually active than he ever had been before," Paul Alexander wrote in his 1994 biography, *Boulevard of Broken Dreams: The Life, Times, and Legend of James Dean*. "If there was a sex act that could be performed (almost always, it had to be a homosexual act), Jimmy wanted to try it. . . . He was probably not aware of it at the time— and maybe he never was—but it seems more than coincidental that as he explored his sexuality, he also began to realize the fathomless potential of his creative talent."

Although he may not have been speaking about his sexuality, Dean would later insist that every actor was obligated to "experience all there is to experience . . . to store away in the core of his subconscious everything that he might be called upon to use in the expression of his art."

Mark Rydell, a friend of Dean's who'd direct a biopic about him in 2001, described Jimmy as a person open to every possible type of encounter: "He didn't let anything go by. I don't think he was essentially homosexual. I think that he had very big appetites, and I think he exercised them."

Yet, he managed to compartmentalize his friendships. As a result, Landau "never saw any indication" of Dean's interest in same-sex relationships. "When we were together, we were two guys together, looking at girls, hitting on girls."

ACQUAINTED WITH THE BUTTERFLIES

At age twenty-one, Dean became the youngest member of the Actors Studio, the exclusive organization of playwrights, directors, and actors. Lee Strasberg, the group's artistic director, said that Dean overwhelmed him at the audition, but "never again performed as well for us."

Strasberg's style of method acting encouraged performers to draw on their own emotions and memories—a philosophy that Dean's fans attribute to his agitated state onscreen. Much of Jimmy's inner torment came from the early demise of his mother. "He talked a lot about the fact that his mother had died and left him," said Arlene Lorca, an actress friend in New York. "He said he never knew what he had done wrong to deserve losing [her] and that's where the guilt feelings came from."

During Actors Studio classes, Strasberg sensed that Dean was on a destructive course. "I always had a strange feeling there was in Jimmy a sort of doomed quality."

Yet, Strasberg did not believe that Dean channeled his emotions properly, and took particular offense to the fact that the young actor didn't solicit the celebrated teacher's advice: "He was sensitive about letting people in too close. He seemed to shy away from people. He was afraid they would get to know him."

But Dean didn't trust Strasberg and was unwilling to blindly embrace his viewpoints just because others had anointed him as a master. To his good friends, Jimmy was the kid he'd been in Indiana—friendly and forthcoming. "He was willing to turn himself inside out to show people who he was," Liz Sheridan said. "And I think that's one of the reasons the world fell in love with him so. Because he was so vulnerable and easy to see."

It was in New York that Dean began to preach to friends about *The Little Prince* as if it were the gospel. When he discussed the book, Dean was neither shameful nor self-effacing, but empowered by his favorite passages:

"All grown-ups were once children . . . but only few of them remember it."

"What we're looking for could be found in a single rose."

"Eyes are blind. You have to look with the heart."

To fortify himself against the difficult personalities he'd meet in the industry, Jimmy would remind himself of one of the most useful lines in the novella:

"I must endure the presence of a few caterpillars if I wish to become acquainted with the butterflies."

A particularly bright light in the actor's life arrived in the form of Jane Deacy. Almost from the moment he met the agent at her New York office, there was a connection. She respected Jimmy's commitment to performing and truly believed that he had the talent to become a top star. Jimmy felt fortunate to find an agent who not only knew the significant players in New York and Hollywood, but also appreciated him as an artist and a person. Given his youth and the uncertainty of his life course, Jimmy was comfortable turning to her for personal as well as professional advice. At one point, Dean even moved into Jane's apartment.

As with Ortense Winslow, Jimmy began calling his agent "Ma."

But that didn't mean that he'd forgotten about his aunt and uncle. Jimmy thought about home often and made it a point to keep track of the Winslows' birthdays, so he could send the family cards. Looking for an excuse to visit his relatives, he decided that he needed a motorcycle to get around the city and made a quick trip to Indiana, where he stopped at the Carter motorcycle shop and traded in his beloved Czech Whizzer for a larger bike. Markie was painting with watercolors at the time, and Jimmy encouraged his younger cousin to express himself through art.

It was cold when Dean left Fairmount, and he tried to insulate himself with a leather jacket and a homemade, black face mask with slits for the mouth, nose, and eyes. He crossed Ohio without incident, but in Pennsylvania, the motorcycle broke down. Rolling into a bike shop, he told the owner his situation and was invited to stay at the man's home. For several days, he remained there, waiting for his agent to wire money and his uncle to send the proper title from Indiana.

Back in New York, Jimmy tried to remain close to the family. Marcus knew that even when Dean wasn't earning a great deal of money, he was applying the ethic he'd learned on the farm in Fairmount, always pushing himself forward. On occasion, the Winslows sent their nephew five or ten dollars. "That doesn't sound like very much now," Markie said in 2005. "But at that time, it meant a lot."

Jimmy also received periodic loans from Rev. DeWeerd, who—despite whatever transpired between them in Indiana—wanted to see Dean realize the ambitions he'd discussed while they were eating on fine china and watching bullfight movies in the pastor's home.

With each month, there was another landmark: an appearance on *The US Steel Hour*, a series of televised plays under the banner of its corporate benefactor; and a reading of Franz Kafka's *The Metamorphosis* at the Village Theatre.

Around Thanksgiving 1952, Jimmy spontaneously decided to visit Indiana another time, this time with Liz Sheridan and his friend Bill Bast. The three took a bus to New Jersey, then hitchhiked to Fairmount. Despite the fact that Jimmy was making a great effort to ingratiate himself into a theater community that could be pretentious and condescending to small-town transplants—and small-town mores—he seemed proud to show off his family and their farm. One day, he stopped by Fairmount High School and ended up teaching Adeline Nall's drama class, pantomiming a bullfight. By all accounts, everyone was having a great time when the

New York theater world interceded—in the best possible way. Over the telephone, Jane Deacy told Jimmy to come back to Manhattan and read for a part in the Broadway show *See the Jaguar*.

The role was that of Willy Wilkins, a sixteen-year-old boy whose abusive mother had kept him locked in an icehouse his entire life. After hitchhiking back to the city, Jimmy pored over the script and instantly felt an affinity for the character.

"To grasp the full significance of life is the actor's duty," he'd say of the challenge of making a portrayal a personal mission, "to interpret it his problem, to express it his dedication."

Jimmy passed the audition. The play opened on December 3, 1952, to grave reviews and closed three days later. But even the harshest critics were effusive in their praise of Dean. The *New York Post* characterized his performance as "believable and unembarrassing." The *New York Herald Tribune* called him "extraordinary."

While everything else about the play was dismal, Jimmy had starred on the Broadway stage and been vaulted into a new category. For the next year, Jane Deacy was able to procure so much work for Dean that his credits from this period are almost too vast to mention. On the stage, he appeared off-Broadway at a Theater de Lys production of *The Scarecrow*. On television, he was featured on such programs as *The Kate Smith Hour:* "Hound of Heaven," *Treasury Men in Action:* "The Case of the Sawed-Off Shotgun," *Campbell Summer Soundstage:* "Life Sentence," and *Omnibus* with Jessica Tandy, Carol Channing, and Alistair Cooke.

"Once, when we were walking down the street after he had done a TV show, we met some other actors," Arlene Lorca said. "They congratulated Jimmy on his performance. He stuck his hands in his pockets and mumbled something. Later, I asked him why he was so rude. 'I felt guilty that I was working and they weren't.'"

Up until this point, Dean's relatives in Indiana had managed to function without the distraction of television. But since Jimmy was now too busy to visit them, Marcus and Ortense purchased one of the first sets in

Fairmount. His grandparents, Emma and Charles Dean, soon bought a television, as well. "The old grapevine got going," Emma said, whenever Jimmy was scheduled to appear on a show. "They'd announce it in school and the neighbors would come streaming in to watch."

Largely because of Dean, television became a part of the culture in Fairmount. Instead of reading, talking, or playing the piano after dinner, families were intoxicated by the medium. Residents would catch a glimpse of Jimmy on TV and "call our house to be sure we were watching," Markie told the Marion *Chronicle-Tribune*, "thinking maybe we didn't know he was on or something. And at that time, you didn't have portable phones you carried around everywhere. So when the phone rang, you got up in the other room and answered the phone. So you'd have to take turns, running back and forth to the phone."

Having only been exposed to people who passed through east central Indiana, Markie thought it was peculiar that the young man he regarded as a brother was on the same small screen as Milton Berle, Jack Benny, and Lucille Ball. Yet neither he nor anyone else in town ever envisioned a time when the bespectacled kid from Fairmount would become one of world's most recognizable figures.

13

NOT SATISFIED WHERE HE IS

After Dean traded in his Czech Whizzer, Fairmount bike shop owner Marvin Carter sold it. But when Jimmy began appearing on TV with regularity, the local entrepreneur had the feeling that he might have traded away a valuable piece of pop lore and bought it back.

Having already acquired the admiration of Broadway critics for his role in the short-lived *See the Jaguar*, Dean distinguished himself again in *The Immoralist*, playing an openly gay character, a manipulative Algerian houseboy who seduces a Frenchman on his honeymoon, creating doubts in the European's mind over his ability to sustain a "normal" marriage. In one scene, Dean danced across the stage in a robe, snipping at the air with a pair of scissors, as if he was cutting away at his lover's facade of heterosexuality.

In years to come, some would wonder whether this scene embodied Dean's defiance of the part he'd play as a Hollywood leading man, squiring beautiful women in front of the paparazzi, while methodically segregating himself from the conventions of the era with each homosexual encounter.

Had Dean decided to remain in New York, he likely would have become a giant of the stage. But on the opening night of *The Immoralist*, he announced that he was taking another direction. As fellow actors clamored around Jimmy to praise his performance, he gave his two-week notice to director Billy Rose, informing him that he was returning to Hollywood to star in Actors Studio director Elia Kazan's adaptation of *East of Eden*.

As Antoine de Saint-Exupéry wrote in *The Little Prince*, "No one is ever satisfied where he is."

In March 1954, with his clothes bundled into a brown paper bag, Dean took his first airplane flight, enjoying first-class accommodations in a seat next to Kazan. In Los Angeles, Jimmy was anxious to introduce the Academy Award–winning director to Winton. When the two met, though, Kazan noticed that Dean's father appeared unmoved by the fact that his son was realizing his dream of becoming a movie star.

It was then that the director was certain that he'd made the right choice, since Dean's Cal Trask character battles his own father in *Eden*. "He *was* Cal Trask," Kazan said. "There was no point in attempting to cast it better or nicer. Jimmy was it. He had a grudge against all fathers . . . a sense of aloneness and of being persecuted. And he was suspicious. In addition, he was tremendously talented."

On the set, there was a natural conflict with onscreen father Raymond Massey, a political conservative who'd openly support Republican candidate Barry Goldwater in 1964 and champion the Vietnam War. "He thought he was stiff and wooden as an actor," Jimmy's friend Lew Bracker says. "He said working with Massey was like working with the Frankenstein monster."

Like Jimmy, who tried to ingratiate himself to Winton by registering for prelaw classes and introducing him to Kazan, Cal can never gain his father's approval in *East of Eden*, leading to combustible exchanges that would tear at viewers' emotions. Interestingly, some of the outdoor scenes were shot in Salinas, where Jimmy was scheduled to race when his fatal accident occurred.

Because he was an unknown in the film community, reporters scrambled to uncover information about Dean. But Kazan isolated them from the actor by keeping a closed set. Still, scribes began describing Jimmy as the next Brando—to Dean's great dismay.

James Dean in 1938 at age seven, after his family relocated to Los Angeles. He would return to Indiana on the same train as his mother's coffin two years later. (Michael Ochs Archives/Getty Images)

In addition to acting, Dean excelled at basketball, once scoring a winning field goal at the buzzer as the Fairmount High School Quakers triumphed over rival Gas City. (Michael Ochs Archives/Getty Images)

With actress Betsy Palmer on an episode entitled "Death Is My Neighbor," part of the television anthology series *Danger*, in 1953, two years before the release of his first major film. (CBS Photo Archive/Getty Images)

MAY 24
WARNER THEATRE
10·30 A.M.

YOU WILL SEE JAMES DEAN

This young fellow will make a lasting impression. His name is

JAMES DEAN

and he becomes a new star in

ELIA KAZAN'S
PRODUCTION OF
JOHN STEINBECK'S

"EAST OF EDEN"

PRESENTED BY WARNER BROS. IN **CinemaScopE** WARNERCOLOR PRINT BY TECHNICOLOR WB

Director Elia Kazan correctly theorized that Dean's conflicted relationship with his father would enable him to portray misunderstood Cal Trask in *East of Eden*, an adaption of the John Steinbeck novel. (Mary Evans/Warner Bros./Ronald Grant/ Everett Collection)

With costars Richard Davalos and Julie Harris in *East of Eden*. Although it was Dean's first starring role, the *Hollywood Reporter* predicted that the young actor might soon be "accepted by young audiences as sort of a symbol for their generation." (Warner Bros./Getty Images)

Dean's timeless role as Jim Stark in *Rebel Without a Cause* has never been duplicated. Strangely, Dean and cast mates Natalie Wood, Sal Mineo, and Nick Adams would each meet tragic, premature ends. (Movie Poster Image Art/Getty Images)

With Wood and director Nicholas Ray on the *Rebel* set. Ray allowed Dean to direct himself, as well as the other actors. Observed cast mate Dennis Hopper, "He was doing things that were just so far over my head, I couldn't comprehend them." (Silver Screen Collection/Getty Images)

A PICTURE OF PROUD PEOPLE. A LOVE STORY. A CAVALCADE--A CONFLICT OF CREEDS--A PERSONAL DRAMA OF STRONG LONGINGS --A BIG STORY OF BIG THINGS AND BIG FEELINGS. THIS IS GIANT!

GIANT

GEORGE STEVENS' PRODUCTION

FROM THE NOVEL BY *EDNA FERBER* STARRING **ELIZABETH TAYLOR** IN WARNERCOLOR

ROCK HUDSON · JAMES DEAN

ALSO STARRING **CARROLL BAKER** · JANE WITHERS · CHILL WILLS · MERCEDES McCAMBRIDGE · SAL MINEO

SCREEN PLAY BY FRED GUIOL AND IVAN MOFFAT · PRODUCED BY GEORGE STEVENS AND HENRY GINSBERG · DIRECTED BY GEORGE STEVENS · RE-RELEASED BY WARNER BROS.

Top: Although he is said to have clashed with Rock Hudson on and off screen during the making of *Giant*, Dean formed a deep bond with Elizabeth Taylor. (Warner Bros./Getty Images)

Left: Despite his youth, Dean had expert command over his character, Jett Rink, who believably transforms into a middle-aged man by the end of the film. (Everett Collection)

In order to play Jett Rink effectively, Dean vowed to live "as a Texan" twenty-four hours a day while making *Giant*. He's seen here in a vintage roadster, petting a horse and balancing a cowboy hat on his feet. (Silver Screen Collection/Getty Images)

"I have my own problems," Lew said.

Dean was earning $1,000 a week and saving a lot of it, since the rent for his room above a drugstore opposite Warner Brothers' studio was fifty dollars a month. Across the hallway was his love interest in *Eden*, Lois Smith. Richard Davalos, who played Jimmy's brother in the film, was on the same floor.

Once again, it was Jane Deacy who'd placed Jimmy in this favorable position. Unfortunately, she didn't have an office in Los Angeles, so—while retaining all New York television and theater management—she arranged for Dick Clayton from the Famous Artists Agency to represent Jimmy on the Coast. Always maternal, Jane was thinking of Jimmy's personal as well as his professional needs.

Clayton had been a child actor and was sympathetic to the struggles Jimmy might encounter in Hollywood. He was good-natured, Bracker remembers, and available if Jimmy needed friendly advice: "He wasn't the kind of person you'd think of as an agent."

With money to spend, Dean purchased a used, 1953 red MG sports car and a Triumph Tiger T110 motorcycle. At Warner Brothers, he loudly drove the MG between the various soundstages, gleefully agitating Jack Warner, who'd forbidden his new commodity from riding the motorcycle there.

To Dean, the studio boss represented an entertainment landscape that threatened to become as mundane as some of some of the look-alike suburban communities being erected outside America's major cities. In 1954, the most popular recording artists included Doris Day, Eddie Fisher, and Perry Como, as well as groups like the Gaylords and the Crew-Cuts (although Bill Haley and the Comets also charted with "Shake, Rattle and Roll," rock 'n' roll was very much in its infancy). Bing Crosby appeared in two top-grossing films, *White Christmas* and *The Country Girl*. James Stewart, Gary Cooper, John Wayne, and Humphrey Bogart were among the biggest names in Hollywood.

Jimmy tended to like older movies. Among his favorites: *Tobacco Road*,

The Grapes of Wrath, All Quiet on the Western Front. Bracker recalls Dean bringing him to a theater that featured exclusively westerns, and another that specialized in silent films. Jimmy would watch these with rapt attention, then, while leaving the theater, talk more about the directing and cinematography than the acting. But he was intrigued by actors he considered kindred spirits, including Montgomery Clift—Jimmy reportedly sat through *A Place in the Sun* twice while living in New York, and was in the midst of his third viewing before he was willing to leave the theater— and Marlon Brando.

Slowly, Dean began to make friends in Los Angeles, including Sammy Davis Jr., who enjoyed watching his grandmother's interactions with the Hollywood newcomer. Sammy's grandmother would pretend to be mad, slapping Jimmy's hand away and telling him to mind his manners. Because they spent time away from other industry people, Davis believed that he and Jimmy had a particularly close relationship. "It was a good friendship because it was an honest friendship," he recounted. Even so, Davis was aware that there were other aspects of Dean's life that he didn't share.

After Dean's death, Sammy noticed that when he spoke about Jimmy with different people, each had his own distinct memories. In fact, one person's tales frequently bore little resemblance to another friend's anecdotes. "If you put it all together," Sammy said, "it almost sounds like you're talking about four or five different people."

Composer Leonard Rosenman characterized Jimmy as a chameleon, who was able to "obscure" his own traits while studying and absorbing the habits of others. Although Rosenman and Dean never discussed the subject, the composer told *Redbook* that he believed that Dean used his interactions with other people as a way to further his education about the human experience.

The two had become friends in New York after meeting at a party and getting into a conversation about little-known composers. Later, Rosenman gave Dean piano lessons. "Jimmy had what I'd call a chapter heading of knowledge," Rosenman said. "He knew a little about almost everything, but he was always trying to fill in the gaps."

When Rosenman was chosen to compose the score for *East of Eden*, their friendship continued in Los Angeles. Although they were just seven years apart, Rosenman believed that Dean occasionally looked to him to fill the void of both not growing up with Winton and having Marcus Sr. so far away. It was a role that Rosenman said that he wasn't prepared to play. The composer neither watched nor participated in sports, but Dean tried to persuade him to get together and play basketball. Apparently, Jimmy asked so often that Rosenman became annoyed and demanded to know why the activity was so important to the actor.

"Well, you know how a fella feels," Rosenman claimed that Dean answered. "You want your father to play basketball with you."

The exchange frustrated Rosenman. He emphasized that Winton Dean was still alive and in the same city as his son. "Why don't you call your father and ask him to play basketball with you?" Rosenman demanded. "I don't play basketball.'"

Eventually, Rosenman was introduced to Winton. In contrast to others who knew Jimmy, the composer described the father as "effusive and warm . . . If this was the real relationship with his father, the warm, loving kind of thing, I don't think he'd want to go out and play basketball with me."

Like Sammy Davis Jr. and Martin Landau, though, Rosenman took Jimmy along to gatherings with relatives. It was through Rosenman that Dean first met Lew Bracker, who lived just minutes from the studio, with his parents. The composer was married into the Bracker family—his wife was Lew's cousin Adele, a pianist—and, because they were the same age and shared an interest in cars, the composer correctly assumed that Lew and Jimmy would become friends.

The first time Rosenman brought the pair together, Bracker noticed how Dean listened intently whenever family issues were discussed, relating the stories to the pleasant memories of his own interactions with relatives in Fairmount. As the three ate lunch at Warner Brothers, Lew observed Jimmy slouching against the wall in the corner of the booth, with his leg up on the seat. Bracker later realized that this was the way that Dean sat when he felt at ease.

Initially, Jimmy was more of an observer. But as the conversation continued, Lew saw the actor's personality emerge. When Paul Newman entered the commissary dressed as a Roman soldier—he was making his screen debut in *The Silver Chalice*—Jimmy smiled and called him over. The pair knew each other from New York, where they'd both appeared on Broadway and studied at the Actors Studio. In fact, Newman had auditioned for the part of Cal Trask in *East of Eden*, but ended up being cast in the historical epic instead. As Jimmy listened, Newman described the film as mediocre—he'd later call it "the worst motion picture produced in the 1950s"—and seemed embarrassed by the role. "You win some, you lose some," Dean joked in a voice that could have been good-natured or sarcastic. "But you do look cute in that dress."

Rosenman and Jimmy also enjoyed talking about Jack Warner, who had a private dining room, at the studio where he'd invite both stars and executives too frightened to decline. "It's like musical chairs," Dean offered. "They fight over the chair on Jack's right and on his left."

The industry talk continued. Although Dean and Rosenman were clearly enthralled by the gossip, they were careful to include Bracker in the conversation. The young insurance salesman was curious about the origin of the term *green room*, the waiting area in a studio or theater that was traditionally painted green. Dean cracked that the room received its name because everyone in the industry was "jealous of everyone else."

Soon, Jimmy was calling the Bracker home regularly, inviting Lew to meet him at Warner Brothers or hang out at night. Besides their interest in cars, Lew and Jimmy had many things in common. Bracker was also born in a small town, Nogales, Arizona, on the Mexican border, where his father distributed local crops around the United States. Then, in elementary school, the family relocated to Los Angeles. Even though he didn't return to his small town, as Jimmy had, Lew retained a connection to a pastoral lifestyle, when his father purchased a ranch seventeen miles north of Santa Barbara. There, Lew rode horses and became as comfortable with nature as he'd be with people in the entertainment business.

"I'd had a lot of friends, in high school and in the army, but never a friendship like this," Bracker says, "where we were so close, where there was mutual trust, where we did things together all the time. We were even talking about going into business together in the future. It was really my first adult friendship. Jimmy roamed in and out of our house. We were like brothers, except we didn't have any rivalry."

In LA, Bracker had gone to school with kids who became actors, and his sister studied the craft and was friends with a number of Hollywood names. So when Jimmy visited the family, there were no questions about movie stars or requests to gain access to events where celebrities might be circulating.

"Jimmy liked our house because my mother made it a family," Lew says. "It was a traditional Jewish family, in that she was always cooking and baking. No one made any demands on Jimmy whatsoever. He was totally accepted. He came when he came and he went when he went. I felt like he would have adopted our family, if he could have."

While Dean was certainly a bohemian, in the Bracker household, he talked about the Winslows and his grandmother and the animals on the farm. When Rosenman was accused of having an affair, Jimmy exhibited what Bracker refers to as "a puritanical streak . . . from his Midwest years. He could be Hollywood or he could be the boy from Fairmount."

Jimmy could have spoken about anything with Lew, including his varied sexual tastes. But the topic of bisexuality didn't come up. In fact, Jimmy rarely, if ever, referred to his period in New York. "And I never asked," Lew said. "I think that's one of the reasons he didn't have his guard up with me. I was never going to pry."

As with Landau, Jimmy and Lew spent much of their time talking about girls. Interestingly, if Dean wanted a date with an actress, he'd ask Dick Clayton to set it up. "He didn't want to go out there in the cold," Lew recalls. "Most girls would have climbed through the phone to get a date with him. But he didn't like to call them direct. He was shy."

At times, at the Warner Brothers commissary, Lew would spot an attractive actress and mention it to Dean. But Jimmy never made an introduction, and Lew never requested one. "I could get my own dates."

Even so, Dean enjoyed mixing Lew with some of his more offbeat Hollywood friends, including Maila Numi, who—dressed in a sexy, low-cut outfit, with black wig and nails—called herself Vampira and hosted a local television show introducing horror movies. Once, Jimmy stormed into one of Vampira's parties, posing as a vice detective and patting people down. Although she was aware of her friend's true identity, Maila—who'd playfully remind her audience to have "a terrible week"—appeared completely entertained by the prank.

Both Maila and Jimmy claimed to have premonitions, little feelings about what might occur in the future. The two may have been drawn together because of their mutual interest in the occult; he told columnist Hedda Hopper that he was curious about whether Numi was somehow possessed by "satanic forces." Maila boasted of psychic abilities, and Jimmy—perhaps because of the loss of his mother—yearned to connect with something beyond the physical world.

Out of nowhere, he claimed, he'd have a strong feeling that someone was trying to communicate with him. There was something out there, something he needed to hear, something he needed to learn. Maybe, one day, he theorized, a medium would help him bond with that force that seemed to pull at him so strongly. Or maybe he'd find it through his art. Never did he think that he'd be the one on the other side—and it would be his fans who'd try to receive that knowledge from Jimmy, long after he was gone.

14

ATLAS HAD A LIGHTER LOAD

Jimmy's romance with actress Pier Angeli remains a source of debate among the various camps of James Dean devotees. Those who focus on his bisexuality describe the Sardinian-born actress—who won a Golden Globe for her lead role in the 1951 film *Teresa* and was working with Paul Newman on an adjoining soundstage in *The Silver Chalice*—as a beard whose relationship with Dean was orchestrated by a marketing machine that included his West Coast agent Dick Clayton and Warner Brothers publicists. But the people who really knew Jimmy insist that he had heartfelt feelings for Pier and wanted to build a future with her, combining their love of acting with the type of family life he romanticized from his years with the Winslows.

Pier had the kind of family that Jimmy craved: a twin sister who was also an actress, and a mother who appeared to be involved in her life. The notion of becoming part of a close-knit Italian clan was appealing to the Midwestern kid who made himself at home while visiting the families of Lew Bracker, Martin Landau, and Sammy Davis Jr. Pier gave Jimmy a St. Christopher medal, which he wore proudly. He brought Pier to visit Winton and his wife—the elder Dean apparently approved of this particular choice—and Jimmy even contemplated converting to Catholicism to satisfy his girlfriend's family. The two went so far as to discuss names of Catholic saints after whom they could name their children. When he told

Jane Deacy about his desire to marry Pier, his trusted agent reminded Jimmy of his youth and blossoming career and advised him to wait.

But, just as Dean was more complex than the farm boy who coveted a nice, Italian wife, Pier's mother wasn't the type who invited neighbors into her home for sweet ricotta cheesecake on Easter. Ultimately, she was a calculating stage mother and didn't think Jimmy was the proper Hollywood husband. He was neither Catholic nor an adherent of conventional male fashion. Pier's studio, MGM, which had loaned her to Warner Brothers for *The Silver Chalice*, was equally disapproving and reportedly conspired with Pier's mother to break up the courtship.

One night, Bracker was babysitting for his younger cousins when Jimmy stopped by and laid out the situation. Things had gotten so bad that Pier and Jimmy could no longer go out in public. If anyone spotted them together, it was immediately reported back to MGM. The only safe place for them was Jimmy's dressing room. Even so, Pier's mother suspected that her daughter was disobeying the order to stay away from Dean.

"Her mother hates me," Dean confessed. "I'm everything she doesn't want in a son-in-law."

Then, exhibiting his signature half smile, he told Lew, "Atlas had a lighter load."

In time, the actress surrendered to the pressure. After *Eden* wrapped in August 1953, Dean went back to New York to appear on an episode of *The Philco Television Playhouse*. When he returned to Hollywood two weeks later, Pier told him that they should start seeing other people.

For a period of time, the pair continued to meet. But Pier's handlers had created the obstacle they needed. At times, Jimmy was told to escort an actress to a premiere, simply to keep his name in the public eye. In September, he was photographed attending the opening of the film *Sabrina* with Terry Moore, who'd been nominated for an Oscar for Best Supporting Actress for her role in *Come Back, Little Sheba* in 1952. As flashbulbs popped, Terry smiled widely, more conscious of the photographers than her date. Sporting a tuxedo, with Terry's arm intertwined in his, Jimmy looked like he'd rather be anyplace else in the world.

"What do you think of Terry Moore," a reporter asked.

"She keeps a clean dressing room," Jimmy replied, hoping to at least amuse himself in an uncomfortable situation.

Eventually, Pier married singer Vic Damone, a well-groomed, polite Italian-American who'd sung in the choir at St. Finbar's Roman Catholic Church in Brooklyn, and knew Jimmy from the Villa Capri. It was a powerful blow that Jimmy didn't take well. The ceremony took place at St. Timothy's on West Pico Boulevard, the very church where he and Pier had discussed getting married. It's become part of the Dean folklore that Jimmy sat across from the sanctuary on his motorcycle, glumly watching the paparazzi photograph the wedding party. Given Dean's posthumous image as a lonely outsider, it's a scene that's easy to visualize. Whether it really occurred is anyone's guess.

Meanwhile, he continued working steadily. In late 1954 he appeared alongside Natalie Wood—his future costar in *Rebel Without a Cause*—and Eddie Albert in *General Electric Theater:* "I'm a Fool," and with Ronald Reagan in *General Electric Theater:* "The Dark, Dark Hours." In the latter production, Dean plays a finger-snapping "hep-cat" who shows up at the home of Reagan, a country doctor, with a wounded friend. At one point, Jimmy engages in the following exchange with the future president, while holding a gun on him and demanding that he perform delicate surgery.

"Oh, no, no, no, Doc. Now, you take out that bullet and stop talking."

"I'm not a surgeon."

"Well, fake it, Dad."

Reagan would remember Dean as "an intelligent young actor who seemed to live only for his work. He was completely dedicated and, although a shy person, he could hold a good conversation on many wide-ranging subjects."

On March 9, 1955, *East of Eden* premiered at New York's Astor Theatre.

An audience comprised almost exclusively of entertainment luminaries sat mesmerized through the first scene, with Dean's Cal Trask character longingly watching his birth mother walk from a bank to the brothel she runs. Once she disappears, he tries forcing his way through the door. When a bouncer stops him, he emits a primal plea, "I just want to talk to her!" Then, turning to the doorman: "You tell her I hate her."

From that moment, James Dean was a bona fide movie star.

To witness this piece of cinematic history, viewers had paid the robust fee of fifty dollars a seat, with the proceeds going to benefit the Actors Studio. Among the celebrity ushers was another Lee Strasberg disciple, Marilyn Monroe. But after initially flying to New York to do advance work, Dean had traveled home, too nervous to sit in the audience at the most critical point of his career.

He might have been more comfortable at a special Tuesday morning screening at the Indiana Theatre in his birthplace of Marion, Ohio. Even before the film was shown—to a special audience that included the Winslows; Jimmy's drama teacher, Adeline Nall; and the senior class of Fairmount High School—*The Fairmount News* was lavishing the production with high praise.

"Homefolks . . . won't be disappointed if they are looking to find a splendid performance and magnificent interpretation by Jimmy," the newspaper predicted. "Fairmount's star has been compared to Marlon Brando and this writer can see some faint similarity between the two. But Dean's is a warmer personality, one that projects itself with a freedom of action that keeps moviegoers on the edge of their seats. . . . Packed houses have seen *East of Eden* every place it has played and, in our opinion, this will be true from Fairmount to Timbuktu."

"Oh, it was something," Markie recalls. "It didn't really seem like he was acting. It just seemed like it was Jimmy up there, and I just couldn't believe that he was in the biggest part of the picture. Right at the very start of the movie, they showed him. It was very surreal."

Nall was similarly enthralled, noting how her former student's "spontaneous laugh" stood out in a way that was "so very natural. It was one of the traits I'd noticed throughout school."

Ann Warr was one of the first Fairmount residents to purchase a ticket. "The film really hit me," says the ninety-three-year-old town historian, turning up her hearing aid. "I was born on a two-hundred-acre farm, not a hospital, so I understood the ways of the [farm] family in the movie. When Jimmy cried, I could feel it. We all could feel it. There were tears in my eyes, and everyone in the theater had tears in their eyes."

Dean did have his share of critics, who didn't understand why he had to slouch on camera or mumble his words. But a larger percentage of viewers accepted the way he chose to redefine his art. Said the *New York Herald Tribune*'s William K. Zinsser, "Everything about Dean suggests the lonely, misunderstood (character). Even from a distance, you know a lot about him by the way he walks—with his hands in his pockets and his head down, slinking like a dog waiting for a bone. When he talks, he stammers and pauses, uncertain of what he is trying to say. When he listens, he is full of restless energy. . . . Occasionally, he smiles unaccountably, as if at some dark joke known only to him. . . . You sense the badness in him, but you also like him."

The *Hollywood Reporter* went even further, characterizing Dean as "that rare young thing, a young actor who is a great actor, and the troubled eloquence in which he puts over the problems of a misunderstood youth may lead to his being accepted by young audiences as sort of a symbol for their generation."

Jimmy hadn't gone to Hollywood to solicit these types of reviews but to realize something in himself. Now that he'd accomplished the task in his first major film, he braced for the backlash—from actors who'd been laboring for years to receive a modicum of the acclaim that the charismatic Hoosier was receiving. Lew Bracker remembers the mood shifting when he'd be socializing with Dean in public. Although no one said anything directly to Jimmy's face, both could sense a "storm of jealousy."

Stories began appearing that Dean was difficult on the set and uncooperative with the media that helped the studios manufacture their marquee names. "I don't understand him at all," an unnamed source was quoted in *Movie Stars Parade*. "Who does he think he is? . . . He isn't even a star yet. And maybe he won't be."

But, although not yet a household name, Jimmy had become a star, and there was little fear that his visibility would falter. Shortly after the release of *Eden*, Bracker noticed the difference when he'd drive around Los Angeles with Jimmy, and strangers would pull up near them and point.

Uncomfortable with living so close to the studio, and the influence of Jack Warner, Jimmy had moved into a small apartment above a garage in Dick Clayton's Hollywood Hills home. The actor was at ease there and would invite friends over to listen to records. At the time, Jimmy was particularly fond of Burl Ives, dubbed "America's Troubador," whose style of folk music would morph into protest songs in the 1960s. He was also a fan of Nat King Cole and took Lew to see him perform.

It was a small venue, and Jimmy appeared charmed by the way Cole interacted with his fans. At one stage, a member of the audience shouted, "Too Young," a reference to the singer's million-selling hit.

"Too loud!" Cole fired back.

Jimmy laughed; it was the kind of comeback he wished he'd come up with himself.

15

GREATNESS IN HORN-RIMMED GLASSES

E ven before *Eden* debuted, Jimmy was preparing for his next and most famous role, in *Rebel Without a Cause*. Assuming that his cast had devoted much of their young lives to pursuing the dramatic arts, director Nicholas Ray arranged for them to take juvenile delinquency workshops, while the wardrobe department soiled hundreds of pairs of jeans for the lead actors and extras.

Ray had become intrigued by the topic of juvenile delinquency following the success of other movies on the topic. But rather than making an exploitation film centered around lust and violence, the director attempted to portray sensitivity in his characters, the way, he pointed out, William Shakespeare had in *Romeo and Juliet*, "the best play written about juvenile delinquents."

In reality, Warner Brothers had been interested in doing a version of *Rebel* for nearly a decade, based on a 1944 study of a young inmate serving time in the Lewisburg Federal Penitentiary in Pennsylvania. At one point, after the studio purchased the screen rights in 1947, Marlon Brando was offered the lead role, but turned it down. The project appeared to have been abandoned until Ray became involved.

Dean had been so busy that he almost had to bypass the opportunity to appear in *Rebel*, having already committed to *Giant*. But when costar Elizabeth Taylor became pregnant, the film was delayed, freeing up Jimmy for his most illustrious part.

The first time that Bracker was invited to the *Rebel* set, he noticed that Jimmy had set up two director's chairs away from everybody else, as if to send a message that they were not to be disturbed. Despite his growing fame, Jimmy needed to feel grounded, even at the studio. While others had begun asking him for favors, Bracker never did. In fact, it was always Dean who requested that Lew join him at the studio.

"Jimmy trusted so few people," Lew says. "So when he'd call and ask me to come over to the studio, I knew he just wanted to talk to someone close, to shoot the breeze. I knew he was bored to death, sitting there, waiting for the hours to pass."

So many of the young performers in *Rebel* would move on to celebrated careers in Hollywood, including Wood, Nick Adams, Sal Mineo, and Dennis Hopper. Much of the on-camera interactions were physical, with the actors hugging, kissing, and grabbing one another to beg for understanding. Reportedly, both Wood and Mineo felt physically attracted to Jimmy, although these fantasies were never realized. Nonetheless, each grew into adulthood with loving memories of the brooding icon.

"It was like a family, and everyone became very tight," Mineo said. "It was almost like a spiritual experience . . . and mainly Jimmy was the focus of it, and we all grew around him."

As the leader of the young group, Jimmy was constantly "testing people," Mineo said, "testing to see how far he could push someone. And if someone stood up to him, he dug it. He respected that."

Wood—whose five-minute crying sequence in the movie would shatter Bette Davis's record in the 1948 film *Winter Meeting*—described Jimmy as "moody and poetic" on the set. "All of us were touched by Jimmy," she said in *James Dean Remembered*, "and he was touched by greatness."

Up until this point, Wood was known as a child actress, best remembered for her role as the little girl who finds the true spirit of Christmas with the help of a department store Santa Claus in *Miracle on 34th Street*. In subsequent years, she was assigned daughter roles in such movies as *Dear Brat*, *Father Was a Fullback*, and *No Sad Songs for Me*. But playing opposite Dean in *Rebel*, she maintained, was "the biggest turning point of my career."

In some ways, Wood saw Jimmy the way his friends in Fairmount knew him: jocular and kind. But, as an actress, she related to the artist in him: "He was a genius, but he never lost his common touch. . . . He had so much to offer, not only as a performer but a person, that everyone who had the privilege of knowing him grew to love him.

"He was greatness in horn-rimmed glasses."

Like Pier Angeli, Natalie was the product of a foreign-born stage mother. The child of Russian immigrants, Natalie had a sister, Lana Wood, who was also an actress. When she was a little girl, Natalie's mother told her that the cameraman pointing his lens at the audience at the end of Paramount newsreels was actually looking at her. Given her background, there was concern that she seemed too innocent to play Judy, the girlfriend of Dean's character, Jim Stark, in *Rebel*. But during the casting process, Natalie, Hopper, and some other teen actors were involved in a car crash that obliterated her previous image. An oft-told tale involves Nicholas Ray coming down to a Van Nuys police station to pick up Wood and hearing an officer refer to her as a "juvenile delinquent."

If the story is true, Natalie then asked the director, "Now, do I get the part?"

Of course, one would have to wonder why, of all the people in Los Angeles, Ray was the one being summoned to the station house. According to at least one biography of the starlet, she was engaged in an affair with the director when she was sixteen and he was forty-three.

Regardless, Ray believed that Natalie had graduated from little girl roles, and possessed the combination of sensuality and underlying sweetness that Judy needed (when Jayne Mansfield did a screen test for Wood's part, the director was so sure that the bombshell was the wrong choice that he reportedly saved money by not placing film in the camera). Likewise, when the director learned that Mineo—the son of Sicilian coffin makers, who'd played the young prince in *The King and I* on Broadway—

had been expelled from his high school in the Bronx, Ray concluded that the exotic young man was suited to play Jim Stark's troubled and fawning sidekick, Plato.

Although he played a minor character in the movie, Nick Adams was very much at home on the set. Born in Nanticoke, Pennsylvania, Nick was the son of a Ukrainian-born coal miner who eventually moved the family to Jersey City, where he worked as an apartment building janitor. Because of the proximity to Manhattan, Nick would roam around New York City and, at age seventeen, happened into an audition, where he was befriended by Jack Palance, whose father was also a Ukrainian coal miner in Pennsylvania. It was Palance who told the teen to anglicize his name—from Adamshock—and sent him to a junior theater company. While still in the coast guard, Adams used his accumulated leave time to play a sailor in the film *Mister Roberts*. After his discharge, his agent secured the role in *Rebel*.

He and Jimmy already knew each other, after meeting on the set of the Pepsi commercial five years earlier in Griffith Park. Along with Natalie and Sal, Nick was one of the few good friends Dean had in the movie industry. Some nights, Jimmy would phone Nick and ask him questions about his mother. The death of Mildred Dean had left such a wide gap in Jimmy's life, Nick concluded, that conversations about a loving mother—particularly one lending emotional support to a son in the dramatic arts—somehow soothed him.

"We would talk until dawn," Nick told *Movie Life* magazine. "He used to ask me about my relatives back in Pennsylvania, about their farm and everything about them. Then, he would tell me about his uncle's farm in Indiana and his grandfather, who he thought was the greatest. He thought all his relatives were the greatest, and he was very proud of them."

By Adams's admission, he and Jimmy were not best friends, but their relationship was a caring one. Once, Dean noticed Nick wearing a Mexican peasant shirt on location and complimented his fellow actor. "Do you want it?" Nick asked.

"I don't want to take your shirt from you."

"It's okay. I can get another shirt from wardrobe to wear home. And I have another shirt at home just like this."

"You really mean it? You sure you really have another one at home? I don't want to take it if you don't have another one."

Recalled Adams, in *Movie Life* magazine, "I gave him the shirt and I never saw him happier. . . . No one has ever thanked me for anything the way he thanked me for that shirt. He kept saying, 'Gee, Nick, no kidding, thanks a million.' He even threw his arms around me and was so touched by what I had done that I thought he was going to cry. . . . A small thing like that meant more to Jimmy than attending all the elite parties in the world."

On the set, Nick and Jimmy would entertain the other actors during breaks, imitating people in the industry. Dean also joked about doing a nightclub act with Adams after the movie was released.

One day, while eating in the commissary at Warner Brothers, Jimmy challenged Adams, "Want to see everybody look at me?"

When Adams nodded, Dean ate his lunch with a cracker in each eye.

Nick described Jimmy as a person who'd go to any length to humor a friend, including jamming carrot sticks in his ears in a restaurant. "If people happened to be depressed . . . around Jimmy, he could always make them feel better by seeing the funny side of their troubles."

His extroversion, however, was balanced by a pensive side that sometimes saw Jimmy withdraw from conversation, playing the bongos and listening to music in his dressing room, as a friend sat nearby in silence.

"A VERY REAL PART OF HIM"

In *Rebel Without a Cause*, Jim Stark appears trapped between the bullies at school—who terrorize him and his friends, luring them further and further into dangerous predicaments—and his parents, who are too concerned with appearances and antiquated values to nurture or help their son. While hiding from the world in an old mansion, Jim and Judy act as mother and father to Plato. But the surrogate family is under siege. Eventually, their enemies and police close in on them, with heartbreaking results.

"I try to imitate life," Dean explained in an interview conducted to promote the movie.

> The picture deals with the problems of modern youth. . . . Parents are often at fault, but the kids have some work to do, too. . . . You've got to show what it's really like, and try to reach (young people) on their own grounds. You know, a lot of times an older boy, one of the fellows the young ones idolize, can go back to the high school kids and tell them, "Look what happened to me. Why be a punk and get into trouble with the law? Why do these senseless things just for a thrill?" I hope *Rebel Without a Cause* will do something like that.

As in *East of Eden,* Dean's character is in conflict with his father. The difference is that, while Ray Massey appears stern and unbending in *Eden*, the father in *Rebel*, Jim Backus—the voice of *Mr. Magoo*, and the future Thurston Howell III on *Gilligan's Island*—is frightened and weak—so much so that, in one climactic scene, Jim Stark hurls him onto the ground and chokes him.

In Lew Bracker's own book, *Jimmy & Me*, Dean's friend makes a parallel between Winton and Jim Backus's Frank Stark: "I understand that Winton was not a strong person. . . . I think that Winton bent with the wind and that was why he shipped Jimmy off to Indiana when his wife, Mildred, died. . . . As I write these paragraphs, it suddenly occurs to me that this was the core problem between the son and the father in *Rebel Without a Cause*! The son was stronger than the father, and the son was anguished that his father was not a stand-up guy."

According to Wood's estimation, Jim Stark "was trying to make the parents into people he could love and into people who could help him."

Ray had made an effort to familiarize himself with Dean before shooting began, meeting some of the actor's friends and getting drunk with him a few times. Once filming started, the pair occasionally rehearsed one-on-one in the director's bungalow. Because of their symmetry, Ray was relaxed when Jimmy improvised on set, confident that Dean was reaching into himself to find things that the script's writers never foresaw.

"When an actor plays a scene exactly the way a director orders, it isn't acting," Dean said. "It's following instructions. Anyone with the physical qualifications can do that. So the director's task is just that—to direct, to point the way. Then, the actor takes over. . . . Without that space, an actor is no more than an unthinking robot with a chest-full of push-buttons."

Because of his friendship with Ray, Jimmy felt a greater obligation to bring his acting to a different level. He'd later say that he could "never take so much out of myself again."

Before one scene, Dean lay down on the ground in the fetal position, as the other actors watched in bewilderment. But when Ray called for action, Jimmy stood and performed perfectly.

While Dean appeared "strange," in the words of his onscreen mother,

Ann Doran, she and other seasoned hands on the set acknowledged that he added qualities to *Rebel* that they hadn't encountered before. Both cinematographer William C. Mellor and Jim Backus were awestruck by the actor's instincts. Backus also asserted that he'd never seen an actor with the same degree of concentration: "The lines were simply not something he had memorized. They were actually a very real part of him."

Doran took the observation a step further, asserting that Jimmy not only directed himself, but much of the cast.

"He was doing things that were just so far over my head, I couldn't comprehend them," Hopper admitted in a 1983 interview with New York director and author John A. Gallagher.

Like Hopper, Mineo had grown to idolize Jimmy. But the adulation was mixed with fear. Mineo claimed that there were times when he was "terrified" of Dean. Jimmy was capable of being "totally awful" on the set, Mineo said, refusing to greet his co-star or engage in conversation for reasons the younger actor couldn't fathom.

"Of course, I felt rejected," Mineo said in *James Dean Remembered*. "And I'd say, 'What did I do wrong?'" This was aggravated by the fact that Mineo was only sixteen years old and "very impressionable and very sensitive. If he didn't say 'good morning' to me, I was a wreck the whole day."

At other times, Dean could be effusively warm, seeking out Mineo and placing an arm around the New Yorker as they spoke. "That was fabulous, "Mineo said. "Because then, I knew he meant it."

"Here was a chance for me to feel what it would be like for someone close, someone that I idolized to be grieving for me, for me to experience what kind of grief that would be," Mineo said. Although they were acting, Mineo felt like Jimmy was legitimately being protective of him. Both actors seemed to be "moved" by the scene, Mineo said, noting that wherever he went on the set that day, Dean appeared to be nearby. "I wanted to do that scene over and over again. . . . It felt nice."

A DESPERATE DESIRE TO WIN

The family dynamics in Jimmy's first two movies conjured up feelings about his own childhood, and while he was still making *East of Eden*, he followed the lead of other actors he knew and began going to therapy—sometimes as often as three times a week. The process seemed to help the performer shed some of his insecurities. "I don't think that, inside, Jimmy thought he was interesting," said Stewart Stern, author of the *Rebel Without a Cause* screenplay. "That's why he tried to fill his life up with so much, to make himself more interesting."

Like Dean, his therapist, Werner Muensterberger, enjoyed slipping into often contrasting worlds, socializing with scientists, power brokers, and artists. He considered Walt Disney, Pablo Picasso, and Andy Warhol friends. Besides Dean, Muensterberger treated future vice president Nelson Rockefeller.

Both psychoanalyst and patient suffered the loss of a mother early on—Muensterberger at age fifteen, inducing what he described as a "reactive depression"—and were bisexual. And, just as Dean spoke of getting married and raising a family, the therapist wed on three separate occasions. Each could relate to uprooting himself from the place where he felt most at home. In Muensterberger's case, that was in the western German region of Westphalia. Because of his Jewish heritage, Muensterberger had to be hidden by a girlfriend during the Nazi era. But he left

Germany two years after the war, building a new life and career in the United States.

Fortunately for Jimmy, Fairmount—and reminders of it—were never as far away.

When childhood friend Harold "Whitey" Rust visited Los Angeles, Dean made it a point to invite him to the *Rebel* set, reminding the visitor to ask security to guide him to Stage Number Eight. For the young Hoosier, the experience was unprecedented. He was staggered by the size of the studio and had a difficult time finding the soundstage. When he finally arrived at the location, filming was underway. Rust looked around the massive set in wonder.

Noticing his friend's bafflement, an amused Dean greeted Rust with a wide smile.

"Hold a lot of hay, wouldn't it?"

As he had with his cousin Markie, Dean fantasized aloud about importing Rust to Hollywood. When his schedule slowed, Jimmy promised, "I'll probably have a job for you."

Given their history, Rust never treated Jimmy as a star and was not shy about bringing up uncomfortable subjects—such as a concern about the hobby the actor appeared to be indulging on the West Coast.

"Be careful with that auto racing," Rust cautioned.

Dean had purchased his first Porsche—a white, 1,500cc, 356 Spyder Speedster convertible—while filming *Rebel*, intent on supplementing his days on the set with race-car driving. In some ways, the lifestyle reminded him of being a kid, flying through the cornfields on his motorcycle.

"Out there on the track and hanging out with the racing guys and mechanics," he said, pausing, then trying to find the words to describe his new companions, "I don't know, they're real."

Hours after he purchased the car, Jimmy stopped at the Chateau Marmont, the West Hollywood hotel modeled after a royal retreat in France's Loire Valley. There, he ran into actor Frank Mazzola, who played the character Crunch in *Rebel,* and offered him a ride up Laurel Canyon.

"He would go around blind curves," Mazzola told CNN in 2004. "I basically grabbed onto the little steel bar on the dash. And there was something weird that came in my mind. We got to the top of Mulholland Drive, and he hit some dirt and we slid. . . . It was right there at the edge of the mountain. And in my mind, this thing, it said, 'This guy's immortal. Nothing's going to stop him. . . . He's not going to die.'"

Nicholas Ray noticed Jimmy's passion for the sport and admired the way that the actor was channeling his energy. The director admitted to *Redbook* that he encouraged Dean to engage in auto racing. Ray believed that the competitions improved both Jimmy's focus and attention to detail.

At the same time, Ray was nervous about Dean getting on the track and competing against professionals. But Jimmy had been testing the Porsche with Bracker on the twists of Mulholland Drive and felt confident. On March 21, 1955, he took first place in a race in Pacific Palisades.

Although he was able to manage turns, Dean described his driving as "all over the place" and conceded that his goal was getting to the flag as quickly as possible.

Five days later, Jimmy was the winner again in the first phase of the Palm Springs Road Races, beating his closest opponent by three hundred yards and qualifying for the finals the next day. In the follow-up race, he came in second, earning the admiration of both spectators and fellow drivers.

While other actors may have viewed a race car as a new toy, Jimmy possessed legitimate skills. Still, he was inexperienced, and some drivers worried that—because he hadn't been in a serious accident—he lacked a certain vigilance on the track. One racer was quoted in *Redbook* as saying that Dean possessed a "desperate desire to win. Jimmy was a menace to himself and other drivers. He wanted to win too much and would take any kind of chance to be first."

Then again, this was the attitude that had catapulted him from farm boy to movie star in a relatively short period.

Despite *Rebel*'s demanding shooting schedule, Jimmy managed to enter another race on May 11, at Minter Field in Bakersfield. He came in third. But when he described the contest to Lew, Dean neglected to mention that he'd lost control of the vehicle and drove into a number of hay bales lining the course.

Perhaps Jimmy was embarrassed, since Bracker had begun racing, too, and Dean regarded them as partners. During one of Lew's competitions, Jimmy insisted on overseeing the pit crew and accompanying his friend for tech inspection, while the tread depth of the tires, lug nuts, coolant overflow tanks, and other components were examined. On another day, the actor went over Lew's house and gave him an autographed helmet.

"Now, I'll always be in the car with you," Dean promised.

Neither young man ever pretended that auto racing lacked hazards. But, to Jimmy, at least, the risk contributed to his sense of self-discovery. Plus, he argued, tracks tended to be safer than freeways, since the drivers all traveled in one direction—and were better skilled than the general population.

"The most dangerous part," he told Lew prophetically, "is driving to and from the track."

READY TO EXPLODE

N atalie Wood and James Dean would sometimes stop at a newsstand together, so Jimmy could comb through the pages of the gossip magazines, looking for stories about himself. "He would read them," she said. "He wouldn't buy them. He was fascinated."

Shortly before his death, Dean asked Lew to meet him at the Villa Capri. There, they were joined by agent Dick Clayton, who drove the pair an hour south to a Huntington Beach movie theater. When the lights dimmed, the friends sat in the rear of the building with Natalie and Nick Adams, along with a number of other actors and Warner Brothers executives. Suddenly, the studio's logo appeared on the screen.

It was a sneak preview of *Rebel Without a Cause*—a film Jimmy wouldn't live to see released.

If the executives were hoping to measure Dean's star power by audience reaction, they had their answer when Jimmy's name appeared on the screen and the teens in the crowd cheered. Lew was stunned. Not only were the girls screaming, but the boys applauded too.

Even at this early stage, James Dean was a teen idol.

By then, Jimmy had also completed his work on *Giant*. The movie was based on the best-selling Edna Ferber novel of the same name, inspired by "Diamond Glenn" McCarthy, the controversial Texas hotelier, oil tycoon, and media mogul. Out of every leading man in Hollywood, Dean had been chosen to play Ferber's McCarthy character, Jett Rink. Because the saga spans three generations, audiences would watch Rink transform into middle age.

This would be Dean's most challenging role, but he appeared to be ready for it. According to one movie magazine quote, he viewed "each succeeding part as better than the ones before. I must always do better. I must improve. I must grow with each year. There is no point in an actor's life when he must feel he has done his best. I always think that my best is yet to come."

Director George Stevens was at the height of his career. In the 1950s, he'd be nominated for the Academy Award for Best Director five times. In 1951, he'd won the prize for *A Place in the Sun*, starring Dean contemporary Montgomery Clift. Dean had studied Stevens closely. Shortly before working on *Giant*, Jimmy had asked Lew to join him at a screening of Stevens's 1939 adventure, *Gunga Din*, then repaired to the Villa Capri, where Bracker listened to his friend analyze virtually every shot.

While preparing for the role, Dean expressed a goal to dialogue coach Bob Hinkle: the actor wanted to "live like a Texan" twenty-four hours a day. During the period when the movie was being shot in Marfa, Texas, Hinkle made sure that Jimmy was always dressed in the attire of the region. When he was off set, he spent time with ranchers and other locals— a pleasurable endeavor for Dean, who always enjoyed being among people who reminded him of his relatives in Fairmount.

The weather was scorching, but Jimmy found ways to entertain himself. In her autobiography, actress Mercedes McCambridge fondly reminisced about a night when the two gorged themselves with junk food. In one sitting, she claimed, the pair consumed a box of crackers, jar of peanut butter, twelve Coca-Colas, and six Milky Way bars.

"He was original," Ferber noted in her own life story, *A Kind of Magic*. "Impish, compelling, magnetic, utterly winning one moment, obnoxious the next. Definitely gifted."

While Jimmy would give everything as an actor, he was acutely aware

that, as his celebrity increased, so did the legions of performers and critics waiting for him to fail. As a result, he was hesitant to let down his
guard. Close friend and *Giant* costar Elizabeth Taylor claimed that Jimmy
was resistant to revealing his true self, "in case it was turned around and
used against him."

In addition to Taylor and McCambridge, Jimmy was able to relax on
the *Giant* set with former *Rebel* cast mates Dennis Hopper, Nick Adams,
and Sal Mineo, who played a typically tragic role in the film—a Mexican-
American who proves his patriotism by signing up for World War II, only
to fall on the battlefield.

Previously, Jimmy had worked with directors who'd allowed him to im-
provise on camera. Stevens had a different perception about how a movie
should be filmed. In Dean's view, a George Stevens movie set was a to-
talitarian state. Stevens dictated every move that the actors made, even
demanding that they appear fully made up on days when they weren't
scheduled to perform. For an artist who pursued his craft because it allowed self-expression, this form of micromanagement was stifling. Jimmy
attempted to assert himself, but this only made Stevens tighten his control. At one point, the director chastised the actor in front of the entire cast.

In *Giant*, the grown-up Jett Rink violently clashes with Rock Hudson's
character, Bick Benedict. Off camera, there was almost as much tension between the actors. As an established star, Hudson may have found
Jimmy's acting philosophy subversive. And, as a closeted gay man, the
older performer is said to have been unnerved by Dean's free-spirited
attitudes.

"One thing that so fascinates about this era, the late forties and early
fifties, especially among the Hollywood elite, is that people lived much
more freely, sexually, than they do in our more conservative time," Mat-
thew Mishory, director of the 2012 film *Joshua Tree, 1951: A Portrait of
James Dean*, told *The Advocate*. "The great difference is that privacy still
existed, so they did so behind closed doors."

But the backstage stress was overshadowed by Dean's ability to convincingly portray Jett Rink from the brash maverick's youthful beginnings to his graying downfall. William C. Mellor, the cinematographer who also worked on *Rebel*, observed that each member of the cast and crew acknowledged that "not even the extreme adjectives of Hollywood" could sufficiently characterize the star's versatility in front of the lens.

"He knew more about acting than any other actor I've met," McCambridge told *Redbook*. "You can forgive a lot of things for talent, and Jimmy was bursting with it."

Concurred Taylor, "He was so bursting with brilliance and genius, I felt he would explode."

The actresses' assessment was not completely figurative. While filming *Giant,* Dean yearned to break away and blast around the banked corners of a speedway toward the checkered flag, as he had when *Rebel* was being filmed. But—after delaying *Giant* once, while Taylor gave birth—Stevens refused to risk losing any valuable shooting days to an auto injury and forbade Jimmy from racing while the movie was still in production.

Irritated by yet another George Stevens regulation, Dean found little ways to dissent. "I'd get set to shoot some cows in a scene in Texas and, suddenly, there was a red Chevrolet in their midst," Stevens said. "I knew without being told it was Jimmy."

But these acts of defiance could only temporarily satisfy the actor. By the time that the film was wrapped, Jimmy was ready to make the same kind of impression on the track as he had in cinema.

Shortly after midnight, on September 16, 1955, Hollywood police officer Eddie Guzak was radioed about a possible break-in at the Competition Motors dealership at 1219 North Vine Street. Guzak drove the two blocks to the location, where he spotted a shadowy figure vigorously shaking the chain-link fence.

When the police cruiser came into view, the person stepped back, placed his hands in his pockets, and began to slump away, moving to the left, then the right, as if to avoid the glare of the headlamps.

Guzak decided to question the man. But instead of encountering a shifty burglar, the officer found himself shining his flashlight on the mov-ie-poster- handsome features of James Dean.

Jimmy was polite and apologetic and had a reasonable explanation.

Competition Motors had recently imported the Porsche 550 Spyder. Jimmy had taken the solitary journey to contemplate the car and ponder the possibilities of himself behind the wheel.

BLOGGING FOR JIMMY

The smell of corn dogs wafts above the booths at the James Dean Festival. Families line up for the Ferris wheel and Super Slide. The Stars and Stripes waves, along with a few Confederate flags. As with other fairs in the Midwest, vendors sell chocolate-dipped cheesecake, elephant ears, and hot Wisconsin cheese.

At a table on Main Street, I meet a fellow New Yorker named Lenny Prussack, selling fifties keepsakes and greeting friends he knows in the Deaner community. The amusement rides imported into Fairmount are familiar to Lenny, who was raised within walking distance of the freak shows and Cyclone roller coaster in Coney Island. Lenny was five when Jimmy died but doesn't remember hearing about it. Nonetheless, the period that Dean would represent was one that Lenny later idealized.

"I was a big fan of the nineteen fifties," he says. "I liked the music. I liked the cars. I'd rather watch an old movie than a new movie. I have an older brother and sister, so I got dragged to all the Murray the K shows"—disc jockey "Murray the K" Kaufman, the self-professed "Fifth Beatle," regularly hosted concerts at Brooklyn's Fox Theater, featuring the Ronettes, Shirelles, Gene Pitney, Little Anthony & the Imperials, and other performers—"and the malt shop. It always looked like they were having such a good time. I got stuck there."

In 1980, he was living in Chelsea and working in the Garment Center when he heard about the James Dean Festival. In late September, he boarded a train to Indiana.

After his first trip to Fairmount, he didn't want to leave. "Having grown up in a city, I thought the whole world was crowded and busy and rushing. And to come here and find this pace of life, where you've just got to slow down and take your time and nobody's in a hurry, I never felt anything like it."

But he had commitments in New York and couldn't relocate immediately. "It wasn't instant," he says. "Amtrak used to go directly from Fort Wayne to Manhattan. There was one train a day. So I'd come out here, hang out, then get on the train overnight, end up in Manhattan, and go to work."

In fact, if it wasn't for his experiences in New York, Lenny might not have ever resettled in Fairmount. It was through his dealings in the Garment Center that Lenny met Dave Loehr. Together, they sold a successful line of rock 'n' roll clothing—a lot of spandex and leather print. But both shared a fascination for James Dean and the 1950s. With the money they made, Loehr invested in James Dean memorabilia, becoming a major collector. In 1987, he told Lenny about a plan to go to Fairmount and open the James Dean Gallery in a seven-room house in a leafy neighborhood at 425 North Main Street.

"He needed help, and I said, 'Yeah, I'll help you.' For a few years, I'd come out here for the summers, but the winters were kind of boring, so I'd go back to New York."

After twenty-five years in Manhattan, though, Lenny felt that he'd had his fill of the city of his birth and wanted to try a different lifestyle. He sublet his apartment for six months and gave Fairmount a chance. "I said, 'I'll see how I like it.' After six months, I loved it."

Eventually, Lenny and Dave became partners. Dave is the gallery's owner and archivist. Lenny owns the Rebel Rebel collectible shop inside the building.

With its large columned porch, the corner location can be mistaken for a funeral home, save for the life-size replica of Dean on the front lawn, in his red *Rebel Without a Cause* jacket. Throughout the day, tourists stop to pose with the facsimile. Inside the gallery, a paper bag has been preserved from a Marion grocery store, with the slogan "Grant County's Own James Dean in *East of Eden*...... Starts Easter Sunday." Visitors can also find a collection of old magazines featuring the actor on the cover, in Spanish, Italian, German, French, Hebrew, and English. A December 1, 1955, edition of the *Fairmount News* bears the headline, "Memorial of James Dean To Be Erected Today."

Emily Kauffelt circulates through the building, fresh from a six-hour drive from Pittsburgh, where she works at the Andy Warhol Museum. With her tie-dyed shorts and boots, she looks like she's still in New York, where she studied fashion design at Pratt Institute. At twenty-three, she doesn't have many friends who empathize with her feelings for James Dean. "But I do have a blog," she points out, "and it has a lot of followers, young people."

Interestingly, at the Warhol Museum, her interest receives acceptance, if not respect. Like Dean, Warhol had provincial roots—his parents were members of the small Lemko ethnic group from present-day Slovakia. And like Nick Adams, Warhol grew up with a father who worked in a Pennsylvania coal mine. When Warhol, the pop artist, considered the link between artistic expression and celebrity, one of the images he invoked was that of James Dean.

It was at Pratt where Emily first discovered the actor, while helping a friend with an assignment about 1950s themes. Out of curiosity, she rented *Rebel Without a Cause* and found herself relating to Jim Stark, "someone who was young and kind of confused and upset with the adult world." From there, she decided to read up on the real James Dean and concluded that she liked him, too.

"He had the same needs I do," she says, "to experience as much about life as possible, and different types of people. I don't want to be judgmental. I want to be open to everything. I've never seen another actor like him, a glamour icon who seemed so human."

As she studied photos of Dean, Emily detected an array of personality traits. She took it for granted that, as an actor, Dean was capable of projecting a variety of personas. But Emily didn't think of the man in the pictures as a performer portraying something he wasn't. Instead, she believed that she was looking at—and bonding with—a person just like her, whose countenance changed with the knowledge gained from each fresh encounter.

"He was kind of a chameleon," she says. "He adjusted to each situation. He was obviously attractive, but in an androgynous way. And that's why he has so many fans, all types of fans."

Before her latest trip to Indiana, Emily was planning on staying at a local inn. When she learned the facility was booked, though, she was put in contact with a fan on Henley Avenue. As soon as the woman on the other end of the phone realized that she was speaking with a fellow Deaner, Emily was invited to stay at a room in the follower's house.

Emily is happy with the arrangement. In Fairmount, no one ever thinks of her interest in Dean as peculiar. "My friends at home are used to it," she says. "But they still tell me I'm obsessed with a dead person. How can I answer that? If you've never loved something like this, you wouldn't really understand where I'm coming from."

The irony, of course, is that she has to go Fairmount to be embraced for something that the people in Pittsburgh and New York will never fully comprehend. In the Hoosier State, her friends consider themselves equally as "weird"—and possessed by the same question of what might have been.

"James Dean was about my age when he died," she says, "and he probably felt a lot like I do right now—on the brink of adulthood, but still very much a silly child. When you think about him, you wonder about the type of impact he would have had. But you also think about yourself. I mean, a lot of us have trouble growing up, and we wonder how it's going to turn out when we really become adults."

For Emily, the fact that Dean never became a middle-aged man—who learned to accommodate different industry types, or compromise his standards by agreeing to mediocre roles—endears him forever.

"He made three movies," she says. "Three great movies. You can watch them over and over, and you'll never be disappointed in him."

20

"YOU'LL BE DEAD IN A WEEK"

Even as Jimmy squabbled with George Stevens on the set of *Giant*, the actor was scrutinizing his nemesis. At times, Dean tried to envision what the celebrated director saw while creating a scene. When Stevens was abrasive on the set, Jimmy noted that, too. It was a mistake that he didn't intend to make.

By the time shooting was completed in October 1954, he had a long-term goal. One day, James Dean would be as vaunted a director as an actor. "For me," he said, "the only true success, the only true greatness, lies in immortality."

Having accomplished his mission to become a successful actor, Jimmy wanted to ascertain that his standing continued to grow. As his power expanded in Hollywood, he pledged, he'd never have to worry about the studio pushing him into the wrong picture or a role that weakened his reputation. All around him, he'd have a band of like-minded professionals devoted to enhancing, rather than diluting, the cinema arts. The most important person on that team would be the man he wanted as a producer, his friend Lew Bracker.

"He took it for granted that there was going to be a lot more fame and a lot more money," Lew says. "And he spent a lot of time thinking about what he could do with all that. I knew Jimmy. I knew what he wanted creatively, but I also knew that he didn't want the responsibility. He wanted someone that he could trust to do things the way he wanted them done."

For his part, Bracker was content selling insurance. He understood the Hollywood mentality, to an extent, and wasn't overly impressed with the industry. But he liked a good movie, and so did Jimmy. Dean spoke about a cinematic version of *The Little Prince*. And he and Lew laughed about their concept of a parody of the popular westerns seen in theaters and on television screens. It wasn't exactly *Blazing Saddles*, but when the film was released in 1974, Lew imagined Dean, rather than Mel Brooks, sitting in the director's chair.

It was always Jimmy who brought up the topic of the two working together, another reason that Bracker believes that his friend trusted him. Although Lew never inquired about the type of money that Jimmy was earning, Dean had asked about a will. He wanted the majority of his money to go to the Winslows, with a sizable amount put aside for Markie's education. He also wanted to ensure that his grandparents Emma and Charles Dean could live comfortably into their old age.

The two spoke about other businesses, too: a restaurant and a Porsche dealership to rival Competition Motors or Europa Motors in Studio City, the place where Bracker had purchased his red Speedster. Invariably, the two forgot about financial issues during these discussions, as they lost themselves conversing about the Porsche's design and performance.

Neither believed there was a better brand in the world.

The man whose name would be most closely associated with the automaker, Ferdinand Anton Ernst Porsche—known to his friends as "Ferry"—was born in 1909, on the day his father, Ferdinand Porsche Sr.—chief designer for the Austro-Daimler company—was taking first place in a race in Semmering, Austria. In 1931, when Ferdinand Sr. and two partners opened the first Porsche plant, Ferry was already engrained into the family business.

Three years later, the company made an important breakthrough, unveiling the Porsche (Model) 60, a compact, affordable family car approved by Adolf Hitler's National Socialist—or Nazi—regime. The name was eventually changed to Volkswagen—or "People's Car" in German. It was the start of a relationship that would later haunt the family. Because the Porsche company worked with Hitler to produce tanks and jeeps—along with race cars—during World War II, father and son were arrested by occupation forces after the Allies prevailed. Ferry paid a large fine—some would call it a ransom—for his freedom and moved the company to Austria. Ferdinand Sr. remained incarcerated until 1947 and was forced to help France's Renault company design its vehicles. By the dawn of the next decade, Ferry would shift operations back to Germany, where he continued marketing race cars and Volkswagen Beetles.

In 1950, the first three Porsches were exported to the United States. Although the 356 Speedster—the company's first sports car—was becoming well known in western Europe, Ferry needed American consumers to strengthen the company and allow it to grow. No one expected the 40-horsepower vehicle—with its slightly souped-up Beetle engine—to become a staple of the United States garage. But, at the cost of a Cadillac convertible, there was the feeling that the discerning American might covet a Porsche as a glamour vehicle.

Slowly, the approach began to work. In 1954, importer Max Hoffman was marketing eleven Porsches a week—up from the thirty-two he'd brought to the United States in all of 1951—in his Park Avenue showroom in New York. Eventually, about 70 percent of Porsche's yearly production would be devoted to the United States. Although the car was considered a graceful accessory to the wide boulevards of midtown Manhattan, in southern California, the sleek vehicles became part of West Coast freeway culture, a remarkable achievement for a company that hadn't shipped a single auto west of the Mississippi River before 1951.

Many of the most enthusiastic buyers were former American servicemen who associated the lustrous cars with the exotic women they'd encountered during their adventures in the European theater. Lew Bracker, for instance, loved the brand, during an era when Jewish-Americans—particularly veterans, like himself—were reticent about buying German products.

"It never occurred to me," he says. "The car was a machine. Porsche was almost a cult in LA. It was revolutionary. The engine was in the back. It looked like an overturned bathtub. It had fantastic cornering ability and a relatively small engine compared to Italian and British cars. Yet, it could whip the hell out of them on corners. And, in the early fifties, Porsche had almost an underdog role in racing, so it was easy to get behind it."

It was Bracker who enlightened Jimmy to the wonders of the automobile—by trading in a large Buick Century convertible for the quirky car. From that point forward, Porsche became one of Dean's fixations. After swapping his own MG for the Speedster Super 1500, Jimmy was known to talk endlessly about the reverse-camber rear wheels, air-cooled, non-radiator engine, and aerodynamic design. As much as Lew liked Porsches, he was taken aback by the austere interior of Jimmy's car—with its plastic curtains instead of windows and a knob on the floor to heat the car with hot air from the exhaust. Bracker noticed that the Speedster lacked not only a radio, but also a clock and gas gauge. But, as Jimmy steered the car back from lunch at a Malibu café one afternoon, Lew had the sense that the pair were rocketing into the future, particularly when he noticed Dean monitoring a tachometer—measuring the engine revolutions per minute—rather than the traditional speedometer.

Soon, the two were driving their Porsches side by side around the turns on Mulholland Drive—late at night, when the road was relatively empty—impervious to the concept of danger.

On Memorial Day weekend, 1955, Jimmy was racing again in Santa Barbara, but, this time, he fell short of his previous success on the track. Intent on winning, Dean shifted his attention away from the tachometer. He was in fourth place when he blew a piston. Not only was he forced to drop out of the race, but the engine would also have to be rebuilt.

Still, he wasn't the least bit discouraged. Now that he had the resources to indulge his hobby, he vowed to acquire the fastest car available. After acquiescing to Warner Brothers's suggestion that others drive him around during the filming of *Giant*, Jimmy was ready to purchase the 550 Spyder.

Bracker remembers the phone call he received from Jimmy after the actor first spied the car through the fence at Competition Motors, the night he was almost arrested.

"I just saw it," Dean said breathlessly.

Later, Lew would recall that Jimmy seemed to be in a rush to end the conversation. Bracker's conclusion: Dean was tired of talking about the 550 Spyder. He needed to buy it and maneuver it onto a racetrack.

"Of course, he crashed, like a lot of us did," fellow driver Joe Playan said in a 2005 National Geographic Channel program about the actor's final hours. "But he always wanted something faster. And the faster he got, the more problems he had, until he got the 550 Spyder."

The car—modeled after a number of personalized vehicles built by Frankfurt-based driver and auto dealer Walter Glöckler—utilized a ladder-style frame more compatible to a tractor than a race car. Taking advantage of aerodynamics and other factors, the 550 was specifically designed to pull everything it could out of its tiny engine—reaching speeds of 124 miles per hour. To lower the center of gravity, the axles were attached to the top, rather than the bottom, of the frame. Anticipating the need for the driver to stop quickly, Porsche equipped the car with extra-wide brakes. But perhaps the most notable innovation was bolting—rather than permanently welding—the center cross member into place, allowing for quicker engine maintenance during a race.

Almost immediately, the 550 Spyder began to overshadow its adversaries. At the one thousand kilometer contest at Nurburgring, Germany in 1953, it defeated competitors from Jaguar, Maserati, and Ferrari. The next month, at the 1953 Le Mans race, the 550 took first *and* second place. Because of its size—the 550 Spyder was so low to the ground that German Formula One driver Hans Herrmann shocked spectators at the 1954 Mille Miglia in Italy by driving under the closed railroad gates—the model was given the nickname Giant Killer.

On September 21, 1955, Jimmy visited Competition Motors during business hours, shaking hands with its owner Johnny von Neumann. In

California racing circles, von Neumann—the son of a Viennese surgeon who'd angered Hitler for refusing to treat him for a larynx problem—was something of a celebrity himself, having already popularized the Ferrari. During the war, von Neumann was an intelligence specialist for the US Army. Then, he relocated to Los Angeles, became a cofounder of the California Sports Car Club, and opened Competition Motors with partner Secondo Guasti, scion of an Italian-American winemaking family. He's largely credited with convincing Ferrari to create its open-top California Spyder, one of the world's premier sports cars, and introducing the Porsche to the state that would become the brand's largest market.

As Jimmy chatted with Von Neumann, the actor's 356 Speedster sat outside. Dean glanced around the showroom, noting that it was stocked with five of the seventy-eight Spyder 550s released internationally in 1955. He studied each car until he found the one that he liked best. Although the Spyder was selling for a hefty sum totaling around $7,000— Lew remembers the precise fee being $6,800—Jimmy traded in his old Porsche and handed over a check for $3,000.

He knew that the car would have to be adjusted to suit his needs, but he was excited to drive it right away. Eager to brag about his purchase, Jimmy sped over to the Villa Capri and sought out the owner, Patsy D'Amore.

Patsy was in front of the restaurant, chatting with Jackie Gleason and Frank Sinatra, when Dean pulled up. Because of his clientele, the restaurateur was accustomed to patrons flaunting their wealth. But the notable price tag for the 550 Spyder staggered him. "Jimmy just buy this car— seven thousand dollars he paid for it," Patsy was quoted in *The Robb Report*. "He pulled up like a bat out of hell and came running in, no necktie on. And he takes me out to show me the car. I didn't like it. I tell him he *die* in that car."

Entering the restaurant, Jimmy spotted Sir Alec Guinness. Dean was a fan of the celebrated British actor and anxious to impress him. So after they greeted each other, Jimmy led Alec out to the parking lot. Guinness was fascinated by the Porsche and began peppering Dean with questions.

But when Jimmy spoke about the speed that he intended to reach on the racetrack, the Englishman was struck with a bad feeling.

"You'll be dead in a week," he blurted.

Joe Playan had the same concern, considering Jimmy's relative rawness on the track: "We all thought it was too much car for him. . . . You get out there and you go these speeds, you get into a problem. You've got to get used to speed."

If Jimmy was frightened by the warnings, he didn't display any outward signs of trepidation. As fans awaited the release of *Rebel Without a Cause* and *Giant*, he looked forward to the bounty he intended to accumulate by taking risks—in front of and behind the camera, and on the racetrack.

21

HOME AGAIN—FOR THE FINAL TIME

ennis Stock came into Jimmy's life almost by accident. The native New Yorker had been discharged from the military in 1951, intent on establishing himself as a photographer. Like Dean, he was possessed with ambition in proportion to his talent and positioned himself to succeed. Months after leaving the military, he took first place in a *Life* magazine competition for young photographers and was receiving the type of exposure others wait decades to receive. By 1955, he was a welcome presence in Hollywood social circles, a photographer who viewed himself as an artist and documentarian rather than a member of the paparazzi.

He and Jimmy met at a party at *Rebel* director Nicholas Ray's house and realized that they had much in common. Because Dennis was unfamiliar with Dean's work, Jimmy invited him to a preview of *East of Eden*.

Stock accepted the invitation. As he watched the film, he was struck by what became known as the bean field scene—Dean surprised director Elia Kazan by doing a spontaneous dance in a bean field, when his character Cal Trask thinks he's rescued the family business by cultivating a new crop—and sat mesmerized for the rest of the film. Convinced that Dean was about to become Hollywood's biggest star, Stock decided to do a story on the actor.

One month before the purchase of his first Porsche, Jimmy decided to return to Indiana and invited Dennis along to chronicle the experience.

But, first, Dean wanted to bring Stock to New York to relive the period of being a struggling actor discovering new concepts and widening his dreams. In Manhattan, Stock photographed Jimmy taking chess and bongo lessons, and dance classes with Eartha Kitt. The camera caught Jimmy at the office of his agent, Jane Deacy, backstage at the theater with Geraldine Page, and alone, walking through Times Square, contemplating the past and future.

From there, the pair disembarked for Fairmount. Interestingly, Jimmy chose not to fly, preparing himself for the journey home by departing the East Coast by train—a mode of transport the actor categorized as appropriately "primitive" for the farm animals that they'd encounter.

At the Winslow farm, Jimmy immediately changed into his work clothes and the type of spectacles he'd worn in high school. In addition to assisting Marcus Sr. with chores on the farm, Dean doted on Markie, fixing his bicycle and attaching a speedometer.

This was a particularly special visit for his paternal grandparents, Emma and Charlie Dean, who never harbored the same cynicism about Jimmy's chosen field that their son had. "He'd got his wish," Emma told *Photoplay*. "He knew he was a good actor."

Yet, it seemed important to Jimmy to remember his background. Not only did he pay homage to his mother's grave, but—with Charlie Dean beside him—the actor also made a point of photographing the headstones of his great-grandfather and great-great-grandfather.

When they returned home, Jimmy reminisced about the way Charlie would hold him on a knee and pretend to auction the boy off to his grandmother. Hoping to recapture the mood of those times, Jimmy gathered Markie and other family members and made a special request:

"Grandpa, do you think you could do some auctioneering?"

Charlie didn't hesitate, entertaining everyone by auctioning Markie's dog back to him.

The next day, Jimmy was with the family again when he burst into a grin, opening a briefcase and unveiling a portable tape recorder. As the relatives examined the high-tech object, Dean clicked a button and re-played the auction over Markie's pet.

With the exception of Jimmy, the family members were unaccustomed to hearing their voices on tape, and Charlie appeared embarrassed. "Hey," he began, with both humor and bashfulness. "You shouldn't have done that without telling me. I used some words that maybe don't belong in polite society."

Jimmy shook his head from side to side. He missed his grandparents, he explained, and the tape would remind him of sitting in their Indiana home. But, one day, he pledged, he was going to convince Charlie and Emma to leave the farm—and move into a house that the actor planned to build in California.

As with every trip home, Dean dropped by Fairmount High School during his Indiana vacation, this time attending a dance, where, according to the *Fairmount News*, he played the drums "mambo fashion."

On several occasions, Dean called his friend from Ward Elementary School, Jim Grindle, beseeching him to go out at night. But Grindle had a baby daughter and resisted. So, Dean turned up at the Grindle home and playfully tossed the baby back and forth with his old classmate. Later, when the child, Jeryl, became a gymnastics instructor, her father pointed to Jimmy's visit as the moment when she developed a fondness for flying in air.

From time to time, Fairmount friends referred to Jimmy as "Holly-wood." But during his time at Grindle's home, the movie business did not come up in conversation.

"We just talked about old times," Grindle, a retired Indiana State Police officer, told reporter Sean F. Driscoll of the Marion *Chronicle-Tribune* in 2005. "I didn't know the actor. I didn't know *James* Dean. I knew *Jimmy* Dean. That was the guy that I could relate to."

Before departing from Fairmount, Jimmy wanted Stock to join him at a stop at the town's only funeral parlor. Looking around, Dean eyed a cof-fin and climbed inside. At first, he was jocular, mugging for the camera.

Then, his face tightened, as he seemed to draw inside himself.

"I just wanted to see how it felt," he explained.

22

A COLD RUSH

hings seemed to be going wrong with the Spyder 550. One mechanic cut his finger on a hose ring. Another was taken to the hospital when one of the doors accidentally smashed his finger. All the while, the "King of Kustomizers" George Barris kept working, inscribing the words LITTLE BASTARD on the side of the vehicle.

There are many stories about why Dean chose this particular slogan. But Bracker is one of the few who knows the actual answer. "Porsches were beating the hell out of the bigger machinery on the sports-car tracks," he explains.

The British Jag drivers with engines ten times the size, they looked down their noses at the Porsches. But when a good driver in a Porsche came along and beat them, they'd refer to us and our Porsches as the "Little Bastards."

That's the main reason why Jimmy put that on. As usual, he was giving someone the finger. It was the same mental attitude he had when Jack Warner didn't want him racing, and he'd roar between the soundstages in his MG, just thumbing his nose at the boss. Jimmy made his presence known in the loudest way possible. So the "Little Bastard" was him just showing off his anti-authoritative side.

When Jimmy finally drove his vehicle out of the Competition Motors showroom on Friday, September 23, his mind was far away from Warner Brothers and almost completely on his next race eight days later in Salinas. The racecourse was actually a temporary track, constructed at the municipal airport. But the location was special, since the outdoor *East of Eden* scenes in Salinas helped transform Dean into a movie star.

As Jimmy once told Judy Garland, "Salinas is where James Dean was born."

For this race, Jimmy was convinced that he had the perfect car and the ideal mechanic. Rudolf Karl "Rolf" Wütherich had been born in the industrial city of Heilbronn, not far from Stuttgart, Germany—the future home of Porsche—in 1927. Although he suffered from a speech impediment as a child, he distinguished himself with his ability to repair engines. When World War II started, he completed an apprenticeship as an airplane mechanic, then joined the *Fallschirmjäger*, the elite paratrooper unit in the German *Wehrmacht*, or military. While other Germans were left broken by the conflict, the war seemed to bring out his best. As the Allies occupied Germany, Rolf took a job with Daimler-Benz. Then, in 1950, when Porsche began its regeneration, he was hired by the Stuttgart company, eventually becoming the second employee in the racing division.

In addition to being a driver himself, Wütherich was an indispensable part of the Porsche pit crew at Le Mans, along with other races, like the twelve-hour endurance contest near Riems, France. Although he'd been in two serious racing accidents in Germany, no one perceived Rolf as an omen of bad luck. In fact, he was considered an asset to any team.

In March 1955, as Porsche attempted to capitalize on its European renown in California, Rolf was dispatched as a field engineer to Competition Motors, customizing the engines of the complicated race cars and training other mechanics on the process. Two weeks after his arrival, he met James Dean for the first time, assisting him with his Speedster. When Dean began contemplating trading in the car for a Spyder, he sought out Wütherich for advice.

At Salinas, Dean anticipated that the engine—which Wütherich repeatedly specified was actually a 547, rather than a 550—would give him the advantage over the other vehicles. But the motor was extremely complex. That's why Jimmy needed Rolf to accompany him to the track. Wütherich was an expert 547 mechanic. It would take him 120 hours to assemble the motor to Dean's specifications, in addition to another eight to fifteen hours to set the timing.

Rolf's concern was that the car wouldn't be broken in by the time the race began. In order for the Spyder to achieve its peak performance level, he advised Jimmy to log at least five hundred miles in the driver's seat. Naively, Dean intended to accomplish this simply by speeding up and down Mulholland Drive and other spots around Los Angeles. In the week before the scheduled race, Eartha Kitt was visiting southern California, and Jimmy gave her a ride in the Porsche. As Dean picked up speed and Eartha's hair blew back, she uttered the same warning that Jimmy had heard from both Patsy D'Amore and Alec Guinness:

"James, I don't like this car. It's going to kill you."

After Pier Angeli, Jimmy's most publicized relationship had been with Swiss bombshell Ursula Andress. But when he attempted to take her on a date in the Spyder, she recoiled. In a 1982 television interview, she spoke of feeling "a cold rush when he drove up. He wanted me to go for a ride in it, but I couldn't even get close to the car."

Invigorated with youthful exuberance, Jimmy wasn't going to let anyone dissuade him from participating in the Salinas race. At the same time, he wasn't oblivious to the danger and made several utterances about the possibility of flaming out at age twenty-four.

All race-car drivers are conscious of the fact that they've chosen a precarious pastime, and a type of gallows humor pervades the sport. Richard Petty, for instance, once joked about the number of times his car went airborne after a collision. "I was a pretty good pilot at taking off," he told the *New York Times*. "But I wasn't too good at landing."

In theory, Jimmy may have attached some romantic allusion to the concept of testing one's fate. At the same time, he never intended to die young. "He may have grabbed too strongly at life," said Natalie Wood. "But I don't think he had a death wish."

Sal Mineo had the same impression: "Never believe that there was a need to destroy himself. There was too much that he would talk about in the future."

In the days leading up to the race, Jimmy tried persuading friends and relatives to join him in Salinas. Among those who received the hard sell was actress Jane Withers. They'd befriended each other while making *Giant*, and Jimmy viewed her as a big sister. Sometimes, he'd stop by her home, and they'd read to each other from plays. Withers also read to Jimmy from the Bible, eliciting a childlike joy in the young actor. Dean was so fond of the way that Withers looked after him that he told Ortense about it. Later, Ortense would send Withers a letter, thanking her for giving Jimmy the mothering he so craved.

"I'd really like you to come to Salinas," Dean told Withers. "I'll even let you ride in the Spyder."

But the mother of three declined.

"I can't do that, Jimmy," she said. "I've got three good reasons. Wendy, Bill, and Randy. You drive too fast, and you scare me to death."

The morning before he departed for Salinas, Dean showed off the Spyder to his friend Bill Bast and talked about the contest. As with the competition in Palm Springs, this was a two-day affair. Dean hoped to qualify for the finals on Day One, then take first place on the second day. At that point, he imagined, the other drivers would truly see him as a peer, rather than an actor with a new leisure pursuit.

Bast inquired about Jimmy's dog, Marcus. Who was going to feed him while the actor was in Salinas?

"I gave him away," Dean answered.

"How come?"

"You know what a crazy life I lead. What if I went away and never came back?"

As easy as it would be to attach meaning to this comment, Dean's agent, Jane Deacy, was convinced that he had no intention of ending his life. On the Friday before the race, he visited her at the Chateau Marmont, where she was staying in a small apartment. The two had enjoyed themselves that week. Although Jimmy complained about his altercations with George Stevens on the *Giant* set, now that the film was wrapped, everyone was looking forward to the praise both men would receive once audiences watched the young Jett Rink transform from youthful wildcatter to middle-aged tycoon. And Jane had also secured Jimmy the male lead in a televised adaptation of *Romeo and Juliet*.

On Saturday, Jane was planning on flying home to New York. Jimmy was grateful for all that Jane had done for him. If it hadn't been a race day, he emphasized, he'd be the one taking her to the airport.

"But it's okay," he added. "I'll be seeing you plenty in New York in a few weeks."

As they parted company, he turned and waved one last time. "See you soon!" he shouted, anticipating nothing but good times ahead.

After meeting with his father and uncle, Jimmy and Rolf Wütherich discussed the arrangements for the rest of the day. Jimmy had not been able to put five hundred miles on the car, as Rolf had suggested, so the two decided that it would have to be driven to the race. This would serve a two-pronged purpose: breaking in the motor and further acquainting Jimmy with the car's idiosyncrasies. Since *Collier's* photographer Sanford Roth and stunt driver Bill Hickman were part of the entourage, they would follow the Spyder in Dean's station wagon, towing the empty racecar trailer. Jimmy intended to steer the Porsche, with Rolf beside him.

It was a situation Bracker says that he never would have permitted. Because cars at the time tended to have long hoods, it would be difficult for a driver to look down and spot the Porsche riding so low to the road. Plus, it would be easy to confuse the silver color with the pavement.

"I think he would have listened to what I had to say," Lew maintains. "If I couldn't have persuaded him not to drive the car, I think I could have at least convinced him to drive behind the station wagon instead of in front of it. That way, the other drivers would have seen the wagon first, and an accident could have been avoided."

The group left Competition Motors at one-fifteen in the afternoon. At Ventura and Beverly Glen Boulevards, they stopped at a Mobile station and filled the vehicles. Then, the four convoyed up Sepulveda Boulevard toward the highway and the long ride north.

Once the group arrived on Interstate 5, the road was akin to "a twenty-mile straightaway," fellow race-car driver Bruce Kessler told the National Geographic Channel. "You could drive as fast as you wanted. . . . You didn't see any traffic."

Hickman, the most experienced driver of the quartet, urged Jimmy to proceed slowly. But this had never been the actor's nature. While riding motorcycles together in LA, friend John Gilmore asserted, Dean liked "to have the bikes running side by side, and he liked to reach out and touch the fingertips of the other person, so that he would feel the pistons working through the energy in the person."

Red lights were apparently meant for others. "The light was not going to stop him," Gilmore said, "and he was not going to pay attention to it. It was just part of his personality. . . . He was almost cold-blooded about it. He just drove straight ahead."

23

APPLE PIE AND MILK

In the 1800s, Santa Clarita—approximately thirty-five miles from downtown Los Angeles—was the epitome of the Old West, known for its gunfights, stagecoach robberies, and range wars. Shortly after the turn of the twentieth century, that history was re-created in the fledgling film industry. "So many of the early westerns were done right here," EJ Stephens, an author, tour guide, and Santa Clarita Valley historian tells me, as we open our menus in the Saugus Café, the longest-operating restaurant in Los Angeles County. "So this isn't only where it happened. It was where it was repackaged and presented to the world."

Residents are proud of that and other distinctions, even if the rest of the planet is largely naïve about them. In 1842—six years before the widely touted detection of gold at Sutter's Mill in the town of Coloma, northeast of Sacramento—the Gold Rush may have actually commenced in the area later labeled "Hollywood's original back lot." "It turns out that the first documented gold discovery in California was right here in Placerita Canyon," contends Santa Clarita Valley Historical Society president Alan Pollack.

The claimant was mineralogist Francisco Lopez. According to legend, he and companions Manuél Cota and Domingo Bermudez were herding cattle on his niece's ranch, when they stopped to nap under an oak tree. It was March 9, his fortieth birthday. As Lopez slept, he apparently had a vivid dream about floating in a pool of gold. When he awoke, the three hiked over a small creek to a grove of sycamore trees and started digging for onions.

"I with my sheath knife," he wrote, "dug up some wild onions, and in the earth discovered a piece of gold, and, searching further, found some more."

That Lopez just happened to be in the region was more than a mere coincidence. He'd studied mining at the University of Mexico and likely heard about other discoveries near the site of today's Magic Mountain theme park. But Lopez took the initiative to have his finding verified by the United States Mint in Philadelphia before petitioning the Mexican governor of California for permission to continue quarrying through the soil. The state, then called Alta California, was, along with Texas and New Mexico, part of the First Mexican Empire. By 1848, 125 pounds of gold had been uncovered.

Pollack believes that Lopez may have embellished part of his tale. If he did fall asleep, it was probably under a sycamore, for instance. Yet, the Oak of the Golden Dream can be found in Placerita Canyon, where it's a historical landmark. Nonetheless, the fact that Lopez identified with Mexico rather than the United States—coupled with the surge into the Golden State after the Sutter's Mill discovery—prevented American historians from giving him the credit that he wanted.

"We're pretty sure there were others before Lopez," Pollack says. "We have some evidence that some gold, found in 1838, was sent to the Philadelphia Mint from here. And we know there were some gold discoveries back in the 1790s. So Lopez may not have been the first. But it definitely wasn't Sutter's Mill, either."

An even more momentous event occurred in the region in 1928, when the St. Francis Dam broke. "They built a dam up the road from here," Stephens says. "Built it in the wrong place, using the wrong materials. Everything's wrong. And it crashes just before midnight. Twelve billion gallons of water sweeps down the canyon and just wipes the place clean.

Luckily, we didn't have a quarter of a million people in this area like we do today. But it kills somewhere between four hundred fifty and six hundred people. They still don't know."

After the San Francisco Earthquake, the dam burst was the state's greatest catastrophe—some still categorize it as "the worst civil engineering failure of the twentieth century"—obliterating the career of LA's water czar William Mulholland, after whom James Dean's beloved Mulholland Drive was named.

"It pretty much destroyed Mulholland's life," Stephens says. "He was a crushed man. And he went from being the most popular guy in LA to a pariah. But LA was a corrupt city, and the Bureau of Water"—now the Department of Water and Power—"wanted the story covered up. So they physically went and destroyed the dam, the rubble. Today, unless you know where you're going, you'll never find any evidence. You've got people who drive next to one of the top twenty disasters in United States history every day. Yet, it's totally forgotten."

Interestingly, the movie industry continued after the tragedy. The last scene of *Modern Times*—in which Charlie Chaplin walks away from the camera with Paulette Goddard—was filmed in Santa Clarita. "I call it the final scene in the silent film era," Stephens says. "*Modern Times* was not a completely silent film. It was a hybrid. But Chaplin had held out for almost a decade into the talkie era. And now there was a big tectonic shift—kind of like the seismic shift the world experienced when James Dean died."

Dean's connection to Santa Clarita, and the question about whether he stopped there on September 30, 1955, remains as ambiguous as the origins of the Gold Rush and the location of the St. Francis Dam.

Claire Landay insists that Jimmy and his companions ate in her family's restaurant, Tip's. The actor is said to have sat at the counter and ordered apple pie and milk.

Although not quite an institution, at one time, there were as many as seven Tip's restaurants in the LA area. The first, opened by Claire's parents, Tip and Ann Jardine in 1925, was situated at Western Avenue and

Sixth Street, and was little more than a counter. Eventually, they expanded to, among other sites, Hollywood and Vine, where actors on Tennessee
Ernie Ford's variety show, across the street, became regulars.

"People loved my father," Claire recounts. "He was quite well known
at the time. My parents had a standing reservation at the Brown Derby"—the Wilshire Boulevard landmark, designed to resemble a bowler
hat—"every Saturday night. They'd bring an autograph book and take it
home to me. I had everybody, from Rita Hayworth to Gregory Peck and
Cary Grant."

In 1955, there were two Tip's locations in the Santa Clarita Valley, one
just southwest of the current intersection of Interstate 5 and State Route
126, the other a much smaller venue that the family referred to as "The
Coffee Shop," the site of a Marie Callender's family restaurant today at
The Old Road and Magic Mountain Parkway.

Claire was not at either of the restaurants on the day Dean purport-
edly appeared. In fact, she was on the other side of the country, attending Mount Vernon College in Washington, DC. Everything she knows
about the stopover came from her family and the restaurant's staff. Yet,
she's certain that Dean visited—despite Rolf Wütherich's contention after
the accident that he couldn't recall pulling over in Santa Clarita, or the
argument that the group may have gone to the other local Tip's. "I'm
seventy-eight years old," Claire points out during our telephone conversation. "I don't know if I sound like it. But I'm in good shape and I remember
everything."

At the time, the area was fairly rural. Claire describes it as "westerly
with a lot of farmland." She theorizes that Dean turned up because "we
were the only place to stop."

Then as now, celebrity sightings in LA were hardly unusual. But after
the accident, the waitress who was on duty at Tip's claimed to vividly
recall every detail of serving the star. "You didn't 'ooh" and 'ah,'" Claire
says of the restaurant's attitude toward its better-known guests. "You let
them come in and eat and enjoy themselves. That's what we're there for."

When Dean finished his snack, the waitress told Claire, Dean and his friends "paid the bill, moved on, and that was it."

As historians, Stephens and Pollack enjoy reevaluating statements others have come to regard as fact. But to this day, the historical society has yet to determine whether the Dean appearance is anything other than an urban legend. "We've never been able to get any solid evidence," Stephens says. "But we have a lot of conjecture."

Says Claire, "I know people are always skeptical. Yes, he was there. Everyone who was around at the time knew that he was there."

At this point, though, validating the visit is almost irrelevant. The fact that it's still debated is testament to the legend that is James Dean.

"Just like Buddy Holly, James Dean took on a lot of his fame after his death," Stephens says. "One of the things I like to do is collect historical newspapers. I have a newspaper with a report of 'the day the music died.' It's about this big." He holds his thumb and forefinger an inch or so apart. "And it's not Buddy Holly they're talking about. It's Ritchie Valens."

Like Dean, Stephens is a native Hoosier, raised about one hundred miles from Fairmount. At eighteen, on a lark, he drove there to see the actor's grave. "I think you can look at his death as a real shift in the way people thought. We were ten years away from World War II. We'd come out of Korea. Elvis was just about to hit." "Heartbreak Hotel" was released almost exactly four months later. "The sixties were coming. You can look back at the whole youth movement, put a stake in the ground, and say, 'This is where it all began.'"

In 2001, Stephens decided to follow Dean's journey up Route 5 into the San Joaquin Valley—on a later trip with his wife, Kim, and Pollack, they'd take a twenty-five-minute detour to the lonely spot where Cary Grant was chased by a crop duster in *North by Northwest*—to the Y intersection where the actor's life ended. That he arrived just after midnight on September 11 magnified the feeling that he was experiencing something whose aftershocks would be felt for generations.

In subsequent years, he's studied other celebrity deaths, and pondered why Dean's means so much more: "Look at someone like Heath Ledger. The guy was fantastic. He'd just starred in an Academy Award–winning role [Ledger received the Oscar for Best Supporting Actor in *The Dark Knight* in 2008]. All the elements were there. But we haven't seen a cult of Heath Ledger like we see a cult of James Dean. Maybe it was the suddenness of James Dean's death. Maybe it was because we didn't live in the Internet era and didn't really know who he was. So we could believe whatever we wanted about him. I don't know."

Either way, Stephens adds, no one could deny the fact that, as the saying goes, Dean left a very pretty corpse.

"I remember when Marlon Brando died, all the articles mentioned how obese he'd become," Stephens says. "I can't remember who said this, but I've heard that the best thing that ever happened to James Dean's career was that he died at twenty-four. The worst thing that ever happened to Marlon Brando's career was that he *didn't* die when he was twenty-four."

"SAVE YOUR SPEED"

After his purported meal at Tip's, Jimmy and his group proceeded up Highway 99 down the Grapevine Grade into the San Joaquin Valley. As he had on Mulholland Drive during his late-night excursions with Lew Bracker, Dean was looking at open road and pressed down on the accelerator. At about three-thirty in the afternoon, he was hitting seventy miles per hour in a fifty-five-mile-per-hour zone. It didn't particularly qualify as reckless driving but was enough to arouse the attention of California Highway Patrol Officer Otie V. Hunter, who was traveling down the four-lane highway in the opposite direction.

"He was going too fast," he said in a video produced for the Santa Clarita Valley Historical Society in 2009. "I could tell that. So there was behind him a pickup truck pulling a trailer. . . . I could tell by the way they were maintaining the distance between them, they were traveling together. So I made a U-turn."

Hunter turned on his siren, pulling both vehicles over to the side of the road.

"Do you know why I stopped you?" he asked Jimmy.

Dean nodded.

"I clocked you at seventy miles per hour."

The actor didn't argue.

The officer began to write a ticket. It was a situation no driver welcomes. Yet, Hunter noted that the occupants of both cars were not only respectful, but also "pleasant." When the patrolman mentioned that the trailer behind the station wagon was empty, Jimmy explained the decision to break in the Spyder on the way up to the race.

"I guess you pushed it a little too much," Hunter observed. "If you don't drive a little slower, you might not make it to the race."

Dean offered no argument, smiling at the officer and shrugging.

Hunter decided to write the ticket for sixty-five miles per hour. "That's not unusual," he remembered. "You can always crop five miles off everything."

A $7,000 race car was an unusual sight on Highway 99, so the officer knew that the driver had money. But Dean wasn't such a big star that Hunter could remember seeing his face. Nonetheless, the patrolman deduced that he was talking to an actor.

Dean was wearing "typical Hollywood dress," Hunter said. "He had an old pair of beat-up, dirty, worn-out jeans, no belt on them." The officer had seen other entertainment-industry types deliberately dressed down. In addition, he noticed that Dean's shoes were devoid of laces—another trend in Tinseltown at that time. "When I saw him, I went, 'This guy's got to be from Hollywood.'"

The hunch was confirmed when Hunter filled in the box on the citation identifying the offender's place of employment. "Where do you work?" he asked.

"Warner Brothers."

What could have been a clash of sensibilities was turning into an affable exchange. There was something about Jimmy that the patrolman liked. Hunter had the impression that the actor came from humble stock. Maybe he even knew a few guys in law enforcement. "He wasn't belligerent or anything like that," Hunter said. "He was just a very nice-talking guy."

The two spoke about the race for a little while. Hunter wished that Jimmy had found the time to break in the Spyder elsewhere. "He probably wouldn't have been speeding up here," the officer speculated. "So it's just an unfortunate circumstance."

Once again, Hunter reminded Jimmy that he'd been going too fast. "Slow down and save your speed for the race up there."

Jimmy nodded deferentially.

The officer handed Jimmy the ticket on a clipboard; it specified that he appear in court on October 17 in Lamont, outside Bakersfield. Dean signed the bottom.

"Good luck in the race," Hunter said, returning to his cruiser.

Jimmy gave the officer a friendly wave as he rolled back onto Highway 99, the station wagon and trailer following behind him.

Later, the traffic ticket would be categorized as "the last autograph."

25

TOKEN FOR A GUARDIAN ANGEL

The time spent on the side of the road had slowed the group down, and Jimmy wanted to get to Salinas early enough to deal with logistics and get a good night's sleep before the race. When the caravan neared Bakersfield, they turned onto Route 166/33 in order to avoid the red lights and traffic of downtown. By the time they switched to Route 466, Jimmy was opening up the car again, leaving the station wagon and trailer in the distance.

He intended to keep going. But at Blackwells Corner—twenty-seven miles from where the journey would unexpectedly end—he saw a familiar vehicle in the parking lot of a rest stop that included a restaurant and gas station. It was a Mercedes 300 SL, and Jimmy knew that it had to belong to fellow race-car driver Lance Reventlow, the nineteen-year-old son of socialite Barbara Hutton. Reventlow was the Woolworth heiress's only child. His Danish father was Count Kurt von Haugwitz-Hardenberg-Reventlow. Barbara would marry seven times, and one of Lance's stepfathers was Cary Grant. "Some people are born with brown eyes," he once joked. "I was born with money."

Steering the Porsche into the parking lot, Jimmy spotted Lance. He was with another driver, Bruce Kessler. Dean pulled over next to the Mercedes and exited. While Rolf wandered over to Highway 466 to wave down Sanford Roth and Bill Hickman in the station wagon, the three competitors talked about their hopes for Salinas.

Everyone seemed to be loose and excited about the next day. Lance had been immersed in the racing world since age twelve, when his mother married Russian prince Igor Nikolayevich Troubetzkoy, the first Ferrari driver to participate in Grand Prix motor racing. Jimmy boastfully showed off his speeding ticket and claimed to have hit 130 miles per hour at one point during the trip up from Los Angeles. After Sanford Roth was introduced to the other racers, he entered the roadside shop and purchased a bag of apples. Jimmy grabbed one and chomped on it while sipping on a bottle of Coca-Cola.

"How do you like the Spyder now?" Roth asked.

Jimmy couldn't see any trade-ins in the immediate future. He expected to keep the auto, he said, for "a real long time."

No car was better equipped for victory. Jimmy was so sure of it that he didn't want to wait for the next day to compete. Looking around the lot, he zoned in on a late-model Corvette and approached the driver.

"Want to race?"

The young man pointed at the Porsche. "Not against that," he said.

How could anyone possibly beat him at Salinas? Jimmy was thoroughly exuberant. After bursting out of Indiana, scrambling in New York, and tolerating envious actors, manipulative studio executives, and controlling directors in Hollywood, this was the life that he was supposed to be living.

Win or lose, Dean and Reventlow wanted to get together after Saturday's contest and decipher the race. They made plans to meet for dinner the next night.

Eventually, Reventlow and Kessler said good-bye, and Jimmy shifted his focus back to his traveling companions. English didn't come naturally to Rolf, so he took a breath and considered his words before offering the actor advice.

"Don't try to be a hero in this race," he emphasized in his thick German accent. "There's a big difference between the Spyder and the Speedster. Be careful."

"Remember, you have bigger fish to fry than racing," Hickman interjected. "You have pictures to make."

Dean looked from one face to the other and smirked, directing most of his attention at Wütherich. "I'm going to be a very conservative driver. Is that okay?" His smile widened. "I'm going to behave myself."

Peering down at his hands, Jimmy slid a ring from his finger. He handed it to Rolf.

"You're my guardian angel. I want you to have this."

No stranger to sentimental gestures before big contests, Rolf thanked Jimmy and slipped on the ring.

Hickman was anxious to get back on the road. It was already five o'clock in the afternoon and, once darkness fell, the Spyder would be difficult to see. If they left now, they could eat a real dinner in an hour, at Paso Robles, then link up to Highway 101 for the final stretch to Salinas.

Returning to the Porsche, Jimmy and Rolf pulled back onto 466, seeing little in front of them but hills and sky. Dean looked around, concluded that the highway was free of patrol officers, and pressed down on the accelerator, hitting eighty-five miles per hour.

26

LOST HILLS

HOMELESS. GOD BLESS.

It's the first image that greets me as I turn left from Route 5 onto 46—466 in James Dean's day—a weather-worn woman with matted hair, seated on a milk crate, a cardboard sign perched on her lap. I'd hoped to coordinate my timing with that of Dean's group on September 30, 1955, arriving at Blackwells Corner at five o'clock in the afternoon, for instance. But, while leaving LA, I became ensnared in traffic on the San Diego Freeway, and I'm running far behind schedule. It's six-thirty in the evening when I pass the homeless woman at the intersection and continue onto the two-lane highway.

It's February, and I know that the sun will be setting soon. An orange glow streams through the clouds over fence-ringed nut fields and silhouettes of oil derricks. Pickup trucks kick dirt off the pavement while passing me on the other side of the highway.

Although the Kern National Wildlife Refuge is nearby, I notice nothing more than horses and cattle in my sightline. There's not much to really look at, and I find myself driving faster—just to get someplace. Blackwells Corner—in the aptly named town of Lost Hills—comes up quickly and is easy to distinguish. Even more prominent than the Texaco sign is an eighteen-foot, wooden paean to James Dean—cut along the perimeter of his body—in his red *Rebel* jacket, towering over the drivers. On the opposite side of the parking lot, facing motorists going south, is another wooden cutout of the icon, equally as imposing. The owner likes to describe it as a billboard. It's cut along the actor's head and shoulders, then pretty much ends. As I drive over to it, I realize that something's been written on the back:

"James Dean"—the actor's name is in red, but everything else is in black—"made his last stop at this corner on September 30, 1955. The young actor died in a car crash a short time later while en route to Salinas for an auto race. Although he appeared in only three films, James Dean remains a legend."

The bust went up in 2004, when an artist arrived at Blackwells Corner and volunteered to put up the billboard for free. The same craftsman installed the other cutout in 2011.

I park and cross past the Texaco pumps, entering the building. The scene reminds me of Fairmount. Oldies music plays. An image of Marilyn Monroe adorns a glass door. A painting of Betty Boop hangs on a wall.

Although the Max Fleischer cartoon made its debut in 1930s, and educes memories of the Jazz Age, I understand why it's there. Like Dean, she represents the past in a way that evokes fondness in people.

In some ways, the place feels like a giant, small-town convenience store. There's a full-size, old-fashioned jalopy on the sales floor, and the aisles are packed with local products: chocolate-covered almonds, garlic-onion almonds, butter toffee almonds, raw walnuts, raw pecans, maple pecans, hickory-smoked pistachios, habanero pistachios, chili-lemon pistachios, crushed garlic pistachios. Below framed posters of Dean and Monroe is a salsa section. The flavors vary from pepper patch to tomatillo to black bean and corn. In the next aisle are the preserves: whole fig, country fruit, peachy peach.

Then, the Dean stuff starts in earnest. A section of the store is devoted to the *East of Eden* Fudge Factory. In the Forever Young diner, the style is 1950s, with spinning seats at the counter, and booths alongside murals of Dean and Monroe eating sundaes, and Elvis standing up and hanging out.

For some reason, there's also a mannequin with a faux automatic weapon in one of the booths. It wears a shirt labeled SECURITY.

The first person I meet is the cashier, Marii Garcia, twenty. She tells me that most of the visitors simply want gas. But, just about every day, someone has a question about James Dean, particularly tourists from other countries who deliberately include Blackwells Corner on their American itinerary. The staff is expected to accommodate them.

"When they ask us where James Dean died, we tell them it's about twenty-five miles away, at the intersection of 41 and 46," she says. "We have to memorize everything."

As with Fairmount, locals tend to be proud of their history. Strangely, some of it can be linked to the dark themes many associate with Dean's demise. For example, George Blackwell, the man credited with starting Blackwells Corner in 1921, was killed in a motorcycle accident three years later, during one of Kern County's worst droughts.

"As summer drew near," reads a display on the wall, "dust replaced air, dead cattle replaced sagebrush." The famine lasted until 1927, a time, the description continues, of abandoned Hudsons, barren soil, crusted earth, and parched bones.

In World War II, the corner was drafted as a PX serving fifty thousand soldiers training with the Ninety-First Division from Lost Hills, many of whom would fight with General George Patton's Tenth Army at El Alamein and the Battle of the Bulge.

Then, nothing happened until James Dean died.

"We have a lot of people call us," owner Kossie Dethloff tells me, "and say, 'Have you see the Little Bastard come by?'"

One afternoon, the phone rang and a woman from Chicago told Dethloff about a rumor that a resurrected Dean had been sighted at the LA Farmers Market and was heading north to re-create his final ride.

"If you guys see him," she requested, "would you give me a call? I want to know."

"We will give you a call, yes," the proprietor assured her. "You'll hear all about it."

There are also regulars who stop in to offer opinions on Dean as well as the state of American society. Dave—he doesn't disclose his last name—wears a cap declaring DYSFUNCTIONAL VETERAN. LEAVE ME ALONE and describes himself as a graduate of the "University of Southeast Asia."

Dave appreciates Dethloff providing him with a forum, and—while he takes issue with most other things—doesn't begrudge the entrepreneur's success at capitalizing on the interest in James Dean. But he doesn't fully grasp why, after sixty years, people remain so obsessed.

"He only made B-movies," Dave insists.

"His movies are great," Dethloff counters.

"He only made three movies. And the only one that came the closest to *not* being a B-movie is *Giant*. And that's because it had Elizabeth Taylor."

I point out that, almost universally, film fans agree that all three movies are pretty good.

"That's because our values are askew. Everything's one-eighty. We take these individuals and put them on pedestals, exalt them, instead of a working stiff like me."

Dethloff is old enough to remember when the cult of James Dean began. He was seventeen years old and headed to boot camp at Lackland Air Force Base in San Antonio when he heard the news on the bus. Kossie was familiar enough with Dean; he'd seen *East of Eden* and was impressed by it. But he initially believed that everyone was talking about Jimmy Dean, the country singer whose first hit, "Bummin' Around," reached the charts in 1953.

That makes sense, considering his background. Like the characters in *Giant*, he's originally from Texas oil country—born in Bridgeport and raised in Burkburnett, just outside of Wichita Falls. When he entered the Air Force, his family had moved across the state border to Lawton, Oklahoma, renowned for its Palm Sunday Passion Play and proximity to the Fort Sill military base.

By the time he was discharged, he was married and making his home in another oil-rich community, Taft, California, not far from Blackwells Corner. After operating a smaller store, fifteen miles south on Route 33, he purchased the rest stop in 1985.

At the time, the location was primarily a coffee shop. Dethloff doubled the size and began featuring local products.

"You're right in the middle of the pistachio-almond capital of the world," he is proud to remind me.

After ten years, though, he was tired of the demands of a seven-day operation and sold. The new owner was, by Kossie's definition, "the worst businessman in the world." But he had at least one idea that resonated.

"He filled the place up with all the James Dean, Marilyn Monroe stuff that you have now. That's what they tried to make their living on. But it didn't work the way they did it. He went down the chute in four years. I had to retrieve it, build it back up and it just started going wild and woolly."

In addition to Dean and Monroe, Dethloff makes sure his customers see a lot of Elvis, along with John Wayne. The wistfulness for another time is comforting and would likely work in another setting. But it's the history that ensures that newcomers keep coming.

"If I could see James Dean in person, I'd thank him," Kossie says. "But I feel like I have. A lot of James Dean look-alikes have been here."

According to some customers, so has the man himself. During a produce-hauling job, a Mexican trucker entered Blackwells Corner, sought out the owner, and pointed at the cutout of Dean in his *Rebel* jacket.

"I don't like that guy," he said.

Kossie asked him why.

"He was coming from Salinas and it was late, after midnight. He was kind of sleepy-headed. And he got to where James Dean had the accident. He was starting up that hill and, all of the sudden, he said, 'That guy, he was there.'"

The trucker apparently saw Jimmy's reflection in the windshield.

But that wasn't all. While pulling over at Blackwells Corner to sleep, the driver claimed that he'd heard someone walking around the truck. He grabbed his tire iron and pulled open the back door but saw no one inside. After returning to the cab and closing his eyes, though, the trucker heard the identical noise.

"Finally, about the third time, he got up and left," Kossie says. "He told me, 'I don't ever stop no more. Not at night.' It kind of bugged him a little bit."

A female customer purported to have her own encounter with Dean in the store's Forever Young diner. "Which one of these booths did he sit in?" she demanded to know.

Recalls Dethloff, "She went to the farthest booth in the back and sat down. Then, she tried every other booth. She got up almost to the front and she sat there and said, 'This is the one. I feel his presence right here.'

"I didn't want to break her heart and say, 'Hey, this place wasn't even here. This is a totally new building.'"

I ask about the most common question he hears.

"'Was he really here?' 'Yes, he was really here.' 'How long was he around? What did he buy?'"

Dave injects himself back into the conversation: "Beer!"

Dethloff doesn't laugh. "I had a customer on the highway patrol, a very good buddy of the guy who gave him the ticket.' And that old boy said, 'If I had known what was going to happen, I'd have took him straight to jail because he was legally drunk.'"

It's a statement wildly divergent from anything Otie V. Hunter ever told the media. But Kossie believes it.

"He might have had a hamburger, but he also had a six-pack of beer," the owner states, perpetuating the very mythology he ridiculed a few minutes earlier.

"In all fairness," Dave cuts in, "a lot of people drank and drove back in the old days. It wasn't a huge deal like today. Today, it wrecks your life."

Dethloff lets the comment register. "I was born and raised in Texas, remember? In Texas, even today, grab me a beer, get in the car, and take off. And a cop pulls you over, he says, 'You got another one?'"

In Lost Hills, California, though, even traffic stops are colored by the legend of James Dean. "Everybody talks about him here," Kossie says. "It's hard to believe. He wasn't here an hour and everybody still talks about him."

27

IMPACT

H ad Jimmy left Blackwells Corner a minute or two earlier, Donald Gene Turnupseed would have never known that he passed a genuine movie star on a winding highway near Cholame, California. The 550 Spyder was another matter. Turnupseed liked cars and would have noticed it as it barreled past him. But both drivers would be going too fast for him to realize that the silver Porsche was being piloted by James Dean.

Turnupseed had been born ninety miles away in the Central Valley town of Porterville, one year before Jimmy. Donald worked at his father's Tulare hardware store as a teen then joined the navy in 1952, during the Korean War. After serving on a hospital ship, he returned home and enrolled at the California Polytechnic Institute—or Cal Poly—on the GI Bill. There, he hoped to meet the requirements necessary to receive an electrical contractor's license.

Despite their contrasting career goals, Donald and Jimmy would have liked each another. Both grew up in environments where the majority of the families made a living from agriculture. While attending Tulare Union High School, Turnupseed bought a Ford Model A and transformed it into a small race car. Later on, he amused himself by building dune buggies.

On September 30, 1955, he was making the one-hundred-mile journey home from his school in San Luis Obispo, a picturesque community where Bishop Peak, the tallest of the Nine Sisters volcanic plugs, gazes over Pismo Beach and other surf towns. He hadn't seen his parents in two weeks and, as his two-tone, 1950 Ford Tudor crossed the Salinas River—close to where Jimmy was scheduled to race the next day—he felt almost as animated as the actor.

One mile from Cholame, Turnupseed was traveling eastbound on 466 when he tried making a left at a Y-shaped junction to enter California Highway 41, en route to Tulare. It was a dangerous spot. Traffic moved fast on 466 and the turn was easy to miss. There was no left-turn lane. The only stop sign at the intersection was for westbound traffic from Highway 41. The road was unlit and had been the site of several fatal accidents before.

Rancher Cliff Hord was in his Pontiac, with his wife, Ruth, and thirteen-year-old son, Ken, traveling westbound on 466. He'd just passed the Y intersection when he spotted Jimmy's Porsche, traveling in the direction of Turnupseed's Ford. He thought that it was going pretty fast.

"Jesus Christ, Ruth," he muttered. "Look at that son of a bitch come."

But Jimmy didn't slow. As Cliff passed the Porsche, his wife, Ruth, claimed to catch a quick glimpse of Dean and Wütherich. According to her recollections, they were smiling—young, bold, and impervious to danger.

Suddenly, Turnupseed cut over the white line in front of the Spyder.

Dean believed that he had the right of way. "That guy's got to see us," he told Wütherich. "He'll stop."

But it was twilight, and the Spyder was roughly the color of the pavement. Although Jimmy had flicked on the headlights, the Porsche was so low to the ground that it was difficult to make out the glare. Turnupseed would later insist that he never saw Dean coming, but his actions indicate otherwise. By the time he became aware of the situation, though, the cars were perilously close. Turnupseed cocked the wheel to the right and stepped on the brakes. Reportedly, Dean tried executing a racing maneuver, using the throttle and turning hard to "sidestep" the Ford's ominous bullet-nose grillwork.

The vehicles collided, practically head-on.

The Ford rotated counterclockwise and slid sideways, about thirty-eight feet east. The impact hurled Donald, face-first, into the windshield. But the car was larger and better fortified than the 550 Spyder. When it came to a halt, his nose was bloody and his left shoulder throbbed. All things considered, though, he was relatively okay.

It was different for the occupants of the Porsche. It left the ground and flipped over several times before stopping forty-five feet away, smoking and mangled, in a gully next to a telephone pole. Rolf Wütherich was ejected from the convertible and landed next to the driver's side of the vehicle. He suffered a fractured skull, a mouth full of shattered teeth and jaw fragments, and an injured hip. His left foot sustained a complicated fracture.

Because of the diminutive size of the Porsche, the movie star's head had hit the Ford's fender. He had a broken neck and crushed left foot, among other wounds. He was slumped across the passenger door, leading to speculation later on that the German mechanic was actually driving.

Paul Frederick and his wife were in a convoy—following his brother, Tom, and his spouse—to a high school football game when they saw the accident from about fifty feet away. Concerned about ramming into one of the vehicles, Tom hit the brakes and watched the two cars spin on the pavement. When they came to a halt, he immediately pulled over, ran to the furrowed Porsche, and contemplated a handsome blond man, caught in the car with limbs twisted. Paul was too scared to touch the victim but wanted to determine if he was breathing.

Paul removed his sunglasses and held the lens under James Dean's nose.

It didn't fog.

28

4EVR COOL

What remains of Route 466 exists in strips of old pavement, covered with dirt and grass in some places, running parallel to the highway that replaced it, California State Route 46. It's now four lanes wide with a divider in the middle. But it doesn't take a great deal of imagination to visualize how the region looked six decades ago. Buildings are far and few. Fencing pens in Jack Ranch cattle. Nut fields stretch into the hills. The road rises and rapidly slopes. If you slow down for any reason, other cars will whiz past you, rattling your vehicle.

Were it not for James Dean, this section of California would barely stand out. Travelers generally pass by towns like Cholame (the proper pronunciation is *Shoal-lamb*) and Paso Robles to get somewhere else. Donald Turnupseed's journey, from college to his parents' house, is pretty typical. Others come from the Central Valley to enjoy the ocean in coastal towns like Morro Bay and Cambria.

For one twenty-three-mile stretch, signs warn motorists to put on their headlights, even during the day. I'm curious about the admonition and want to ask the locals about it. So I pull into the Jack Ranch Café, just yards from the spot where Dean died.

In 1955 it was the garage where both the 550 Spyder and Turnupseed's Ford Tudor were towed. Given the dearth of businesses in the area, it also doubled as a grocery store.

It's an unassuming, Old West–style building with paneled walls and a deliberate scorn of anything too sleek or modern. Instead of a hostess greeting guests, visitors encounter a tin sign, charging them to PLEASE SEAT YOURSELF in blue paint.

As with Blackwells Corner, the building's history is posted on the wall: "At the turn of the twentieth century, this business had the first drive-through window (in the area). Farmers and ranchers would holler their order to the clerk, and he would scoot the supplies down a board running to the customer. . . . Now, the building is rustic. We call it character. The characters serving you may be a little rusty, but we're glad you're here."

In reality, no one seems particularly enraptured about the prospect of meeting another tourist. Still, the owners have made a great effort to accommodate them. Images of the film star are everywhere. There are photos of Dean, the Porsche, and the garage where it was hauled. A poster for Jimmy advertising a cola called Kist is displayed. At the register, patrons can grab a Dean magnet or postcard, or one of many books written about the legend, while paying the check. Dean's final speeding ticket is blown up and framed, along with the special edition of the *Fairmount News*, announcing his death. License plates abound, all bearing the actor's countenance and variations of the same theme: LIVE FAST, AMERICAN LEGEND, 4EVR COOL.

A stand-up, paper cutout of the box-office sensation occupies a prominent spot in a separate dining room. It's accompanied by a photo from *Giant* and a very realistic illustration of Marilyn Monroe resting her head on Jimmy's shoulder, as he guides his motorcycle in the afterlife. A poster reads LEGENDARY CROSSROADS—the artist is listed as Chris Consani—featuring Jimmy, Marilyn, and Humphrey Bogart lounging in front of a diner, as Elvis sits on the bumper of a vintage car, strumming his guitar. Another Cosani work depicts a place called NORMA JEAN'S ROADSIDE DINER. James Dean fills his Porsche with gas outside. Through the windows, we see Bogart, Marilyn, and Clark Gable.

Besides James Dean, the Jack Ranch Café specializes in pie: apple-peach, boysenberry, chocolate cream, coconut cream, banana cream, blueberry cheese, and cherry.

Tom Smith and his wife, Gretchen, are kindergarten teachers in Bakersfield, sweethearts who met as education majors at Fresno State. For years, they've driven past the café and read the annual stories commemorating Jimmy's death. But this is the first time that they've ever ventured inside.

They invite me to sit at their booth. I do and immediately ask why drivers on 46 are instructed to turn on their lights.

"The road's only been widened recently," Gretchen explains. "It's a very vindictive road. When it was a two-lane highway, people would pass the slow trucks very fast and come up a hill without anyone on the other side knowing they were there. The lights help. But it's just very dangerous."

In fact, the road is so treacherous that even in Dean's day it was called Blood Alley. In 1959—after nearly four years of adverse attention—the highway was reconstructed. The lanes were broadened, and a safety island was inserted between north- and southbound traffic. But misfortunate continued. Between 2000 and 2010, there were thirty-eight fatalities on the single ribbon of highway. At one time, a billboard was erected along the green hills, exhorting motorists, DRIVE WITH CARE. LIFE HAS NO SPARE.

The Smiths are easygoing and cerebral, able to analyze central California culture with a degree of detachment. If Dean had to die so suddenly, they concede, it helped places like Blackwells Corner and the Jack Ranch Café, where the majority of customers appear to genuinely like the actor and view him through a timeless prism.

Gretchen motions at a framed poster of Jimmy, sitting in a director's chair with his legs in front of him and balanced on a stepladder. He gazes into the camera, as if staring through time. "Look at him," she says. "He's so good-looking. I mean, he's even wearing Converse. Those are very stylish now. And he has those round glasses. It's more than sixty years ago and—just look at him—he's still so hip."

29

NOT VERY ALIVE

The ambulance braked to a halt next to the Porsche, facing the opposite direction of the road. While his partner, Collier "Buster" Davidson, checked on Rolf Wütherich, emergency medical technician Paul Moreno— who also happened to own the garage in Cholame, where the damaged vehicles would be towed—looked down at James Dean. The young man was still alive, but barely.

It was going to be difficult to remove him. Dean's foot was caught in the clutch and brake. The damaged Spyder had concaved on the movie star.

Someone at the garage called the police. California Highway Patrol officer Ernie Tripke answered the phone. After writing down the details, Tripke went outside and found fellow officer Ron Nelson. After both serving in World War II, Tripke and Nelson were among eighteen thousand applicants—many of them veterans—for one thousand jobs available on the California Highway Patrol. Each was accepted and assigned to the freeways around Los Angeles. Eventually, the two were transferred to San Luis Obispo where they met, frequently working the night shift together out of a base set up at the Paso Robles station. By September 30, 1955, they considered each other friends.

Outside the building, Tripke told Nelson about the accident report. "I don't have anything to do," Nelson replied. "I'll follow you out there and assist you."

The officers entered separate cars and drove to the scene at about one hundred miles per hour. At about six-twenty in the evening, Tripke pulled up. He'd be the lead investigator in the case. Nelson arrived immediately afterward, placed flares on the road, and looked for witnesses to interview.

"Ernie and Ron were relatively young men at the time, but they didn't know who James Dean was," says EJ Stephens of the Santa Clarita Valley Historical Society, who interviewed both officers several times while researching James Dean's final ride. "And he was alive. They told us that, definitely, he was alive when they got there."

From covering other crashes, Tripke instinctively knew that Dean had a broken neck. "He was not bloody or mangled like I have read," he said.

When Jimmy's traveling partners, photographer Sanford Roth and stunt driver Bill Hickman, arrived at the location, they noticed flashing lights and Donald Turnupseed's Ford Tudor. They'd hoped to catch up with Jimmy at some stage, but now, an accident was holding them back. Would Dean realize that he'd lost his companions and pull over to wait for them?

They stopped to investigate the damage. Before they even left the station wagon, they were confronted with the painful truth. There was Jimmy, still trapped in the wreck. Hickman ran over to the actor and held him, shouting his name to rouse Dean from his apparent slumber. It wasn't working. Roth would tell *Life* magazine that he went into journalistic mode and photographed the carnage. Later, he'd deny this, while his wife maintained that he only took the pictures to assist with any insurance claims that might be filed.

Reportedly, Hickman raged, "You son of a bitch! Help me!"

Eventually, Moreno managed to untangle Jimmy's feet from the gears in the car. Both EMTs hoisted the body, placed it on a gurney, covered it with a blanket, and fastened it with straps.

Roth took another photograph.

Nelson was directing traffic. "I didn't get a good look at [Dean], but I could hear him, and he was breathing hard," the patrolman said. "I speculated that his head had actually made contact with the front of Turnup-seed's car, and that he had suffered severe brain damage."

The entire time, Turnupseed stood by his car, seemingly eager to answer whatever questions the authorities had. To Nelson, the student "seemed to be all right. I think he hit his head on the windshield." Nelson asked him to describe the accident.

"He was making his turn. I didn't see him coming until the last split second, and it was too late."

The story sounded plausible. Neither officer thought that the college student deserved to be placed under arrest. With his car no longer oper-able, he hitchhiked to Tulare, where his family lived.

Dale "Blackie" Kimes picked him up. "He seemed like such a nice, caring kid," the driver told the San Luis Obispo *Telegram-Tribune* in 1995. "He kept saying over and over again, 'I hope [Dean's] going to be all right." At Tulare District Hospital, Turnupseed was treated for a scraped nose and bruises, then went home to rest in his old bedroom.

Back on 466, Dean and Wütherich were slid into the same ambulance. Jimmy's gurney occupied the bottom position, Rolf's the top. Dean "wasn't very alive," according to Tripke, "but he was still alive."

On the way to Paso Robles War Memorial Hospital, though, the ambu-lance experienced a head-on swipe with another vehicle. The damage was insignificant. But the ambulance driver, Paul Moreno, still had to exit to exchange addresses, phone numbers, and insurance information with the other motorist.

Around this time, Wütherich would later tell the German magazine *Christophorus*, he briefly regained consciousness and realized that he couldn't move. It would be days before he'd be notified of Dean's condition.

"Dean was in very bad shape," says Stephens. "But you still have to ask yourself if history would be different if they hadn't had to stop the ambulance."

When the ambulance finally arrived at the hospital, Wütherich was wheeled into the emergency room and quickly examined by Dr. Robert

Bossert, who'd been called at home and told about the crash. The physician noted a broken jaw and leg, and chest injuries, along with scratches and bruises. But those could wait. With resources limited, he walked briskly to the ambulance to check on Dean.

The actor's feet were peeking out of the ambulance. "There were minor facial injuries," Bossert, then ninety-four, said in 2005. "I couldn't see any severe destruction except that he was totally unresponsive in every way."

James Dean was pronounced dead, the county's twenty-seventh auto casualty that year. As Bossert turned and reentered the hospital to help Wütherich, Moreno closed the ambulance door and drove the body to the Kuehl Funeral Home, down the hill at Seventeenth and Spring Streets.

In a room thick with the odor of formaldehyde, mortician Martin Kuehl assessed the cadaver. He wrote, "The left side of the face was more damaged than the right side. Upper and lower jaws multiple fractures, broken neck, possible basal skull fracture. Both arms multiple fractures."

Martin Kuehl's father had opened the family mortuary in 1929 and passed the business down to his son. He was accustomed to seeing sights as gruesome as the dead actor and had witnessed a lot worse: dead babies, charred bodies, corpses rotted by disease or decomposition. "If you try to remember everything of everybody, you'd be in la-la land," he later confided to the San Luis Obispo *Tribune*.

At the accident scene, the dispatcher radioed the patrolmen, asking when they'd be completed with their assignment. This was unusual. Officers were generally allowed to finish their tasks in the field before they were contacted about other matters. "But they called me several times," Tripke said. "And I told them, 'I'll let you know when I'm through here, but I'm not through yet.' . . . When I finally did have the chance to talk to the dispatcher, he said that he'd been bombarded with calls and the hospital had been bombarded with calls. Everybody wanted to know something."

But no one could deliver an answer until Tripke and Nelson returned to their substation at the Paso Robles Police Department and provided details.

"The dispatcher had gotten word that there was James Dean in the accident," Tripke said. "And the only way . . . he could find that out is that night the Paso Robles football team was playing the Bakersfield High School football team. And the two men that owned the Paso Robles radio station came through the accident scene shortly after it happened, and they found out it was Dean, and they called in to the station. . . . Once the news media got ahold of it, everybody knew."

Sadly, Jimmy's wasn't the only traffic fatality case that Tripke and Nelson encountered that night. "There was a young man in the military who was also killed," Tripke said. "But that was quickly forgotten due to the James Dean crash."

In order to properly field the telephone calls that were pouring into the police station, the officers on duty asked anyone who knew anything about James Dean for background data. Someone at the funeral home had a copy of a *Saturday Evening Post* that included a story about the actor, and Tripke quickly scanned it, digesting pieces of information to use with the media.

"I didn't know who it was," he said. "I thought it was Jimmy Dean the sausage maker. . . . I'd never heard of him."

Jimmy Dean, the country singer, didn't form his food company until 1969, but Tripke would innocently tell this anecdote so frequently that it no longer matters. It would be among the least sensational falsehoods about the tragic legend. Once the mythology started, one story begot another in a chain that never ended.

30

LIKE SEEING A GHOST

With the exception of Turnupseed, there were few eyewitnesses who could tell police exactly what occurred when the Spyder collided with the Ford. But the media continued to call, hoping for nuance and elaboration. At one point, Ernie Tripke returned to the hospital and asked Dr. Bossert if Rolf Wütherich had revealed anything noteworthy.

"No," the doctor replied. "I can't seem to get anything out of him. Maybe it's because he's from Germany. I don't know how much English he speaks."

Tripke decided to talk to the Porsche mechanic himself. When the officer spoke English, he was met with a glassy-eyed stare. Tripke switched to German—the language the officer had spoken at home with his parents. The life returned to Wütherich's eyes. He was relieved to find someone, in this remote, American hospital, who could communicate in his tongue.

The problem was that Wütherich's memories were hazy. Tripke remembered Rolf telling him "just that they had an accident, and he didn't know too much about it. You see, he couldn't talk much. He was in a state of shock, with a broken jaw and everything else. . . . So I didn't push it, with him being in injured condition."

In all the chaos, the hospital operator was instructed to call Warner Brothers studios. A night watchman answered the general number and was informed that James Dean had died in a car accident.

The officer phoned *Giant* producer Henry Ginsberg, who called Jimmy's LA agent Dick Clayton. Jane Deacy had yet to leave for New York. Clayton got her on the telephone at the Chateau Marmont and delivered the tragic news.

They agreed that they didn't want Winton learning about his only child's death through the media. Clayton drove over to Reseda to tell the elder Dean in person.

Now the burden was on Winton to tell the family in Indiana. Haltingly, he called Markie's older sister, Joan Peacock, at home. Ortense and Marcus Sr. were in transit from their California road trip, and wouldn't learn about the loss of their surrogate son until they pulled onto their property and saw Joan—sad and anxious—waiting for them. By then, everyone in Fairmount knew.

"It's hard for us to understand why Jimmy's life had to end so soon," his grandmother Emma Woolen Dean said in *Photoplay*. "Seemed like he was just beginning to give other people the same kind of pleasure he had always given his family."

At a charity function in Hollywood, the WAIF Whisper Ball, Jane Russell, in a glittering white dress, introduced the master of ceremonies, comedian Bob Hope. An audience that included Clark Gable and Fernando Lamas chuckled at the one-liners. Suddenly, a murmur started. Someone had heard that James Dean was dead.

It seemed preposterous. Dean was twenty-four years old and in perfect health. Rumors like these circulated all the time. Still, the gossip spread around the room and across the street to where the Makeup Artists Ball was being held.

At Warner Brothers, director George Stevens was in a dark screening room, viewing a rough cut of *Giant*. Suddenly, the phone rang, interrupting the session. It was Henry Ginsberg. Stevens listened then ordered that the lights be turned on.

"I've just been given the news that Jimmy Dean has been killed," he told the people assembled in the room, including Elizabeth Taylor. Taylor immediately burst into tears. Despite their battles on the set, Stevens cried too.

Lew Bracker's mind had been on USC football. He ate at Julie's, a restaurant the school's alumni and coaches frequented, before the game. Then, when USC defeated Texas, he drove over to the Villa Capri in celebratory spirits.

"I was in the mood to have a drink, even though I wasn't a drinker," he says. "I thought maybe I'd have a cappuccino."

Lew was driving a Porsche, like the Speedster Jimmy had previously owned. As he pulled up in the parking lot, about eleven o'clock that night, the restaurant's public relations representative, Sam Wise, was smoking outside. The sight of the Porsche appeared to unnerve him.

"Oh my God," he said, "I thought I was seeing a ghost."

Lew was visibly confused.

"You haven't heard?" Sam asked.

"Heard what?"

Sam didn't feel qualified to convey the information himself. He gently took Lew by the arm and led him into the building. Owner Patsy D'Amore and Nicco Romanos, the maître d' and Jimmy's landlord, were among a group of somber men standing by the bar. When they noticed Bracker, they rushed toward him and sat him down. Patsy ordered someone to bring Lew a glass of wine.

Lew knew that something terrible had occurred.

"Jimmy was killed in a car crash in his race car," Patsy said.

This was impossible. The race was the next day. Something had to be wrong.

Lew called his parents. They'd heard about the accident on the news and asked their son to come home. Patsy and Nicco were worried about Bracker driving by himself. But he needed to be with his family. He felt like he'd lost a brother.

At the house, Bracker's mother gave him a sleeping pill. He went into his bedroom and stayed there for the next two days, playing the score

East of Eden over and over. It had been composed by his cousin's husband, Leonard Rosenman, and brought back memories of laughing with
Dean on the set and at the Warner Brothers commissary. "I seemed to
find comfort in that score," he wrote in his book, *Jimmy & Me.* "Perhaps
it reminded me of the beginning."

In Salinas, the race continued as if nothing unusual had occurred. No
one spoke about James Dean because the news hadn't traveled to the
auto-racing crowd. JP Kunstle, who'd taken second place in Bakersfied
on May 11—just ahead of Jimmy—won the competition on Saturday to
advance to the finals the next day. Just behind Kunstle was Ray Ginther.
Both drove 550 Spyders.

On Saturday night, Lance Reventlow and some friends waited for Dean
to join them for dinner. When Jimmy didn't show up, they were mildly disappointed. But Jimmy was a busy guy, a movie star. The assumption was
that he'd been sidetracked, maybe even found something more compelling to occupy his time. It didn't really matter anyway. There were plenty
of people around who wanted to talk about the race.

Lance would catch up with Jimmy on another day. He was certain
about that.

Claire Landay was in her dorm at Mount Vernon College in Washington, DC, watching television in a common area. Everyone in her social
network, it seemed, was already a fan of James Dean.

"Oh yes, God," she recounts. "At that time, I hung out with a lot of actors, and some of them knew him. We all knew he was one of the great
movie actors of our time. For us, it was James Dean or Marlon Brando."

It would be several days before she'd hear that Dean and his entourage
had made an appearance in her family's restaurant, Tip's. As bewildering
as that seemed to be, though, she never imagined that she'd still be discussing Dean's purported order of apple pie and milk well into the next
century.

"Every time somebody writes about this, somebody contacts us," she
says. "It's an incredible thing that people are still fascinated by this. Some-

one's always getting ready to write a book. We've been closed since ninety-five and, here we are, part of history."

On Monday, Lew finally felt well enough to leave his parents' home. He phoned Jimmy's landlord, Nicco, and asked to visit Dean's apartment. Bracker's concern was that some fanatic would break in and steal everything of value.

Nicco agreed with Lew. But Bracker couldn't bring himself to open any of the drawers. Jimmy kept certain things to himself and, even in death, didn't deserve to be violated. Instead, Lew gathered every important item he saw and carefully placed them in a cardboard box.

For more than forty years, Lew held on to the box, ensuring that Jimmy's personal items remained in the possession of someone he trusted. Eventually, he concluded that the contents humanized his old friend and should be shared. So he sent the material to the place where Jimmy would want them to be.

Today, the materials are at the Fairmount Historical Museum, available to the pilgrims who've devoted themselves to James Dean.

With Ursula Andress at the Thalian Ball—named for the Greek muse of comedy—at Ciro's on August 29, 1955, one month before James Dean's death. When the pair met, Ursula was nineteen and dating Dean's cinematic rival, Marlon Brando. (Michael Ochs Archives/Getty Images)

Dean with girlfriend Pier Angeli on the *East of Eden* set in 1954. The actor contemplated marrying the Italian actress and converting to Catholicism, but he claimed that her mother and her studio, MGM, conspired against them. Friends deny the rumor that Angeli was a "beard" used to distract fans from Dean's bisexuality. (Michael Ochs Archives/Getty Images)

Following his mother's death, Dean was raised by his aunt and uncle, Ortense and Marcus Winslow Sr., and came to regard their son, Markie, as a younger brother. Markie would remain on the family farm and manage James Dean's estate. (Dennis Stock/Magnum Photos)

During a visit back home in Fairmount, Indiana, in February 1955, Dean brought *Life* magazine photographer Dennis Stock to the town's only funeral parlor and posed inside a coffin. Later, fans would use this photo as proof that the actor had a death wish, but according to Dean, he "just wanted to see how it felt." (Dennis Stock/Magnum Photos)

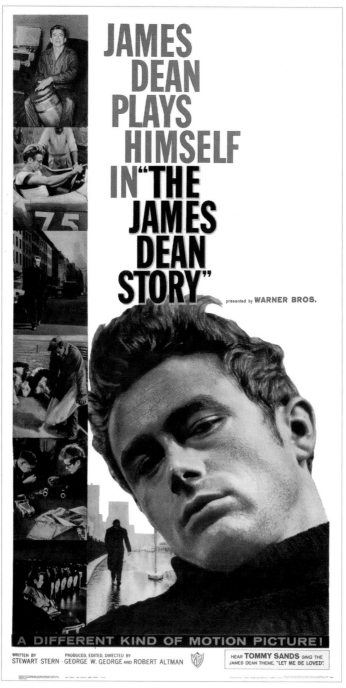

As the public clamored for any information about James Dean after his death, Warner Brothers released the documentary *The James Dean Story*, in 1957. (Everett Collection)

Dean with two of his racing trophies. Because of his working class upbringing, Dean enjoyed the banter among the pit crews at the racetrack. He hoped to become accomplished enough at the sport that his fellow drivers would view him as something other than a hobbyist. (Popperfoto/Getty Images)

After trying a number of other race cars, Dean became infatuated with the Porsche 550 Spyder. He was driving it to a race in Salinas, California, when he was killed. (Warner Bros./Getty Images)

After the accident that claimed his life, the wreckage of the 550 Spyder was displayed around the United States. Following a series of fatal mishaps, owner George Barris concluded that the car was cursed. (Hulton Archive/Getty Images)

The nondescript nature of Dean's gravesite reminds visitors of his understated Quaker upbringing. This has not prevented more zealous fans from attempting to steal or vandalize the tombstone. (Michael Ochs Archives/Getty Images)

Six decades after the release of his last film, James Dean still inspires. His most loyal devotees—known as Deaners—regard themselves as an international community committed to creativity and self-realization. (Everett Collection)

31

BY A TINY TWIST OF FATE

On her website, Pamela Des Barres describes herself as "legendary groupie, author, journalist." While still a teenager, she babysat Frank Zappa's children and used the opportunity to meet some of the rock stars she'd later chronicle in autobiographical tomes like *I'm with the Band* (1987) and *Let's Spend the Night Together: Backstage Secrets of Rock Muses and Supergroupies* (2007). As "the world's most famous groupie," she boasts of her sexual liaisons with names like Mick Jagger, Keith Moon, Jimmy Page, and Waylon Jennings.

She also counts Don Johnson and Woody Allen among her celebrity lovers.

In 2013, she started her own clothing line, Groupie Couture.

But before the Who and the Stones, Pamela loved James Dean. "I became a fan at eight years old," she says. "Fanatical. I compared every boy at school to him. Because he was a rebel. I was always interested in people who were trying to break the norm, people who were shaking things up.

"I've always wanted to turn heads and make a statement."

Because of Jimmy, she claims, men learned "to be sensitive and vulnerable, and to weep. It's a huge gift he gave the world by just being who he was."

Pamela has been to all the Dean landmarks within driving distance of her Venice Beach home. But she's just as contented on Main Street in

Fairmount as she is on Santa Monica Boulevard. On a Friday afternoon, as she's preparing to do a writing workshop at the James Dean Gallery, she navigates the town, her flaming red hair adorned with a garland of roses, and a pair of pink-tinted glasses providing an Aquarian view of the pickup trucks and American flags.

Like other Deaners, Pamela blends her affection for Jimmy with other fifties icons. Tattooed on the back of her neck is a James Dean signature, just above a rendering of Elvis. "My segue from Dean and Elvis into sixties rock guys is a pretty seamless trajectory. The people I went out with, they were definitely walking along the edge there."

Still, Dean is the one who continues to own her heart. "I carried a picture of his gravestone in my wallet in school," she says. "I mean, I was obsessed. Before there were VCRs, I'd set my alarm so I could wake up and watch *Rebel Without a Cause* on TV. I did it forever and ever. I know every line of every movie. I've wanted to come here my whole life."

When she finally did arrive in Fairmount—while researching a book that she wanted to be "from the heart"—she was greeted by Lenny Prussack and Dave Loehr, the proprietors at the Gallery. Not only were they honored to meet the Queen of the Groupies, but they also related to her yearning to seek out the place that gave the world James Dean.

"Welcome home," they each told Pamela.

At times, she envisions Dean in the 1960s, smoking a little pot, playing his bongos, adding to his record collection, maybe even attending the same concerts that she did. "He would have fit in with all the sexual experimentation, too. People were just open to everything and trying everything. It was like a tiny twist of fate that he wasn't there."

And when people argue that maybe it was good that they didn't see Jimmy age into the same type of troubled character as Marlon Brando, she counters that Dean would have been more like Paul Newman: socially aware, professionally vital, as handsome as a senior citizen as he'd been as a teen.

Because residents have seen every variant of fan, a person like Pamela is recognized in Fairmount for the sincerity of her convictions, and—notoriety aside—made to feel welcome. She now visits between two and three times a year and is considering purchasing a second home in Indiana.

"I'd rather be here more than anywhere else," she says. "*Anywhere* else. It's just so comforting and peaceful. I go sit at his grave and commune with him, sit on top of his bones and commune with him. I know everything there is to know about him. I've had plenty of dreams about him. I mean, I just feel connected to him. I talk to him. I know this is going to sound very, very weird, but I let him look through my eyes when I'm here. He likes to look around. I believe there's no separation between souls. Of course, that's another conversation. But part of it is just being with him. When his fans are here, he is here."

32

"THE HOTTEST PROPERTY WE HAD"

I n the wake of Jimmy's death, sympathy cards for members of the Dean and Winslow clans family flooded the Fairmount post office. The *Fairmount News* informed Jimmy's former neighbors that the former guard for the Fairmount Quakers had left behind an estate worth a remarkable $105,000. Almost immediately, the weekly newspaper sold out. Hundreds of more copies were hastily printed. These, too, instantly disappeared.

As a result, the publisher opted to create a special edition "to try and meet the public's demand." Above the broadsheet's masthead, the words IN MEMORY OF JAMES DEAN appeared in a black box in seventy-two-point type.

"We, as members of the staff, would like to take this opportunity of expressing our sympathy to the bereaved family of James Dean," read an item situated on page one, to the left of a posed portrait of Jimmy at UCLA, likely procured from one of his Fairmount relatives. "Words cannot begin to express emotions during periods of time such as this, but Jim Dean and his influence on Fairmount will never be forgotten."

The writer had no idea how true that statement would be.

In the halls of Fairmount High School, a mood of "unbelievable sadness" pervaded the student body, according to the newspaper. "The students feel they knew Jim well because he spoke before them in convocations whenever he was home and visited classrooms, especially speech classes. Because he was a Fairmount graduate, the students felt especially proud when he came back to the school, with his greatness never making them feel small or unimportant."

As much as the article emphasized the gratification that locals derived from having one of their own achieve celebrity stature, it was acknowledged that Dean wasn't quite like most of the people in town. Jimmy, the story stressed, was "an interesting person, not afraid to be different, but with a personality all his own."

But the accident had fused the varied aspects of Jimmy's life. Along with stories about native sons home from the military on leave and events at the American Legion Hall, the *Fairmount News* beat now extended to Hollywood. "Dean was the hottest property we had," a Warner Brothers official was quoted in the newspaper. "We had great plans for him."

Said James Bacon, Hollywood correspondent for the Associated Press, "Dean could well become Hollywood's first posthumous Academy Award winner for his role in *East of Eden*."

In its editorial that week, the weekly celebrated Dean's career, exercising a touch of the same creativity that Jimmy applied to his acting. "His path," the newspaper said, "to those who knew him best, was steep and rugged and was covered with sandpaper instead of velvet." Yet, his accomplishments were "as bright as a meteor which flows like a golden tear down the dark cheeks of night.

"By the law of averages, it was most unusual for a lad twenty-four years of age to leave a rural environment . . . and go so far and fast in so short a time. . . . He made his living by acting, by his own definition, 'behavior of and for other people.' For a little period of time, he made the lives of many more entertaining, more interesting, and, in some cases, more bearable. Such a life is not suddenly wiped out in the wreckage of a car in California."

It was Winton who came up to Paso Robles to claim his son's body. Just as Jimmy accompanied his mother's coffin back to Indiana sixteen years earlier, Winton flew with Jimmy's casket to Indianapolis. When the flight landed—four days after the accident, at ten-seventeen at night—a hearse was waiting to transport the corpse the seventy-odd miles to Hunt's Funeral Home in Fairmount.

Once Marcus Sr. and Ortense received the news about Jimmy's death, their house became the gathering place for friends, relatives, and others hoping to convey their condolences. The responsibility of opening up their home, in the midst of grief, was overpowering, and the decision was made for Joan Peacock to keep her brother, eleven-year-old Markie, in her guest bedroom for the next several days.

"There were people coming into town from everywhere," he recalls. "You didn't know from one day to the next what was around the corner. We knew that Jimmy was a movie star, but we didn't know how big of a movie star he was. You have to remember that *Rebel Without a Cause* and *Giant* weren't even out yet. It was something we'd never seen before."

Because the Back Creek Friends Church, where Jimmy had attended services, was relatively small, the family decided to hold his funeral at the Fairmount Friends Church, which seated six hundred. But by the morning of Saturday, October 8, more than double that number had already lined up for the ceremony at two o'clock in the afternoon. Fearing a disorderly scene, the Winslows asked that speakers be wired in front of the building for the mourners outside.

It was the largest crowd ever to gather for a funeral in Grant County, estimated at somewhere between two thousand and three thousand. An additional five hundred waited at Park Cemetery for the burial. Despite the size, even the most fervent fans maintained their discipline. When the public address system failed, groups positioned themselves in the churchyard, along the outside walls, and in the building's nursery room, where an audio transmission of the service could be heard. If there were complaints, the Winslows never heard them.

• • • •

The only funeral to which the media could draw a parallel was that of Rudolph Valentino, twenty-nine years earlier. Valentino, cinema's first sex symbol, was an Italian immigrant who'd worked as a ballroom dancer—

and, reportedly, a gigolo—under the moniker Signor Rodolfo in New York before continuing to southern California. After a series of bit roles, his dark, good looks, combined with a general air of mystery and danger, propelled him to distinction in the fledgling silent film industry. In 1921, the movie *The Sheik* launched the Valentino craze. Noted Bette Davis, "A whole generation of females wanted to ride off into a sandy paradise with him."

The movie tells the tale of an aristocratic woman, Lady Diana Mayo, who decides to explore the Algerian desert alone. From afar, she's detected by Valentino's character, Sheik Ahmed Ben Hassan, an Arab guide. So overcome with lust is the sheik that he cannot contain himself from abducting the visitor and whisking her away to his tent.

"Why have you brought me here?" she asks.

"Are you not woman enough to know?"

In the novel of the same name, the sheik takes Lady Diana by force. But, in the culture of the time, his motives are depicted not so much as those of a sex criminal but an experienced lothario who knows exactly what women like this really want. While James Dean's movies challenged the conformity of the 1950s, *The Sheik* appealed to the permissiveness of a time later labeled the Era of Wonderful Nonsense. The fact that Ahmed Ben Hassan is not exactly white played to the titillating concept of breaking boundaries. Yet, in an effort to appeal to the status quo, the story ends with the comforting revelation that the sheik was never an Arab at all, but a European adopted by the exotic tribe.

The movie was so successful that it earned an extraordinary $1 million, five times more than the cost of production.

Like Jimmy, Valentino led a complicated private life. Despite rumors about his sexual inclinations, he married twice. His first wife was said to be a lesbian. An aspiring actress, she allegedly wed Valentino to remove herself from a love triangle involving two other women and immediately regretted her choice, locking him out of the bedroom on their wedding night. By many accounts, the marriage was never consummated. Nonetheless, when he married a second time, to set designer Natacha Rambova, he was arrested and charged with bigamy. Valentino's fans would criticize Rambova for exerting too much influence on his career, encouraging him to take roles that diminished his reputation and make decisions that alienated him from power brokers in the industry.

In 1926, at the age of thirty-one, Valentino collapsed at the Hotel Ambassador in New York and was rushed to the hospital. Doctors performed immediate surgery for appendicitis and gastric ulcers, but, during his recovery, he developed peritonitis. The newspapers covered the story as if the patient were Calvin Coolidge or Henry Ford. Thousands gathered outside New York Polyclinic Hospital, praying for the screen idol. Despite the supplications, Valentino passed away on August 23.

The reaction to his death was more extreme than the hajj to Fairmount that followed Jimmy's accident. The estimated number of mourners lining the streets leading to the Frank E. Campbell Funeral Home was somewhere between thirty thousand and one hundred thousand. Windows were smashed, and police on horseback chased down flappers and other female devotees, hauling them to jail. The press maintained that dozens of fans committed suicide.

Yet, Valentino's movies did not speak to future generations the same way that James Dean's did. To quote Alice Terry, female lead in the 1920 Valentino movie *The Four Horsemen of the Apocalypse,* "The biggest thing Valentino ever did was to die."

• • • •

The family was exhausted, emotionally and physically, from the parade of strangers converging on the town and seeking them out. Even friends and neighbors felt besieged, as well as obligated to assist those who'd come to Indiana with good intentions. Because there were so few vacancies at nearby inns, pallbearer Bob Middleton opened up his Marion home to Nick Adams for several days.

Lew Bracker never expected to encounter the mob he saw surrounding the church and was worried about missing his friend's funeral. When he expressed his concern to photographer Dennis Stock, the lensman maneuvered his way into the building and came out with Marcus Sr. Lew had never met Jimmy's uncle, but Marcus had evidently been told about the way the Bracker family provided sanctuary for Dean in Los Angeles. To Lew's astonishment, Marcus led him back into the church and insisted that he sit among Jimmy's relatives.

Crammed in at the front of the room, with people clogging every exit point, Markie felt claustrophobic. "As a child, it seemed like the funeral was awfully long," he told the Marion *Chronicle-Tribune* in 2005.

Rev. Xen Harvey, pastor of the Fairmount Friends Church, addressed the throng, scolding any "idle curiosity seekers" who came for the "excitement of a movie star's burial." He tempered those remarks by welcoming "those who came with genuine sadness for the loss of a friend or relative."

Act One, according to the pastor, comprised the years Jimmy spent in Fairmount, followed by Act Two, the acting career for which he'd achieve a level or prominence no one in town ever envisioned. Act Three, Harvey continued, centered on "the new life into which he has just entered."

To the people in Fairmount, Jimmy would forever be the intense, endearing kid on the Winslow farm—the child in Act One. "We loved him as a small boy," Harvey said. "We loved him when he was fast breaking with the basketball team." And, because the people in Fairmount knew him so well, they also loved James Byron Dean "in the lean, hungry years of his career" and when he became a celebrity in Hollywood.

This affection was born of sincerity, and the grief that pervaded the town was authentic—as was the disdain Harvey felt for people who "in the emptiness of their lives and the littleness of their spirits," had journeyed to Fairmount to gawk at the doleful proceedings that day. He also resented the "amateur psychologists" who clung to folklore and untruths about Jimmy, entitling themselves to analyze a young man they didn't know. "Because we knew him as a normal boy, who did the things normal boys do. . . . He was not brooding or weird or sullen or even odd. He was fun-loving and too busy to be sullen."

Harvey described Jimmy as "an actor in the noblest meaning attached to the term," a person who occupied the hearts of the characters he represented on the film and television screens. Because of the heightened sensitivity that came with his vocation, "he suffered when they suffered, brooded when they brooded, and rejoiced when they rejoiced."

Returning to the theatrical analogy, Harvey outlined his belief that the body was a "stage property" employed in the physical world. And whether death occurred through a sudden accident or a long, degenerative illness, each human set down his or her "stage property," and moved on to the next world. "It does not affect the existence of a person any more than it affects an actor to lay aside one stage property used in one act of a play, and go on to another act. . . . The career of James Dean has not ended. It has just begun. And remember, God himself is directing the production."

The speech left the majority of attendees uplifted. Harvey appeared to understand Jimmy and his eternal impact. But there was another clergyman on the podium, as well: Rev. James DeWeerd, now a religious broadcaster on popular Cincinnati radio station WLW, who'd flown into Marion for the event—and was escorted to town in a State Police cruiser.

"Dr. DeWeerd, who served on the local school board during the formative years of the young actor, pointed out that he was not a problem boy," the *Fairmount News* summarized the sermon, "but simply a boy with problems who knew how to seek counsel from men older and wiser than himself."

Because of Jimmy's proclivity for compartmentalizing various aspects of his life, Bracker knew little about DeWeerd. But the minister made Lew uneasy. Just as Harvey compared Jimmy's life to the theater, DeWeerd referenced the fast-paced lifestyle most people associated with the acting field. Quoting the poet Edna St. Vincent Millay, DeWeerd intoned, "My candle burns at both ends; it will not last the night; but, ah, my foes, and, oh, my friends, it gives a lovely light."

The suggestion that Dean's heedless choices were responsible for his demise—even if they lent a romantic glow to the actor's reputation— deeply offended Lew, particularly in front of Winton, the Winslows, and

Jimmy's grandparents. Bracker knew about Jimmy's plans to direct films and start his own production company. He'd spoken about buying a house in Los Angeles for himself and his grandparents, and, eventually, helping Markie find work in the film industry—essentially re-creating the familial contentment that the actor had known in Indiana to the city where he made his living. Yes, he liked fast cars. But, by Bracker's assessment, Jimmy was becoming more settled.

Lew never communicated his disenchantment to DeWeerd personally. But the "burning the candle at both ends" quote irritated Bracker whenever he remembered it.

"JAMES DEAN IS NOT DEAD"

As Lew feared, Jimmy's apartment was burglarized after his death. Although his personal papers were safely in Bracker's possession, the intruder took a 16-millimeter camera, tape recorder, bongos, and a drawing that the actor had made of himself—lying prone, surrounded by candles.

Meanwhile, Rolf Wütherich was transferred from War Memorial Hospital in Paso Robles to White Memorial Hospital in Glendale, less than ten miles from Hollywood. He was in unbearable pain and sedated most of the day. For the next several months, he remained in bed, his shattered bones held together with plaster casts and wire. Other surgeries awaited: a bone-grafting operation and a procedure that involved reconnecting his hip bones with nails and screws.

Feeling depressed and guilty, he'd tell Germany's *Bild* magazine, "I never should have let James Dean drive the car."

Since Jimmy was no longer around to advocate for the mechanic whose counsel he'd valued, Lew took it upon himself to do so. With Ursula Andress, he drove to Glendale to visit the ailing passenger. Using Ursula as a translator, Bracker asked if Wütherich had any visa or legal issues that needed attention. He didn't and thanked his visitors for their consideration.

Feigning a Nordic stoicism, he vowed to manage his own tribulations.

At Warner Brothers, studio executives closely monitored Dean's transformation from movie star to cult figure. "The situation was tense," Warner producer Lou Quinn was quoted in *The Robb Report* in 1990. "After all, he only had one movie out. Should they release *Rebel* right away or wait? They had a lot of money tied up in it. Finally, they decided to go ahead. But everybody was nervous."

From a business standpoint, the decision was a wise one. From the moment that *Rebel Without a Cause* opened on October 26, 1955—less than one month after Dean's accident—Jimmy became the hero of the cynical, the unconventional, and the disenfranchised. *Variety* called the movie "exciting, suspenseful, and provocative," while the *New York Times* described *Rebel* as "violent, brutal, and disturbing." The release triggered debate about larger issues: the proliferation of rebellious youth in a time of postwar prosperity, poor choices, and the obliviousness of parents who refused to acknowledge problems festering in their own households.

Even the most artful publicist could not have generated this type of attention. Over the next twelve months, Warner Brothers would receive more than fifty thousand letters praising James Dean. On both sides of the Atlantic, the film's success inspired other movies about teenagers in trouble: among them, *High School Confidential!* and *West Side Story*—starring Natalie Wood—in the United States, and *The Loneliness of the Long Distance Runner* in the United Kingdom, sometimes referred to as the British *Rebel Without a Cause*.

Despite its triumph at the box office, even the most profit-driven studio executive understood that there would have been more money to make had Jimmy remained alive. And the collateral damage of the ill-fated crash was profound. Collier "Buster" Davidson, the ambulance attendant who'd been riding with Dean when he died, rarely discussed the incident. But less than twenty-four hours after the tragedy, he made a decision that changed the course of his life.

"He wasn't going to drive the ambulance again," his daughter, Helen Hopper, told the San Luis Obispo *Tribune*. "It was too much for him. I guess the sight of what they found and the whole situation just bothered him. It was horrible."

Ken Hord, who—as a thirteen-year-old passenger in his father's Pontiac—had seen Dean's Porsche on the highway moments before the crash, would never fully understand why the wreck held so much fascination for people who weren't there. Ken himself had seen Jimmy's body after the accident. And there was nothing to romanticize.

"It's unfortunate," he said. "He had a terrific career in front of him. It's just lucky that he took himself out and nobody else."

At the Winslow farm, day-to-day activities were irrevocably altered. Now, when Markie stepped outside, he noticed not just cattle or sheep, but cars lined along the road, and people rushing toward him with cameras in hand. "I remember being in our basement on the weekend, looking up at the window and seeing feet walk by," he says. "It changed our life. There isn't any way around it."

At first, the family theorized that the interest would wane after two or three years. But it never did. "I've heard losing a child is the hardest thing," Markie told the Marion *Chronicle-Tribune*. "Mom and Dad were in love with [Jimmy] like one of their own. They were constantly reminded of him. I think it's harder—how do you say it?—harder to let them go when you're constantly reminded of it. . . . He's just always there."

Sometimes, visitors were obnoxious, trying to talk their way inside and touch Jimmy's bedroom set. Most of the time, though, the fans were polite, conscious that they were intruding on the family's time and grateful for a handshake or quick exchange of conversation.

"It just became a way of life," Markie says. "My parents were very proud of Jimmy, and they felt that, if these people were coming here from all over the world, Jimmy would want us to be friendly to them. And my parents were very generous with the fans over the years. They let them come on the farm. They even invited some of the nicer people into the house."

As a rule, the guests' behavior confirmed that they were worthy of the courtesy. "We've been very fortunate over the years. We never had anything stolen out of the house. The closest we came was, soon after Jimmy's death, Mom and Dad sent photos to some magazines. They asked the reporters to send them back, and some of them never did. But, you know, nothing real drastic. Most of Jimmy's fans have always tried to be respectful. We just haven't had a lot of problems."

Residents displayed a similar civility toward the family, abstaining from opportunities to cash in on the tragedy. Motorcycle shop owner Marvin Carter—who'd reacquired Jimmy's old bike when the actor began appearing on television—had been hoping that the Czech Whizzer would become a collector's item one day. Although the value increased after the accident, Carter no longer wanted the motorcycle. Instead, he gave it to the Winslows.

· · · ·

In November 1955, *Collier's* magazine ran Sanford Roth's photographs of James Dean's final journey, along with a firsthand account of the calamitous trip. Fans were mesmerized and, soon, other publishers were churning out issues specifically devoted to the late actor. Ideal Publishing, the company that regularly produced *Movie Stars Parade* for newsstands, came up with a *James Dean Album.* A summary of Jimmy's life began with the headline THE BOY WHO REFUSES TO DIE.

"In the months since the life of 24-year-old James Dean was so suddenly snuffed out," the story read,

> an uncanny thing has happened. In the history of Hollywood tragedies, there has never been anything like it. It is almost as if from somewhere in the Great Beyond, with the same intense fire that always burned bright in him, James Dean is defying the fates that took his life before it really begun, defying them to make him die.
>
> We see it very clearly now: James Dean is not dead. He is not going to die. We know because we have the evidence—in many ways. Most poignantly, in the letters and phone calls that are pouring into our office every day. Of course, a certain amount of such interest was to be expected. But after an interval of

mourning, it would normally stop. *It hasn't stopped.* And, much more significantly, *the people do not speak of Jimmy as if he were dead.*

The magazine devoted a section to analyzing Jimmy's love interests. "With Pier Angeli," one section began, "it was real love. . . . With Vampira, it was friendship." A paragraph followed explaining how Dean was attracted to the horror movie hostess for "her eccentric charms. . . . He'd go to her apartment for advice, professional and romantic—nothing more. Contrary to an article in a recent scandal magazine, which tried to paint a sordid picture of their dates, the only relationship they had was on a platonic basis."

His liaison with Ursula Andress was described as tempestuous. "Though they fought like cats and dogs, Jimmy admitted it was fun making up. . . . When she felt it wasn't working out, she switched her affections to [director] John Derek. Moody and sullen, Jimmy dogged her footsteps for weeks afterwards, peering in car windows at her and John, confronting them in restaurants, calling her at odd hours. But he was left in the cold."

In the same issue, a woman who identified herself only as "Jeanne"—an alleged actress who'd met Dean in New York while he was taking classes at the Actors Studio—was credited with this analysis: "Jim was afraid of love. He seemed to feel that if he fell in love, he would have to lose the object of his heart. I'm sure that has to do with the fact that he lost his mother when he was nine. Although I'm no psychologist, the pattern was obvious. But it was more than that, too. Jim had no time or energy for love. He wanted to save his emotions and his feelings for his work."

Even at this early stage, the folklore had begun, with purported associates—some undoubtedly invented by pulp magazine writers—filling in the blank spots on the canvas with expressionistic strokes.

On their first Christmas without Jimmy, his relatives trudged to his grave, a short distance from the Winslow farm. When they arrived, they saw that numerous fans had preceded them to the headstone, leaving behind their own symbols of dedication. "We counted fourteen wreaths, a cross, a vase of fresh flowers, a vase of bittersweet, and a big basket of red roses," his grandmother Emma Woolen Dean was quoted in *Photoplay*. "We are touched that Jimmy earned such devotion."

34

NOT OF THE WORLD

The official investigation into James Dean's death occurred a week and a half after the accident. Donald Turnupseed's lawyer, Peter Andre, would later say that both motorists played a role in the crash; Turnupseed should have watched where he was going, and Jimmy should have slowed when he noticed the Ford making the turn. Comparing the time of the stop at Blackwells Corner with the time of the crash, coroner Paul E. Merrick estimated that Dean was traveling at either eighty-five or eighty-six miles per hour. From his hospital bed in Glendale, Rolf Wütherich "categorically denied" witness reports that he was actually the one behind the wheel of the 550 Spyder.

Either way, at a coroner's inquest on October 11, 1955, Turnupseed was absolved of any wrongdoing. And the customary blood test the state performed on all deceased drivers failed to reveal even a hint of alcohol in the actor's system.

"It was never established whose fault it was," CR "Budgie" Sturgeon, a partner at Turnupseed's insurance company, Spuhler and Sturgeon, later told the driver's hometown newspaper, the Tulare *Advance-Register*. "It just died."

Nonetheless, the romanticized perception of Dean became that of a wild iconoclast, with little regard for traffic laws and possibly less for his own safety. Despite this, Natalie Wood took it upon herself to dispel this image. "Much has been printed about Jimmy's carelessness," she said in one interview. "He was not driving recklessly the night of the accident. This accident could have happened to anyone."

She knew this, she claimed, because when she'd been injured after her own car accident, Jimmy was the one Hollywood friend who called to scold her for the example that she was setting for impressionable fans.

"As actors," she maintained that Dean told her, "we belong to our public and not to ourselves."

While the world moved forward, the captivation over the crash never vanished. As late as 2009, the first officers on the scene were still having their opinions on September 30, 1955 dissected. In an interview with the Santa Clarita Valley Historical Society, Ron Nelson disputed the coroner's appraisal of Dean's travel velocity: "If he'd been going (close to) ninety miles per hour, I don't think there'd be anything left of the car or even the mechanic that was with him."

Said Ernie Tripke, "There are so many stories that have started with that accident. Even in our local newspaper several years ago, they were talking about the fiery crash. . . . There wasn't a spark in the whole thing, let alone a fiery crash."

The pair continued working together for the next several months, until Tripke was promoted to sergeant and transferred to Eureka, the largest coastal city between San Francisco and Portland, Oregon. "I was sorry to see him go," joked Nelson, "because that meant that all the phone calls fell to me."

With Dean no longer competing with him, Paul Newman stepped into roles that almost certainly would have gone to Jimmy, including boxer Rocky Graziano in *Somebody Up There Likes Me* and Billy the Kid in *The Left Handed Gun.* Yet, Dean remained very much a part of the scene. At the twenty-eighth Academy Awards, he was nominated for Best Supporting Actor for *East of Eden,* while Sal Mineo and Natalie Wood were considered for their supporting roles in *Rebel Without a Cause*, and Nicholas Ray was a contender for Best Director. Although none of them won, Jo Van Fleet did receive an Oscar for Best Supporting Actress in *East of Eden*.

As the attendees were leaving the RKO Pantages theater after the ceremony, they seemed to be fixated on two topics: the movie *Marty*—which had taken the prizes for Best Motion Picture, Best Director, Best Actor, and Best Story and Screenplay—and James Dean.

So was much of the public. When *Modern Screen* magazine held its Audience Award for 1955 at the famed Cocoanut Grove nightclub at LA's Ambassador Hotel—the same Ambassador Hotel where presidential candidate Robert F. Kennedy would be gunned down in a very different America, thirteen years later—Natalie Wood accepted the Best Actor award from future Monaco princess Grace Kelly on behalf of Jimmy. Watching from the audience were Winton Dean and his second wife, Ethel.

"Nothing would make us happier than to be able to have his award to treasure forever," the couple wrote the publication. "Do you think this would be possible? Do you know who has it now?"

The plaque was located in the Warner Brothers trophy case and turned over to the pair.

A letter to the editor from James Dean's father was a coup for *Modern Screen*, and the magazine proudly published it, alongside the general fan missives. "I must say that I was very pleased when I saw that James Dean received an award," wrote one young woman." "You just don't know how happy it's made me that our so-called 'rude monster' has some fans after all. . . . I'm not going to deny that [the accident] knocked me for a loop, nor am I going to deny that I've cried every night since his death . . . and go to sleep on sixteen mags containing articles about him. I can't deny those things and, under no circumstances, will I ever."

Farther down the page, another female admirer addressed *Giant* director George Stevens directly:

I read every story on Jim. Now, I want to let out my feelings about him.

He went out with girls who didn't understand him, yet those girls were very lucky to be with such a wonderful guy. If I could have only been with him for a moment, I would learn to understand him. He was a very lonely boy who felt he wasn't wanted. . . .

I know this is asking too much of you, but can you please ask Jimmy's father if I may have Jimmy's medal that he wore in some of the books [it's unclear if she meant the St. Christopher medal given to Dean by Pier Angeli or the National Forensic League Award he'd won in high school]. Thank you very much for trying to understand my letter.

Stories of Jimmy's interest in the occult abounded. Even Jimmy's friends, in their efforts to sympathetically explain his eccentricities, contributed to the frenzy. In one interview, Patsy D'Amore asserted that Judy Garland had told him about an all-night séance in Dean's apartment. According to the tale, Jimmy lay in a coffin while the other guests surrounded it, attempting to help him reach the spirit of his late mother.

"I was put *on* this world," he apparently stated. "But I'm not *of* this world."

The anecdotes greatly irritated Dean's family. "All those magazines would come out and say he had a death wish and all this kind of stuff," Markie says. "We knew that wasn't true. But it's hard to fight something like that. You just have to go with the flow, I guess, even if you don't like it."

Every month, the newsstand articles became more fantastic. As the first anniversary of the accident approached, the publishers of *Filmland*—cover lines generally included fare like SEE JOAN COLLINS IN A BUBBLE BATH, and DEBBIE AND EDDIE'S MIXED MARRIAGE BABY, a reference to the impending birth of Carrie Fisher, daughter of Jewish singer Eddie Fisher and Christian actress Debbie Reynolds—put out an issue that reportedly included Dean's "own words from beyond."

The entire magazine was devoted to a single article, told from the perspective of a former Dean girlfriend named "Judy"; her name is changed, the writers point out, "in order to avoid possible embarrassment to her family and her employers."

According to the fable, one day, Jimmy confides to Judy about a dream. In it, he dies "in an auto smash-up." But he appears unafraid. "If I'm doomed," he assures her, "some time, somewhere, I'll come back to you."

After the accident, Judy is overtaken with an urge to write. But as she looks at the page, she becomes aware that neither the words nor the handwriting are hers. "Yes, Judy," she reads, "I can speak to you this way. But I needed your belief to do it. Your belief is like a magnet, giving me the force to be able to speak to you. If your belief ever faded, I would have to be silent again."

Dean knew that his dream was a premonition, he discloses. Yet, he did nothing to circumvent the inevitable. When he began driving to the race in Salinas, he was looking forward to facing a personal challenge.

> What I thought of then as "death" . . . added excitement and spice to my life, my life that was becoming just one big glare of publicity.
>
> . . . The crash itself was nothing. I felt no shock, no hurt . . . I could see myself lying there, and I should have been feeling the pain of my broken body— and yet, here I was looking down on that other person who was Jimmy Dean. . . . I watched with amazement and wonder, and the realization gradually sank into me—this is what we called death.
>
> But it wasn't death. I had never felt so full of life. My head had never been clearer. I wasn't conscious of any worries or troubles. . . . I heard a voice call my name, and I seemed to be a small boy again, hearing my mother call me.
>
> But Judy, about us . . . you were the only one I wanted to come back to. You believe me, don't you, Judy?

Before she can answer, though, the writing stops. She stares at the pencil in her hand and realizes that James Dean "would always be here."

• • • •

The extensive profile of Dean in *Redbook* would have a far greater impact. While Judy never existed, Rev. James DeWeerd did. And his alleged opinions about Jimmy's spiritual, cultural, and intellectual alienation from most of his Fairmount neighbors—the story mentioned that the "worldly" pastor and Jimmy discussed, among other topics, "the limited way of life" in Dean's hometown—hurt feelings and provoked anger.

On September 16, 1956, the *Fairmount News* ran an article about the controversy. The newspaper noted that a number of facts were incorrect in the *Redbook* story. For example, DeWeerd had been the minister of a local Wesleyan church, not a Wesleyan *Baptist* one, as *Redbook* reported. Defending the pastor, the *News* editorialized, "Anyone who knows Jim DeWeerd realizes that any comments he might make certainly would not be of the nature as related in the magazine. . . . He believes now, as always, that a greater stress should be placed upon spiritual values and broader views about world conditions."

According to DeWeerd, he was about to embark on a world tour when he received a call from *Redbook*. Rushed and preoccupied, he admitted exhibiting far less eloquence than he did at the pulpit. "For some time, my policy has been a refusal to discuss my friendship with James Dean on the basis that whatever knowledge I had of him was 'privileged communication.' Because of my utter nausea from much of the garbled publicity, released posthumously, I decided to grant interviews requested by reputable firms. Apparently, instead of painting the unknown or little known phases of Jim's inner life in its true light, I have only added to the confusion, for which I am heartily sorry."

All appeared to be forgiven. When the one year anniversary of Dean's death was commemorated in Fairmount less than two weeks after De-Weerd's mea culpa in the local press, he played a key role in a ceremony that culminated with Ortense Winslow placing an immense wreath—sent from the movie star's German fans—on her nephew's headstone.

At least five hundred cars—containing some two thousand participants—filled a parking area near the cemetery. An oil painting of the actor—by his friend California artist Robert Ormsby—was unveiled. The Short Ridge High School chorus sang "Father, in Thy Mysterious Presence Kneeling" and "Breath of God."

"We are grateful, as the citizens of Fairmount, that from our town, in our state of Indiana, and in our times, James Dean, one of our young men, has earned world acclaim in his chosen field of dramatic arts," said DeWeerd, accompanied once again by Fairmount Friends Church Rev. Xen Harvey.

The minister told the crowd that, despite the actor's remains buried below him, he preferred thinking of Jimmy as existing in "in the hearts of everyone," and continuing to use his influence to better his generation.

It was a generation that was slowly moving toward the sixties, displaying the early signs of insurgence in destructive activities like drag racing. The week before, the press reported, two carloads of young people in Tampa had participated in one of these unsanctioned contests. When one of the vehicles slammed into a telephone pole, a passenger, as well as a bystander, was killed.

Wrote the *Fairmount News*, "It's pretty obvious that drag racing . . . is becoming a critical problem and is highly dangerous. The merits of drag racing on supervised strips, which some people advocate, is also highly questionable. It seems that the time is about at hand where authorities will have to crack down on young offenders if they persist in drag racing after adequate warning."

At the gravesite, DeWeerd cited a number of reasons for the apparent surge in juvenile delinquency: the baby boom, as well as the media's depiction and sometimes glorification of deviant behavior. But, DeWeerd counseled, troubled teens could reverse course by emulating James Dean's drive to set goals and achieve them.

Because space was limited at the tribute, those who could not attend cavalcaded through Park Cemetery into the night, slowing as they passed Jimmy's grave. With so many visitors from out of state, the ones who remained overnight rented rooms from Dean's former neighbors in Fairmount.

Hoping to capitalize on the public's fixation with the actor, Warner Brothers released a documentary, *The James Dean Story*, in 1957. In addition to interviews with Dean's friends and family, there were re-creations of his final drive—with Lew Bracker steering the 550 Spyder.

The family was satisfied with the tone of the film, and Lew never harbored any guilt about exploiting his friend's mishap. He did, however, regret not spending enough time with Marcus Sr. and Ortense Winslow when they visited Los Angeles. "I was tied up with racing and I was dating someone, and I wished I'd concentrated on them," he says. "I really should have brought them up to the house to spend time with my family. I should have brought them to the Villa Capri and Hamburger Hamlet. That's really what Jimmy would have wanted me to do. I still think about that. If there's one thing I could do over—other than persuading Jimmy not to drive the Porsche on the highway, of course—that would be it."

35

BODY DOUBLES

Eighteen-year-old Trai Pelletier turns a corner in Fairmount, dressed in a red leather jacket over a white T-shirt, his sandy hair combed back in a pompadour, a cigarette tucked behind his ear. Three months from now, he starts US Marine recruit training. But right now, the resident of Bourbonnais, Illinois, is hoping to win the James Dean look-alike contest, a highlight of the festival dedicated to the late actor.

"I've been doing this my whole life," he says, referring to his habit of impersonating Jimmy for an audience. And he means it. Pelletier was four months old when his grandmother Linda Sue Pelletier first entered him in the Little James Dean competition that precedes the look-alike tourney. He continued returning every year, winning twice as a child. Now, he's in the adult division—at least until the military shears his locks.

Night has fallen on the town, but the screeches from the amusement rides are heard in the distance, as a crowd packs itself into a square between two downtown buildings, waiting for the challenge to begin. Some people sit on portable chairs, others on blankets. Many stand, spilling out backward from the staging area onto the street, the merriment of the contest mixing with the music blaring from the other attractions at the fair.

Twenty-eight-year-old Haley Robinson takes a position against a brick wall at the side of the stage, her hair a blazing red, her arms and upper chest adorned with tattoos. When the sun is up, Haley works as a hairdresser, but her true love is burlesque dancing. On the stage at the White Rabbit Cabaret in Indianapolis, she calls herself Gurl Haggard, "the only burlesque dancer to be pardoned by Reagan." Her sense of humor, as well as inspiration, comes directly from Jimmy. She refers to her routine onstage as "classic burlesque through a snarl."

"The aesthetic is similar," she observes. "Working man's entertainment. And there's an Indiana element to it too. James Dean was a native Hoosier, just a kid from a really small town in Indiana, who became this powerful creative force, an icon who's completely untouchable."

On this night, the Little James Dean contest is won by three-and-a-half-year-old Wyatt Most, who strolls across the stage in a cowboy hat with a pack of cigarettes jutting from his pocket. An older woman rushes forward to hug him.

"This is great," says the child's grandmother, "because we're also from Fairmount."

"Are you one of James Dean's relatives?" she's asked.

"Oh, no. But we are good friends with the Winslows."

Before the main look-alike competition, six members of the Class of '49 are announced as judges, along with Lew Bracker. The senior citizens seat themselves on the stage, chattering with one another but taking the task seriously. As airy as the mood may seem, this is still about Jimmy.

Each of the dozen contestants marches past them, posing and bending forward into the arbiters' personal space. Mostly everyone is costumed as Jimmy in *Rebel*, except for one—Phil Timos from Australia—who portrays an older Jett Rink in *Giant*.

In the end, though, the judges pick Trai. There's something about the teen, they conclude, that captures the essence of the young man they knew.

Pelletier raises a hand, responding to the audience's applause. He nods and becomes introspective. It appears that he's not only imitating the way that James Dean looked but understands the way that he felt.

"The guy lived every day like it would be his last," Trai comments. "He didn't waste any time. He took life to the fullest, which is what everybody should do."

36

THE JINX

R olf Wütherich's final Hollywood moment occurred at the premiere of *Giant*. James Dean's passenger was an honored guest, posing on the red carpet in crutches, as Elizabeth Taylor wept beside him.

Privately, Wütherich was a tormented man. Not only was he in enormous pain, but the allegation that he'd actually been driving the Porsche also continued to follow him, provoking hateful messages from Dean's more unbalanced devotees. While he attempted to recover from his injuries, his wife had been talking to the press and providing them with erroneous quotes that she attributed to her husband. Unaware of this, Rolf was shocked to read his alleged firsthand accounts of the accident in magazine stories under lurid titles like "My Deadly Journey with James Dean."

Once a darling of Competition Motors, Wütherich became a distraction. Celebrity customers avoided him, too nervous about his association with James Dean's demise. Physically limited in the garage, Rolf was an ornery presence. Coworkers treaded lightly in his company, hoping not to provoke a long, German-accented rant. In 1956, Johnny von Neumann fired Wütherich for being "unruly" at work.

Because of his reputation, Rolf was still able to earn a living as a freelance Porsche mechanic. But his psychological problems, combined with legal entanglements, persisted.

Although Jimmy had intended to draw up a will designating that his earnings be distributed among a number of relatives, there was no official document at the time of his death. As a result, his next of kin, Winton Dean, inherited his son's wealth; showing their characteristic decorum, Marcus Sr. and Ortense did nothing to contest the arrangement. When Rolf learned this, he sued Jimmy's father, then Donald Turnupseed, seeking compensation for the injuries incurred in the crash. Motions were filed and hearings were delayed. Turnupseed reenlisted in the navy, while his insurance company wrangled and ultimately settled with Jimmy's.

Rolf received nothing. Six years after the accident, a judge dismissed his lawsuit. By that point, Wütterich had left the country.

Although inoperable, the wreckage of the 550 Spyder endured its own trials, leading believers in the occult to conclude that the vehicle was cursed. In fact, some have argued that the Porsche that carried James Dean up Route 466 was directly linked to another foredoomed vehicle, the six-passenger, 1910 Graf and Sift double phaeton that was carrying Austro-Hungarian Archduke Franz Ferdinand and his wife, the Duchess of Hohenberg, through Sarajevo on June 28, 1914. Earlier that day, the royal couple had survived an assassination attempt when a hurled bomb bounced off the convertible's folded roof and into another car in the imperial entourage. Although the duke and duchess were unhurt, their enemies correctly predicted that they'd attempt to visit the wounded in a nearby hospital. Assassins positioned themselves in the vicinity, hoping to ambush the monarchs.

As the twenty-eight-foot vehicle slowly navigated the narrow, twisted streets, the chauffeur, Leopold Lojka, made a wrong turn and pulled to a halt. Gavrilo Princip, a violent Serbian nationalist, happened to be standing just six feet away.

Princip's plan had been to pull out another bomb and toss it into the car. But the crowd around him was so dense that he lacked the capacity to extend his arms. Instead, he reached for a pistol and held it forward.

"Where I aimed," he later testified, "I do not know."

The gun discharged. One struck the duchess in the stomach, the other hit the heir to the Austro-Hungarian throne in the jugular vein. Despite the haphazard circumstances of the shooting, Princip accomplished his goal. Both died instantly.

World War I was underway.

Meanwhile, General Emil Potiroek of the Fifth Austrian Corps gained possession of the Graf and Sift. Despite its luxurious interior—it was lavishly decorated with Venetian crystal bud vases, Aubusson carpet, and African mahogany woodwork—his wife was frightened of the general's ostentatious acquisition.

"That car is evil," she opined.

Potiroek was unfazed by such superstition, and, five days later, took his first drive in the vehicle. Cruising at high speed, he plowed into two Croatian peasants, killing them, swerved into a tree, and died.

After the end of the war—and the dissolution of the Austro-Hungarian empire—the Graf and Sift was passed on to a governor of the newly created republic of Yugoslavia. Within a four-month period, he'd been in four separate accidents and lost an arm.

The next few owners fared even worse. A doctor was crushed to death when the car flipped over. A jeweler committed suicide. Another doctor lived but lost his clientele, who were too fearful of the curse to continue retaining his services. A Swiss race driver died when he was involved in an accident and hurtled over a stone wall. An affluent farmer was killed when the car overturned a sharp bend in the road.

In 1923, a garage owner named Tiber Hirshfeld came into possession of the historic artifact. Lovingly, he repaired and painted the car. One day, he was proudly piloting the vehicle, taking six friends to a wedding, when it slipped off the road down a mountainside, claiming the lives of every occupant. Some witnesses claimed that Hirshfeld was attempting to pass another auto. Others said that the car suddenly took off by itself.

At this point, it was generally agreed upon that nobody should be driving the Graf and Sift. Eventually, the car was rebuilt at government expense and sent to the Vienna Museum of Industrial Development. During World War II, Allied bombs destroyed the building.

But the story—and the spell—apparently continued.

In 1968, Dr. Karl Unster from the University of Vienna traced the vehicle's remains to a junkyard outside of Stuttgart. When the Porsche company was rejuvenating itself after the end of World War II, Unster contended, Ferdinand Porsche Sr. and his son, Ferry, visited the dump and purchased several consignments of recyclable steel to make their new models. And according to one theory, James Dean's doomed 550 Spyder was molded from the vestiges of the archduke's cursed car.

• • • •

Four weeks after the crash, "King of Kustomizers" George Barris paid $2,500 for what was left James Dean's Porsche, salvaging the tires, transmission, and most of the engine. The first sign of trouble occurred while the vehicle was being delivered to its new owner. The remnant of the 550 Spyder slipped off its trailer, breaking a mechanic's leg.

A few days later, Barris sold the engine parts and transmission to Burbank doctor William F. Eschrich, who'd raced against Dean at several events. Reportedly, Eschrich installed the engine parts in his own Lotus XI race car chassis and would race at least a half dozen times in the refurbished vehicle without incident. He lent the transmission to his friend and fellow racer Dr. Carl McHenry. McHenry was looking forward to the advantage that the addition would give him. With Eschrich, he enthusiastically drove to his next competition, October 24, 1956, at the Pamona Fairgrounds.

"Aren't you superstitious about using parts from a car that somebody was killed in?" a friend asked McHenry.

The question seemed laughable. As a medical professional, McHenry's perspective was modern and logical, not hysterical and folksy.

But midway through the fifth lap, the doctor motioned at his pit crew that something was wrong with the car. A few seconds later, he spun into a tree. At that moment, Eschrich, the leader in the race, came around a turn in his own car—replenished with parts from the Little Bastard. Out of nowhere, he seemed to lose control and flip over. Eschrich was paralyzed. McHenry died.

Those who received other items from the 550 Spyder had their own frightening experiences. On one car, two tires from the Porsche are said to have malfunctioned *simultaneously*. As the car ferociously shook, the motorist gripped the wheel hard and managed to steer the car to the side of the road on its rims.

Even thieves who attempted to tamper with the Porsche's spare parts paid some type of price. A man trying to rob the steering wheel cut himself on a piece of jagged metal, slicing open his arm.

Still, Barris couldn't bring himself to part ways with the car he'd helped prepare for James Dean's final drive. Working out a deal with the California Highway Patrol, he began exhibiting the vehicle at high schools, alongside signs with slogans like "James Dean's Last Sports Car" and "This Accident Could Have Been Prevented."

"I guess you could say that's when the curse started showing itself," he said in *The Robb Report* in 1990. "Ever since I started having anything to do with the car, I had felt bad vibes coming from it. It was bizarre. But I didn't really think too much about it until later when *really* odd stuff started happening."

In between tours, the object was stored in a Fresno garage. But in March 1959, a fire ignited in the building, burning everything except the Porsche.

The road show continued. There was a plan to finally bring the car to Salinas, the place that Jimmy had been trying to reach when he died. But just outside the city, the truck carrying the vehicle crashed, propelling driver George Barhuis from the cab onto the roadway. That's when the Porsche became detached from its trailer, falling on top of the trucker and killing him.

Barris found another driver. In a possible effort to break the curse, a decision was made to display the car outside the Golden State. But bad luck persisted. In Detroit, on the fourth anniversary of Jimmy's death, the bolts holding down the 550 Spyder snapped, sending the car careening from the platform. This time, it hit a fifteen-year-old boy, breaking his hip. The kid had been dressed like James Dean in *Rebel Without a Cause,* in jeans, a white T-shirt, and a red leather jacket.

At each stop, fans picked at the vehicle, taking home shreds of metal, rubber, and glass. As a result, on at least three more occasions, the car broke into pieces while being transported on the highway, causing at least one more traffic fatality.

In 1960, while displaying the car in Florida, Barris decided that it was better to keep the Porsche away from the public. It was loaded into a box-car, sealed, and shipped back to Los Angeles. A team of Pinkerton detectives rode along to prevent the larceny of this slice of Americana. When the train arrived in California five days later, the seal was said to still be intact. But the car had disappeared.

"It's hard to believe in curses," Barris said thirty years later, "but this has always baffled me. Even today, I get letters from people who claim they've seen the Porsche somewhere. Who knows? Maybe I'm lucky the thing disappeared."

• • • •

Just as the Porsche appeared to be blotted by its connection to Dean, so did at least one location that he apparently passed on the last day of his life. On April 6, 1970, four California Highway Patrol officers were fatally shot at the site of Tip's, the restaurant where Jimmy may have ordered apple pie and milk before his northward trek. The incident was dubbed "the Newhall Massacre," and accounted for what at the time was the deadliest day in the history of California law enforcement.

Ironically, Jimmy's affiliation with the Porsche 550 Spyder has added to the model's allure. Authentic 550 Spyders have been sold for more than $1 million. Home-built kits, which include modern flourishes, can cost about $50,000, and are among the most replicated cars among collectors.

Even without James Dean, Ferry Porsche became one of the most

esteemed figures in auto manufacturing, earning the gold cross for distinguished service from the Federal Republic of Germany twice. From
its original car, the Porsche 356, the company would produce thirty current models. In 1983, Porsche drivers claimed the first, second, and third
places at the Daytona 500. The same year, the Porsche 928S became the
fastest car ever sold in North America. At the time of his death, in 1998,
the company was about to celebrate its fiftieth anniversary, a commemoration of its feats on the track and the marketplace, as well as a sense of
style that might not have been possible—at least in certain quarters—
without the association with James Dean.

37

TREE OF HEAVEN

F inding the precise spot where James Dean died is a perilous undertaking. Despite the alterations made to what today is California State Route 46, the highway still rises and dips dramatically, and traffic moves frantically through the desolate region. Signs for landmarks like Antelope Road and Cholame Creek fly by, as if they never existed. When I spot the green marker with white letters reading JAMES DEAN MEMORIAL JUNCTION, I have to pull over to the side of the road to study it. Two big rigs immediately blow by me, rumbling past sagebrush and fencing before vanishing into the hills.

I try to envision Donald Turnupseed making his turn. Everything's moving so fast, I can understand why he didn't touch the brake pedal until it was too late; this isn't a place where people slow down. I also have a sense of why James Dean kept going. Although so different than my native New York, I empathize with the urgent feeling here to get somewhere else.

Besides, another few seconds on the front or back end and Jimmy and Turnupseed could have avoided the crash, moving on without ever remembering the near miss.

But that's not how it turned out. And so here I am, engaging in the morbid pastime known as the "death ride." "It's actually a very soulful thing to do," says EJ Stephens of the Santa Clarita Valley Historical Society. "You're doing the same thing as James Dean on the last day of his life. And you have all these parallel universes that you think about. What if he'd swerved and gotten around Turnupseed? Would he have died in another crash? Was it meant to turn out that way?"

Subscribing to this possibility, I wonder what might have occurred if Dean had died in a wreck a few years later. Perhaps by that point, he might have made a bad film, blurted out an embarrassing remark during a movie junket, or been "outed" by a British tabloid. Would the stain to his reputation stick and prevent him from achieving the immortality that he now enjoys? Would Seita Ohnishi, the Japanese hotel owner who calls himself the world's biggest James Dean fan, have purchased the collection of Sanford Roth's photos of the final ride and erected the monument to the actor that now stands next to the Jack Ranch?

After failing in his initial attempt to build a memorial at the literal intersection of 41 and 46, Ohnishi contacted Cholame's aging postmaster, Lily Grant, in 1975 and asked for her assistance. At first, Grant was unmoved. She liked Errol Flynn, Clark Gable, and Douglas Fairbanks. To her, James Dean represented a generational mentality that she couldn't comprehend. But Ohnishi was sincere, not only in his admiration for Dean but the nation whose spirit the actor embodied on screen.

"He said he's not a movie buff or anything," his San Francisco lawyer, Yuji Mitano, told the San Francisco *Chronicle*. "But he's always loved America and thought highly of Americans."

In particular, Ohnishi was entranced by the way that Jimmy's onscreen characters represented the relationship between fathers and sons. "In Japan, that is traditionally an important relationship," Mitano continued. "[Ohnishi] was very impressed that Americans could express these feelings."

Ultimately, Grant grew to appreciate the hotelier's mission and embrace it herself. "She basically felt kind of an obligation," her grandson, Mathew Grant, told the *Chronicle*. "She knew that a lot of people were James Dean fans, and she figured that the least she could do is provide a place to come for information."

With the postmaster's help, Ohnishi spent $15,000 to install a metallic sculpture around a tree—surrounded by a bed of rocks—alongside the Jack Ranch Café in 1977. In raised lettering, the memorial reads JAMES DEAN, 1931 FEB 8–1955 SEP 30 PM 5:59. Pennies are jammed between the metal characters. The letters are stolen and replaced on a regular basis. But, on a highway with very little else to offer, the site is a tourist destination.

Many of the visitors know little about the circumstances of the accident and ask if Jimmy perished by crashing into the tree. "That's the main misconception," Jack Ranch owner Sandy Warner told Marion *Chronicle-Tribune* reporter Rachel Kipp in 2005.

The monument's inscription helps provide the answer. "Tribute to a Young Man," it begins. "James Byron Dean. He was an actor. He died just before sundown on September 30, 1955, when his Porsche collided with another car at a fork in a road not 900 yards east of this tree, long known as the Tree of Heaven. He was 24 years old."

The shrine then lists some of Jimmy's plays, as well as his movies, before continuing, "Before he was in the grave, James Dean was already a legend. Every day, somewhere in the world, at the cinema or on television, James Dean lives on. Cinema is no longer just celluloid."

What follows is Ohnishi's interpretation of Jimmy's pathology:

He was a youth yearning for one precious touch of warmth between parents and their offspring. He was an individual struggling in this huge land of infinite promise and many races. He was a rebel searching for the cause we must all possess. This young man, seemingly ordinary, yet possessing talent and individuality that were unique in their combination, has come to personify a generation awakened. . . .

James Dean is more to us today because his life was so fleeting. In Japan, we say that his death came as suddenly as it does to cherry blossoms. The petals of early spring always fall at the height of their ephemeral brilliance. Death in youth is life that grows eternal.

The plaque was installed on the twenty-second anniversary of Jimmy's

death. At the ceremony marking the occasion, Ohnishi eloquently articulated his passion in heavily accented English: "This monument is not
intended to be merely a tribute to James Dean. It is also meant to be a
reaffirmation of the value of all life . . . to serve both as a memorial to
this young man I so admired and a reminder to all that life is a precious
gift to be preserved at all costs. . . . Having transported this monument
across the Pacific Ocean from Japan, where it was designed and made, I
have had it erected on this day. For me, there is no greater happiness. . . .
To the people of this area, for their friendship and cooperation, I offer my
deepest gratitude."

After the commemoration, Ohnishi traveled home. But the legacy of
James Dean—and the spot on the side of the highway—remained in his
thoughts. As satisfying as the ceremony had been, there was more that
he wanted to say. So on July 4, 1983, a second tablet was mounted next to
the original:

"This monument stands as a small token of my appreciation to the
people of America, from whom I have learned so much. It celebrates a
people who have over the years courageously followed the path of truth
and justice, while expanding the limits of mankind with their boundless,
pioneering spirit. It also stands for James Dean and other American rebels who taught us the importance of having a cause.

"For those who helped this stranger from Japan realize his dream of
erecting this monument, I express my heartfelt thanks."

A number of those facilitators are then mentioned, along with "the
people of this community who warmly extended their kindness and cooperation. And, naturally, to all the James Dean fans who have carried this
torch throughout the years, thank you."

On the West Coast, the memorial tree instantly took on the same type
of sanctity as Jimmy's grave in Fairmount. Fans came, leaving offerings
of cigarettes, beer, and money. On the night of September 29, 1986, a
stranger placed a license plate at the monument. It read, "To James Dean.
From Elvis."

As the years passed, Ohnishi's dedication to the movie star grew. For the fiftieth anniversary of the accident, the businessman created a now-defunct website, *OscarForJimmy.com*, hoping to start a grassroots movement to sway the Academy of Motion Picture Arts and Sciences to confer the honor that eluded Dean in 1956. It included the Sanford Roth photos, and such copy as, "Young rebel, passionate actor, American icon. These are the images we remember of the rising young star whose life tragically ended in a car accident on September 30, 1955. . . . Despite his 'rebel' image, Jimmy really did want an Oscar. The dream now is to keep the hopes of an Oscar for Jimmy alive in the hearts of all his fans. . . . We hope that you enjoy these images of Jimmy and help keep the hope alive for an Oscar for Jimmy!"

38

T-SHIRTS IN MOSCOW

I t was hard not to look at Donald Turnupseed and think of James Dean. His associates knew better than to bring up the subject. Doing his best to put the incident behind him, Turnupseed—with the help of his parents, Harley and Ruth—built a successful electrical contracting business. In the decades after the collision, Turnupseed Electric, in the city of Tulare, would expand and open branch offices in Bakersfield and Fresno and generate annual assets of $15 million. Specializing in preventative maintenance programs, the firm's clients grew to include Häagen-Dazs, Kraft Foods, US Cold Storage, and California Milk Producers.

As president of the San Joaquin Valley chapter of the National Electric Contractors Association in the nineties, Donald was a well-known figure in his field. Fellow business owners, as well the company's approximately seventy-five employees, described Donald as fair and likeable, but circumspect over what he revealed. He'd been quiet even before the accident. But the crash, and the publicity it generated, "more than likely" drew him further inward, Al Paggi, owner of rival Paggi Electric, told the Tulare *Advance-Register*. "You could never get close to Don."

By contrast, Marcus Sr. had taken it upon himself to speak for the memory of his nephew. At one point, the family concluded that interest in the accident was dwindling. When Marcus died in 1976, his son moved into the farmhouse, expecting to live in relative tranquility. He soon realized that the prospect would be difficult to achieve. An anniversary, a magazine story, or a broadcast of one of Jimmy's movies would often provide just enough of an impetus to send fans into Fairmount, seeking out the family.

"The responsibility began to come my way," Markie explained to the Marion *Chronicle-Tribune*.

The year that Marcus died, the Broadway show *Come Back to the 5 & Dime, Jimmy Dean, Jimmy Dean*—about a James Dean fan club reuniting in the 1970s—premiered. Jimmy's drama teacher, Adeline Nall, attended the opening night festivities, squired into the theater by Dustin Hoffman.

Clearly, Dean's former instructor relished her connection to the screen icon. In 1979, she was given a prominent place on the memorial committee when Martin Sheen organized the first large-scale James Dean Festival in Fairmount.

Jimmy's old friend Sammy Davis Jr. understood why people remained sentimental. "Years have passed. Why should people have kind of a thing about him?" he asked rhetorically in the ABC television special *James Dean Remembered*. "He had something to say to the youth of America. They believed him because he dealt honestly with it . . . and they felt him up there on that screen."

At times, Davis imagined how Jimmy would react to the uproar caused by his untimely death: "I think he would give it that half smile of his . . . because that's the kind of cat he was to me. That's the side I saw of him."

Dennis Hopper thought a lot about James Dean, as well, particularly while traveling through Europe. "James Dean never saw Europe," Hopper said. "And yet, I see his face everywhere. There's James Dean, Humphrey Bogart, and Marilyn Monroe—windows of the Champs-Élysées, discos in the south of Spain, restaurants in Sweden, T-shirts in Moscow. My life was . . . disoriented for years by his passing . . . the great films he would have directed, the great performances he would have given, the great humanitarian he would have become. And yet, he's the greatest actor and star I have ever known."

Late one night in 1988, a luxury tour bus rolled into Fairmount and stopped at the Winslow farm. One by one, a group of cosmopolitans trooped down the stairs. They tried to be quiet and discreet. But when a vehicle that large kicks up the gravel on your property, you hear it. Markie and his wife went outside to inspect.

After a few moments, they realized that they were staring at Bob Dylan. He didn't want to invade their privacy—after all, he knew how that felt—but he couldn't drive through the state without seeing the place where James Dean grew up.

"He'd had a concert in Indianapolis," Markie told the *Chicago Tribune*. "He came out here for a few minutes."

Dylan was respectful, but—like any fan—excited, too. Markie knows that they engaged in a brief, pleasant conversation, but that's where the exchange blends together with every other one he's had with people who felt entitled to drop by the farm in the middle of the night.

"I don't even remember," he said. "My wife recognized one of the ladies with him. The others were just band members, I suppose. They seemed nice enough."

A DOOMED CAST

Near the Capitol Records tower in Los Angeles—built the year of Jimmy's death and designed to look like a stack of discs on a record player—James Dean fans seek out his terrazzo and brass star on the Hollywood Walk of Fame. Nearby are the stars for Jimmy's onscreen fathers, Raymond Massey from *East of Eden* and Jim Backus from *Rebel Without a Cause.*

Dean died before he had the opportunity to make his mark among the approximately two hundred handprints, footprints, and autographs in the concrete nearby, on the grounds of Hollywood's TCL Chinese Theatre—previously Grauman's and Mann's Chinese Theatre. When *Giant* was released, his costars Rock Hudson and Elizabeth Taylor, and director George Stevens, smiled for the paparazzi and sank their hands in the cement. Even at the time, they realized that most visitors who saw their prints would also think about Jimmy.

Despite their complicated lives later on—Taylor was married eight times to seven men, while Hudson, a closeted homosexual, succumbed to the AIDS virus—Dean was the first *Giant* actor to meet a sad, premature end. However, an examination of the way his other costars lived and died suggests that the curse of James Dean may not have been limited to his car.

"Jimmy really believed in this stuff," said Sal Mineo in the magazine *After Dark* in 1966. "'We're all cursed. We are the young ones put on this earth to make the old ones wake up.' He had some sort of odd idea that since Natalie and I were getting close to him, we would be cursed, too . . . all die violent deaths."

In the months after the accident, Nick Adams overdubbed some of Dean's lines in *Giant*—specifically, Jett Rink's rambling speech in the climactic scene in the ballroom of his new hotel—and gave frequent interviews about his departed friend. "He ignored the people he thought were insincere," he told *Movie Life* magazine. "But if you were a friend of his, he was the nicest, kindest, humblest guy you would ever want to meet."

When the topic of the accident arose, Nick would stridently defend Jimmy's decision to drive the 550 Spyder up 466 toward Salinas: "Jimmy always did say what he felt and believed. . . . Whatever he did, he did because he wanted to do it. He died driving the car he wanted to drive. But at least he was honest with himself and did what he felt was right. Fate or whatever you call it just stepped in and Jimmy lost his life. But Jimmy was doing what he enjoyed most, and I'm sure . . . if he knew he had to go, he would have wanted it the same way in the car he loved."

But Adams's critics accused him of capitalizing on Dean's death. With photographers in tow, Adams posed with a tearful group of teenage females, grieving for Jimmy, and at Dean's grave, holding flowers. Hoping to evince the "die young, leave a beautiful corpse" philosophy attributed to Jimmy postmortem, Nick bragged about his own love of reckless driving: "I became a highway delinquent. I was arrested nine times in one year. They put me on probation, but I kept on racing."

He also claimed that one of Dean's most besotted female admirers had now switched her obsession to *him.*

Rock 'n' roll was becoming part of the public consciousness, and Nick was closely watching the trends. Elvis Presley's associates later maintained that Adams used his friendship with Dean to ingratiate himself to The King. Despite the fact that their visages often appear alongside each other on murals, T-shirts, and posters, Elvis and Dean never met each other. This may have been one of the great regrets of Presley's life, according to Frank Mazzola, who appeared in *Rebel Without a Cause* and later met Elvis through a mutual friend.

"All he wanted to know is about Jimmy," Mazzola told CNN. "He was doing Jimmy's dialogue from *Rebel Without a Cause*. . . . It seemed like he knew the whole script. He knew my dialogue. But I got the sense that Elvis wanted to be Jimmy in a strange kind of way."

Adams met Elvis while the singer was in Hollywood making his first movie, *Love Me Tender*. In some ways, their friendship was manipulated by studio executives and Elvis's manager, Col. Tom Parker, who believed that his charge's image would be enhanced if the public believed that he and the now-mythical Dean shared the same associates. Nonetheless, once Adams had his entrée, he worked diligently to ingratiate himself to the rock star.

Elaine Duddy, the author of the 1985 book *Elvis and Gladys*, about The King's relationship with his mother, claimed that the camaraderie Nick enjoyed with Elvis served Col. Parker in a multitude of ways. Allegedly, Parker maintained control of his crown jewel by planting paid informants in Presley's inner circle, who reported back about the singer's movements and moods. By Duddy's estimation, Nick was little more than a "brash, struggling young actor whose main scheme to further his career was to hitch his wagon to a star, the first being James Dean. . . . This made it easy for Parker to suggest that Nick be invited to join Elvis's growing entourage of paid companions."

Both Nick and Presley shared an interest in motorcycles and would ride together—in one well-circulated photograph, Elvis steers while Adams sits behind him—as well as privately agonize over the challenges of celebrity. Reportedly, the two would also consume prescription drugs while socializing backstage at shows or in the private quarters of Graceland.

One of Elvis's early girlfriends, June Juanico, took an instant dislike to Adams, asserting that Presley spoke about Nick incessantly and his affiliation with James Dean. Taking advantage of the gift Jimmy had bestowed on him, Adams would drop in on Elvis uninvited, but was always welcomed into the room. This apparently annoyed June, who was convinced that Nick was competing with her for the singer's attention.

Even Gladys Presley, the woman Elvis idealized above all others, had reservations about Adams's persistent behavior, remarking, "He sure is a pushy little fellow."

Yet, Nick remained a central figure in the Elvis camp for several years; when Adams's daughter, Allyson, was born in 1960, Col. Parker was named the godfather. "I would have preferred Elvis," she later joked.

Unbeknownst to Elvis, Adams was writing a manuscript about their friendship. It was never published but kept in a box along with a typewriter and scrapbook Jimmy had given him, and movie magazines that included his accounts about Dean, Natalie Wood, and other friends in Hollywood.

In 2012, the items were discovered by Allyson—named for her godmother, actress June Allyson—and self-published under the title *The Rebel & The King*. In particular, the book chronicles an eight-day period Presley and Adams spent together in Memphis and a "homecoming concert" in the singer's birthplace, Tupelo, Mississippi, in 1956. According to Allyson, Nick admired Elvis for many of the same traits that Dean possessed.

"My father wanted to be noticed and accepted, and Elvis did that," she told the Elvis Information Network website. "Elvis wasn't jealous about others' success like other people in Hollywood, and that was so refreshing to my father. Also, Elvis had the ability to see a movie once and repeat all the dialogue verbatim, plus act out all the parts, and was that way with music, too. Elvis had uncanny, natural gifts."

In his memoir, Adams paid attention to tiny details about The King, including the food he ordered from room service. "Elvis had four slices of a Crenshaw melon," Nick wrote, "a grilled cheese sandwich with butter, six slices of bacon burned to a crisp, mash [*sic*] potatoes, gravy, and four milks."

Allyson acknowledged that her father was "really young and starstruck." But even Presley "had no idea what was coming down the pike," she told the *Los Angeles Times*. "It's a rags to riches to fame as a bad habit. Elvis had too much fame, and my father didn't have enough."

After *Rebel Without a Cause*, Adams worked steadily—appearing in movies like *Picnic, No Time for Sergeants*, and *Pillow Talk*—but leading roles eluded him until 1959, when he starred in a show he cocreated, *The Rebel*. Although his character—a tough, ex-Confederate soldier who wanders from one adventure to the next—was the apparent inspiration for the title, Adams was likely also playing off of his affiliation with Jimmy's most famous film.

In its promotional material, ABC referred to Nick's Johnny Yuma character as a "Reconstruction beatnik." A *Los Angeles Times* review exploring Adams's character sounds more like an analysis of Dean in *Rebel Without a Cause* than a leading man in a TV western: "He is a symbol of rebellious youth, a loner seeking something to hang his life on."

The Rebel, the newspaper predicted, would "be a show that teenagers will dig."

Hoping to benefit from his relationship with Presley, Nick recommended that Elvis sing *The Rebel*'s theme song. He was overruled, and Johnny Cash was chosen instead. Still, the song became a hit and, even after its two-year run ended, *The Rebel* remained popular in reruns.

Elevated by the exposure, Nick's memorable performance as a murder suspect in the 1963 courtroom drama *Twilight of Honor* garnered him an Academy Award nomination for Best Supporting Actor. But his next film, *Young Dillinger*, was panned by critics, summoning up the feelings of self-doubt that had trailed him since the beginning of his career. By 1965, he was taking work outside the United States, in productions like the Japanese science fiction movie *Frankenstein Conquers the World* and the Godzilla film *Invasion of Astro-Monster*—marketed in the United States as *Monster Zero*. In England, he costarred with Boris Karloff in the science fiction movie *Die, Monster, Die!*

As with Jimmy, there were always rumors about Nick's sexuality. Gossip columnist Rona Barrett asserted that Adams was affiliated with "a group of salacious homosexuals." Gavin Lambert, author of a 2004 book about Natalie Wood, maintained that the studio had arranged for her to be Adams's beard at public appearances, the way Dick Clayton and Warner Brothers apparently orchestrated Dean's relationship with Pier Angeli. In his 1981 biography, *Elvis*, Albert Goldman claimed that Nick "offered himself to the shy, emotionally contorted and rebellious Dean, as a friend, a guide . . . a homosexual lover—whatever role or service Dean required." Goldman wrote that, after Dean's death, Adams replicated the role with Elvis Presley.

Adams also had a wife, former child actress Carol Nugent, whom he met when she appeared on an episode of *The Rebel*. But the marriage was a disorderly one. The first time they separated, he is said to have made the announcement during a television appearance, without informing her beforehand. They briefly reunited, split again, then, in 1966, announced a reconciliation on the local TV show *Bill John's Hollywood Star Network*. In less than a year, though, divorce proceedings continued. Although he won temporary custody of their two children, within a few weeks, he agreed to let Carol raise them. To their son, Jeb, the entire exercise had become a "competition" for his father.

By this stage, Nick was a classic Hollywood has-been. After finishing the Mexican movie *Los asesinos* (*The Assassins*) in 1968, he flew to Rome at his own expense. He believed that he was about to start work on another science fiction project. But when he landed in Italy, he learned that the production had been cancelled.

Disheartened, Adams returned to his house in Beverly Hills. On February 7, 1968, after he failed to show up at a prearranged dinner with a friend, the man drove to the house and noticed that a light was on and the actor's car was still in the garage. After busting through a window, the friend found the thirty-six-year-old Adams slumped against the wall, dead.

Officially, Adams overdosed from a combination of sedatives. Authorities were unable to determine whether he'd intended to take his own life. His best friend at the time, Robert Conrad, insisted that the death was an accident. Allyson Adams also claimed that her father would never commit suicide. "He always bounced back," she said. "I know my dad could go low, and he was having a terrible time in his life, personally and career-wise, but he was a fighter."

A number of acquaintances told reporters that they suspected murder, since one of the drugs mentioned in the coroner's report, paraldehyde, could not be located in the house. Adams's physician brother, however, disputed this argument, telling investigators that he'd been the one who'd prescribed paraldehyde, a medicine used to treat alcoholism as well as various nervous and medical conditions.

On Adams's headstone is a silhouette of a Confederate soldier, a tribute to his one starring role on American television. But the inscription also conjures up memories of James Dean.

"Nick Adams," it begins. "The Rebel. Actor of Hollywood Screens."

• • • •

Of all the male actors in *Rebel Without a Cause*, Sal Mineo seemed most qualified to step into the position that Dean was building for himself in Hollywood. With his dark, exotic features and soulful eyes, Mineo appeared complex and thoughtful, handsome but vulnerable. Regardless of the role that he was playing, viewers tended to feel that his emotionality was authentic, and they were somehow looking at the real person on the screen.

His performance in *Rebel*, climaxing with his heart-wrenching death at the end of the film, had endeared him not only to audiences, but the industry's decision makers. Although edged out by the multifaceted Jack Lemmon—who plays indolent Ensign Frank Thurlowe Pulver in the navy film *Mister Roberts*—for the Best Supporting Actor Oscar in 1955, he'd be nominated again for his part in *Exodus* in 1960.

Both Sal and Jimmy were almost as ardent about their love of music as their acting. In 1957, Sal recorded an album that included a song, "Start Movin' (In My Direction)," that reached number nine on *Billboard*'s pop chart. Two years later, he was chosen for the lead role in *The Gene Krupa*

Story. While the celebrated big band and jazz drummer provided the soundtrack himself, Mineo adeptly played the bass drum and cymbals on camera.

By examining Mineo's career at this stage, one can imagine the impediments that Jimmy might have faced. Because of his nervous energy and youthful features, Mineo tended to be typecast as a troubled teen and had to consistently prove himself to his critics. Hence, the satisfaction when his portrayal of militant Zionist Dov Landau in *Exodus*—a film about the creation of the State of Israel—was hailed by the *New York Times* as "absolutely overwhelming."

The acclamation should have sustained him as he attempted to further his career in the 1960s. Yet, although he was in his early twenties and still looked young, Mineo appeared to be "aging out," like a teen pop star. The problem continued for years—even after his triumphant depiction of Uriah in George Stevens's 1965 Biblical epic, *The Greatest Story Ever Told.* Reportedly, Mineo was so intent on playing Fredo, the weak-willed brother in *The Godfather*, that he waited outside of director Francis Ford Coppola's house, hoping to appeal to his fellow *paisan.* But Coppola chose John Cazale, who put on a memorable performance.

In the book *Conversations with My Elders,* Sal told celebrity journalist Boze Hadleigh, "As I get older, the range of roles for me will hopefully open up. But I'm sick of waiting, and they still think of me like I only did a couple of roles, and the rest of my career was all reruns." Sounding embittered, he added, "No kid star ever becomes an adult star. The ones that do are all girls."

But what Mineo found particularly galling were interviewers who sought him out, only to ask a litany of questions about *Rebel Without a Cause* in general and James Dean in particular.

His efforts were complicated by the fact that, in the late 1960s, Sal came out as a gay man. Despite the freedom of the times, homosexuality still carried a stigma. Police regularly raided gay bars and harassed the patrons. In public, at least, personalities like Rock Hudson, Tab Hunter, and Paul Lynde were still in the closet; television star Raymond Burr had even invented a story about a deceased wife and son. But Mineo appeared proud of his choice, appearing in the play *Fortune and Men's Eyes*, which dealt with the themes of homosexuality and sex slavery in prison, in 1969.

Sal maintained that the gay subtext in *Rebel Without a Cause* was obvious, describing his character, Plato, as "the first gay teenager in films. You watch it now, you *know* he had the hots for James Dean." Because of Dean's bisexuality, "it's like he had the hots for Natalie [Wood] and me."

As a result, he continued, Mineo's character had to be "bumped off," drawing Dean's Jim Stark and Natalie's Judy closer together, as a solution to the lovers' triangle.

After his final film role—as the chimpanzee Dr. Milo in *Escape from the Planet of the Apes* in 1971—Mineo seemed most at home in theater, which had a strong gay culture and audience. In 1976, his performance in the play *P.S. Your Cat Is Dead* generated the type of positive feedback he hadn't received in movies for more than a decade. The show started in San Francisco—where Mineo's portrayal of Vito, a bisexual burglar, set a standard for subsequent actors who played the part—then moved to Los Angeles.

Sal was back in Hollywood, feeling optimistic, as well as nostalgic about the time he spent with Jimmy. Like Dean, Mineo was fascinated by the paranormal and convinced that he'd established contact with his old friend after the deadly car accident. In the *James Dean Remembered* television special, Mineo maintained that he'd felt his old friend's presence and was certain that he and Jimmy communicated in some way.

Despite this, he was given no indication about how soon they'd apparently meet again.

At about ten o'clock at night on February 12, 1976, Sal was attacked in an alley behind his West Hollywood building. As he screamed for help, his assailant thrust a knife into the actor's chest. The blade pierced the heart, causing the internal bleeding that led to Mineo's death.

Immediately, the tabloid press linked Mineo's homosexuality to the murder. Some said he'd been working as a male prostitute and been stabbed by a "trick." Another rumor had Sal being killed by a potential "rough trade" sex partner he'd just met. In other stories, he was knifed repeatedly, as if the killing was a fetishistic act.

The truth was that he was simply returning home from rehearsal.

"The story lines concerning gay characters often end in tragedy, the subconscious message being that if you are gay, you will suffer and be punished for your 'sin,'" wrote Michael Gregg Michaud—who spent ten years researching his book, *Sal Mineo: A Biography*—in *The Advocate*. "Sal Mineo did not die because he was gay, or because he compromised his own safety with a stranger in an alley, or because he picked up a violent gay 'killer.' He was killed in a robbery gone wrong by a young man who didn't even know who he was. Being gay is not punishable by death."

The killer's name was Lionel Ray Williams, a pizza deliveryman responsible for at least ten other robberies in the neighborhood. His identity would remain a mystery until 1979, when he apparently boasted about Sal's killing to some fellow inmates in a Michigan jail. In between, an actress named Christa Helm was also stabbed to death in West Hollywood, under similar circumstances.

Her murder was never solved. Besides the details of the actual crime, authorities know that she was killed one year to the day that Mineo was attacked. Just as Sal's killer was oblivious to his identity, though, this appears to be a coincidence, rather than part of a sinister pattern.

Still, it seems unusual that both Christa Helm and Sal Mineo happened to die on the week of James Dean's birthday.

· · · ·

For the first few years after *Rebel Without a Cause*, Natalie Wood's career was uncertain. Would she age gracefully into adult roles, fall into obscurity, or end up in average films that would do little to develop her acting skills? In 1961—against the advice of associates convinced that Natalie was on the same path as Sal Mineo—*East of Eden* director Elia Kazan cast Wood in *Splendor in the Grass*, as a teenager struggling with the puritan values of her isolated Kansas town. Upon its release, the *New York Times* praised the "poetry in her performance." Onscreen, the review continued, Natalie's eyes "bespeak the moral significance and emotional fulfillment of this film."

For the first time, she received an Academy Award nomination for Best Actress.

But unlike Mineo, whose striking performances in *Exodus* and *The Greatest Story Ever Told* were five years apart, Natalie followed up her triumph with perhaps her most memorable role, Maria, in the New York City gang film *West Side Story.* Although she lip-synched her songs—the actual vocalist was Marni Nixon, who also dubbed the tunes in *The King and I* and *My Fair Lady*—Wood radiated from the screen, helping viewers relate to her inner conflict as she falls in love with the boy who killed her brother.

Invariably, though, parallels were made to *Rebel.* In a racially polarized neighborhood, the Puerto Rican Maria's relationship with Tony (Richard Beymer)—a white gang member yearning to break free from the tribal warfare—is reminiscent of the outcast she becomes in *Rebel* by forming a surrogate family with James Dean and Sal Mineo.

Still, Natalie needed to emancipate herself from teenage roles. She escaped in 1962 by playing the sultry title role in *Gypsy*, a musical about a burlesque dancer who, like Wood, is raised by a stage mother. In *Gypsy*, Natalie seems confident, fully unleashing her sensuality on camera. In the eyes of the viewing public, she'd finally blossomed into an adult.

The next year, in the film *Love with the Proper Stranger*, her portrayal of Angie, a salesclerk who becomes pregnant after a brief affair—leading her to contemplate options like abortion and a marriage of convenience—led to her second Best Actress nomination.

In total, Wood appeared in fifty-six cinematic and television movies. But her choice of roles were uneven. Her 1965 film *Inside Daisy Clover,* for instance, was a critical failure, although it later gained a cult following. In 1966, the *Harvard Lampoon* awarded Natalie the Worst Actress prize "for this year, next year and the following year." Rather than cower with embarrassment, she surprised the editors by accepting the award in person.

Because of this attitude, she always managed to remain vital and was able to maneuver a deal in which she received ten percent of the profits from the 1969 comedy *Bob & Carol & Ted & Alice*, a box office hit in which she portrayed a swinger. And in 1980, she received a Golden Globe award for Best TV Actress for her role in the miniseries *From Here to Eternity*.

Offscreen, her personal life was as turbulent as her career, characterized by stops and starts. She first married actor Robert Wagner in 1957—after going out with him on a studio-arranged date on her eighteenth birthday—but they divorced in 1961. In 1972, they married again.

"We were such a romantic couple, actually," Wagner said after her death. "The highlight of our lives was when we got back together. And then, this horrible tragedy . . . good God."

On November 28, 1981, Wood and Wagner left for Santa Catalina Island, twenty-two miles off the coast of Los Angeles, on the sixty-foot yacht *Splendor*. Natalie had been shooting the science fiction thriller *Brainstorm*, and her costar, Christopher Walken, was the couple's guest. Also on board was the boat's captain, Dennis Davern.

After anchoring the yacht in the water, the three actors took a dinghy the rest of the way to the island, where they had dinner at the Harbor Reef Restaurant, known for its fish caught in local waters. Champagne was ordered, and the waitstaff later reported that the trio became loud and intoxicated.

At about ten-fifteen at night, they returned to the dingy and once again boarded the yacht.

On the boat, Wagner claimed, the group continued drinking, exacerbating existing tensions within the marriage. When he'd visited her on the *Brainstorm* set, he told *The Times* of London in 2008, she was so immersed in her work that she appeared distant. Although he said that he did not believe that she was having an affair, he characterized her attitude as "emotionally unfaithful." As they discussed this on the yacht, Wagner and Walken had a loud argument. According to Wagner, Walken advocated that Natalie devote herself completely to her craft, even if it compromised her relationship with her husband and children.

Eventually, Wood left to return to the bedroom of the master cabin, Wagner said, while the two men lingered together. In his 2008 book, he speculated that she might have been trying to flee the argument. After the departure, Wagner maintained that he and Walken calmed down. According to Wagner, the two men were civil to each other when they said good night, and Walken left for his own cabin. Wagner said that he remained alone for a while, then went to the master cabin himself. When he arrived there, he asserted, Natalie was missing.

The next morning at eight o'clock, Natalie's body—her feet pointing at the bottom of the sea, and her hair and red down coat splayed out in the water above her—was found floating a mile away, a victim of both drowning and hypothermia. Her blood alcohol level was nearly twice the legal limit, 0.14 percent, and the painkillers and motion sickness medication in her system almost certainly added to her intoxication.

After examining the partially digested food in her stomach, authorities determined that she'd died around midnight.

The Los Angeles coroner ruled that the death was accidental. There was no history of suicide attempts or threats, and she hadn't left a note. Wagner told *The Times* that he believed that the dinghy had become loose, knocking against the side of the yacht, and Natalie went up to the deck to secure it. At that point, he theorized, she might have slipped.

Despite her other abilities, she was unable to swim.

"I have gone over it so many millions of times with people," Wagner said. "Nobody heard anything."

As with the Mineo murder, numerous conspiracy theories surround Natalie's death. In a 2013 article, the *National Enquirer* quoted a member of the lifeguard team who searched the waters for Wood. He claimed that one scenario detectives considered was Natalie walking in on the two men engaged in a sexual act, setting off the events that led to her curious demise. Other media have raised the possibility that Wood and Walken were the ones having an affair.

In 2011, the case was reopened after the yacht's captain said that he'd initially lied to authorities about what he'd witnessed on the ship. Dennis Davern now claimed that the couple had been fighting for hours. At one point, he told the television show *Inside Edition*, Wagner smashed a bottle of wine on a coffee table and yelled at Walken, "What are you trying to do, fuck my wife?"

Disputing the statement that Wood had returned to the cabin alone, the captain said that Wagner was with Natalie until the moment that she went overboard. In fact, he'd tell CBS's *48 Hours* and NBC's *Today* show that he heard not only arguing, but a physical struggle after the two returned to the master cabin.

The *48 Hours* report also revealed audiotapes from an interview author Suzanne Finstad had done with the actress's sister, Lana Wood, for the 2001 book *Natasha: The Biography of Natalie Wood*. Lana told the writer that, in a drunken phone call, Davern confessed that Wagner had accidentally pushed Natalie off the yacht, then did little to help her: "He said it appeared to him as though RJ [Wagner] shoved her away and she went overboard. Dennis panicked and RJ said, 'Leave her there. Teach her a lesson.'"

On the *Today* show, Davern expressed remorse about not doing enough to save Natalie's life: "We didn't take any steps to see if we could locate her. I think it was a matter of: 'We're not going to look too hard. We're not going to turn on the searchlight. We're not going to notify anybody right now.'"

According to autopsy report, Wagner placed a radio call to report his wife missing at about one-thirty in the morning, some ninety minutes after she died.

An attorney for Wagner claimed that the neither the actor nor his daughters had anything new to add to the inquiry, and accused Davern and others of sensationalizing an old case. "Mr. Wagner has fully cooperated over the last thirty years in the investigation of the drowning of his wife," said Blair Berk. "Mr. Wagner has been interviewed on multiple occasions by the Los Angeles Sheriff's Department, and answered every single question asked of him by detectives during those interviews."

After considering some of the revised version of events, Los Angeles County Chief Medical Examiner Dr. Lakshmanan Sathyavagsiswaran amended the death certificate from accidental drowning to "drowning and other factors." Apparently, the circumstances that led to Wood falling into the water were "not clearly established."

But the coroner's report did make special mention of the bruises on Natalie's body: "The location of the bruises, the multiplicity of the bruises, lack of head trauma, or facial bruising support bruising having occurred prior to entry in the water."

After Natalie's death, the ending for *Brainstorm* was rewritten, and key scenes had to be reshot, with a stand-in replacing the lead actress. "It actually became the most difficult thing I ever had to do—get that movie finished—and so, it never really was anything it was intended to be," director Douglas Trumbull told the blog Archive Seven in 2009.

When production was completed, he quit the industry. "Getting the movie done was extremely heartbreaking and difficult, and that was when I decided I just have to get out of here," he said. "I have to hang out my shingle doing something else."

The lurid coverage of Wood's death was among the inspirations for Don Henley's song "Dirty Laundry" about the irresponsible nature of the tabloid press.

It was not Henley's first time writing about an unfortunate actor from *Rebel Without a Cause*. In 1974, while he was performing with the Eagles, the song he coauthored about James Dean being "too fast to live, too young to die," reached number seventy-seven on the pop singles chart.

40

"THE DEATH OF AN IDOL BECAME MY CURSE"

n 1956, Pier Angeli played Norma Graziano, wife of boxer Rocky Graziano, in *Somebody Up There Likes Me*. Although her costar, Paul Newman, had put on a performance that solidified his future as a perennial leading man, he'd been the studio's second choice. Were it not for the events of September 30, 1955, Pier would have been playing opposite her old boyfriend, James Dean.

In 1958, she and Vic Damone divorced, engaging in a vicious custody battle for the next several years over their son, Perry—named for his godfather, bandleader and television host Perry Como. At one point, when Damone took Perry back to California from Pier's mother's home in New York, the actress had the singer arrested for kidnapping.

As her film career faltered in the United States, Pier attempted to start fresh in her native Italy, billing herself by her birth name, Anna Maria Pierangeli. She tried finding happiness, marrying film composer Armando Trovajoli and having a second child, but the luster of her early days in Hollywood was gone.

For much of the 1960s, Pier struggled with tax problems, clinical depression, and other personal issues. At one point, a wealthy businessman was accused of holding her hostage for two weeks in Rome. Like Nick Adams, she was relegated to the genre of poorly done monster films. Her last movie, *Octaman*—about a seven-foot, half-human octopus—would eventually become a cult favorite to people amused by the silly story line and cheap production values.

But by then, she was dead.

On September 10, 1971, at age thirty-nine, Pier died of a barbiturate overdose. Although she'd been financially destitute—her body was found by a much older roommate in the apartment they shared in West Los Angeles—her friends and family did not believe that she committed suicide.

Like so many people associated with James Dean, Pier Angeli was a victim of bad luck.

• • • •

Even some of the peripheral characters who'd crossed paths with James Dean were destined for misfortune.

Lance Reventlow, the heir and fellow driver who chatted with Jimmy at Blackwells Corner, appeared fated for great things. A charming lady's man, he'd marry two actresses, Jill St. John and Cheryl Holdridge, a former Mouseketeer on television's *Mickey Mouse Club*. Although he could have lived off his inheritance, he continued to indulge his automotive passions, winning the International Grand Prix and Governor's Cup in Nassau, Bahamas, in 1958, and racing Cooper Formula 2 cars in Europe for a season. In Venice, California, he started a company building open-wheel cars powered by Chevrolet 283 CI V-8 engines. Because of its beetle-like shape, the car was called the Scarab. Competing against Jaguars, Ferraris, and other premium vehicles, the Scarab entered races in the United States, Europe, and Australia, finishing first in several contests.

Reventlow and a group of investors also planned to develop a ski resort near the home he owned in Aspen, Colorado, where he taught skiing each winter. On July 24, 1972, he was aboard a Cessna 206, scouting locations, when the airplane flew into a blind, wooded canyon during a thunderstorm. Despite Reventlow being a commercial pilot who'd spent thousands of hours in the air, an inexperienced student pilot was at the controls. As the Cessna turned around, the engine stalled. Lance, thirty-seven, and the three other people on board were killed when the airplane plunged straight down.

That Reventlow saw Dean on his final day induced the inevitable discussions of the pestilence that even seemed to consume the driver who, moments before the crash, spotted Jimmy going too fast on Route 466.

On March 31, 1991, eighty-five-year-old Cliff Hord was going down Highway 46 after an afternoon of branding cattle. At about eight o'clock in the evening, at the Green Valley grade, his vision was obscured by the fog that shrouded the car. "He couldn't see," his son, Ken—who, at age thirteen, had contemplated James Dean's body trapped in the 550 Spyder—told the San Luis Obispo *Tribune*. "He got in that fog and just run off the road, up the bank, and turned over."

Thirty-six years after the accident that claimed Jimmy's life, the eyewitness perished on the same road.

· · · ·

In 1959, Rolf Wütherich made the decision to move back to Germany. Despite his falling out with Johnny von Neumann at Competition Motors, Porsche offered him a job at its factory in Stuttgart, working in the testing department. Yet, even in his homeland, it was impossible to put the accident behind him. In some ways, the German fans seemed more fanatical about James Dean than the American ones. Rolf received threatening letters in his native language, blaming him for the screen idol's death. When he'd attempt to walk around Stuttgart, teenagers would stake him out, then follow and shout questions at him about both James Dean and the crash that claimed his life.

Reporters found Wütherich, just as they had in America. He accommodated them by telling the story of the tragedy over and over again. Rolf had taken to saying that he didn't even remember the accident. He'd fallen asleep, he claimed, because the ride up 466, past the nut fields and oil derricks, had been so boring.

The job in the testing department didn't last. He was fired—due to his eroding interpersonal skills—pledged to find something different, then rehired by Porsche. All told, Wütherich had ten jobs after the accident. He would also marry a total of four times. Associates worried about him. Was the fabled mechanic going insane?

Yet, whenever it seemed like he was about to implode, Rolf found a way to rebound. In 1963, he was the codriver in Gunther "Bobby" Klass's Porsche 356 when the racer finished ninth in Wiesbaden International Rally. The next year, he was with Klass again when he took fourth in the Tour de France.

Given his technical knowledge and driving skill, auto-racing insiders were frequently able to overlook Wütherich's personality quirks. In 1965 at the Monte Carlo Rally, he was the navigator for driver Eugen Böhringer in the factory-sponsored 904 GTS Porsche. They placed second overall, but first in their class. In 1966, he teamed with Klass again in a Porsche 911 S Coupe, finishing fifth overall and again first in class. But in 1967, Klass left Porsche to compete for Ferrari.

Over the past several years, Wütherich had grown close to the driver, and was disappointed about their separation. But he also understood that circumstances changed quickly in auto racing, and hoped to work with the Stuttgart-bred racer again.

On July 22, 1967, Klass was driving his space-age-looking Ferrari Dino 206 SP, practicing on the sixty-six-kilometer (forty-one mile) Circuito del Mugello course, near Florence. While speeding downhill from Giogo Pass toward Firenzuola, the vehicle smashed into a tree on the driver's side of the road and burst into flames. Caught behind the steering wheel, Klass suffered fatal chest and internal injuries.

More than anybody, Wütherich understood that racing was a dangerous undertaking. But the loss of yet another close associate demoralized him—at a point when his other problems had once again risen to the surface.

Nearly three months earlier, on May 1, 1967, Rolf had stabbed his wife, Doris, fourteen times. He'd tried killing himself in the past, he explained, and was feeling suicidal again. This time, he hoped to go in the company of his spouse. "I wanted to end it all," he'd tell a reporter in German, "and I wanted to take my wife with me."

Believing that Doris agreed to the pact, he prepared a dual suicide note. But at the final moment, he claimed, she changed her mind. Not wanting to die alone, he opted to kill her first. But it wasn't as easy as it had been for Sal Mineo's killer, who'd been able to slay the actor with one thrust. Doris fought back. Rolf continued stabbing and stabbing until he was apparently too emotionally spent to slash himself.

Fortunately for both parties, Doris survived. The marriage did not.

The German press covered Wütherich's 1968 trial, viewing it not as an isolated occurrence involving a man who may have suffered brain damage in a car wreck but an opportunity to conjure up the specter of James Dean. With little other recourse, the defendant's lawyer mentioned the actor as often as possible. Rolf Wütherich was a complicated and confused man, the attorney claimed, caught up in events far bigger than him. Because of Jimmy's death, the argument went, Wütherich felt not only guilty but persecuted by the fans who continued to hold him responsible for their idol's passing. However—also due to Dean—he'd become something of a celebrity. As a result, he'd cultivated a small band of sycophants who indulged his erratic behavior to the point where Rolf was barely aware of the difference between right and wrong.

In contrast to the United States, the German courts were not obligated to declare a visibly unstable defendant not guilty by reason of insanity. Wütherich was an intelligent, accomplished man, the judge concluded, who bore some accountability for his violent actions. Yet, at the same time, he wasn't really "normal." According to German law, the judge ruled that Rolf was "partially responsible" for the assault and demanded that he be placed in a psychiatric facility in Weissenau.

He remained there until doctors determined that he'd come to terms with his behavior, showed sufficient contrition, and was "healed." But this was not the same Rolf Wütherich who painstakingly reassembled the motor for Jimmy's 550 Spyder. According to the German media, he was a "broken person" dependent on antidepressants. As soon as he was re-leased from the hospital, he began drinking heavily, mixing alcohol with the prescribed sedatives.

Even though his affiliation with the company stretched back eighteen years, Porsche no longer wanted Wütherich anywhere near its factories. In 1969, he received a termination letter directly from Ferry Porsche. The automotive titan had known Rolf personally from the days after the war when Porsche was preparing itself to eclipse the giants of the racing scene, and the letter reads more like a message to a friend than a cold, corporate document. For more than a decade, it suggested, the death of James Dean had haunted the mechanic. Whenever Rolf saw the word *Porsche*, it served as a reminder of the traumatic event. Perhaps, Ferry Porsche advised, Wütherich would feel better if he were working for an-other company, where his memory wasn't constantly jogged about the crash that had become the source of his psychological problems.

For most of his life, Rolf had considered himself a city person, enjoying the large crowds at the racetrack as much as the excitement of the contests, and appreciating the diverse assortment of characters he met while living in Los Angeles. But now, he felt a need to retreat. Holing up in an attic apartment in the small town of Kupferzell—in the state of Baden-Württemberg, about an hour from Stuttgart—Wütherich's primary confidant was a cat he'd named Romeo. The stuttering he'd conquered as a child returned. Severe migraines would force him to dig his head into the pillow. When the pain receded, he'd look up at the arched walls above his bed. He'd decorated the room with photographs of the women he'd loved.

In 1979, he found work at a Honda dealership in Hohenlohe, near his birthplace of Heilbronn. He appeared overjoyed at first, looking forward to his time alone with a complicated engine, and talking to the other employ-ees about innovations in new vehicles. At night, he could appear gleeful, buying drinks at the pub and flirting with women. But, when he returned home, alone, to his apartment, he was bombarded with mail from James

Dean fans—particularly now, with the twenty-fifth anniversary of the actor's death approaching—leading to memories of the accident and the troubles it had caused him.

His efforts to ignore the missives didn't work. Logically, he understood that the writers were frequently too young to remember James Dean, and the only reason that they had chosen to correspond with him was that Jimmy was no longer around to receive their mail. It might have been healthiest for Rolf to discard the letters in the trash. Yet, the sight of his name on the envelope made him curious—and entitled—to read what was inside. In moments of isolation, he even wrote back, establishing friendships with a number of teens.

"I want to say thank you for your friendly phone call," began one letter later found in a leather briefcase in Rolf's apartment. "I don't know what I can believe. The newspapers are saying so many different things. That's why I wrote you in the first place. And that's why I'm writing you now. Because I know you're not going to throw out my letter." The writer then asked about the ring Jimmy had taken off his finger and given to Wütherich at Blackwells Corner. "What did you think when James Dean gave you that ring? What do you think of when you look at it now? Can you send me a photo of you and James Dean? I hope you like your . . . apartment."

Another letter starts with a fourteen-year-old thanking Rolf for a previous letter. "After twenty-four years, you must be sick of all these questions about James Dean," it continues. "But you can rest assured, I'm not one of these people. I'm not going to ask any questions. I think people who say that James Dean is just imitating Marlon Brando are crazy. They just don't want to admit that he was just as good as Marlon Brando. Since I believe in life after death, I am sure that you are going to meet James Dean again when you die."

Despite all attempts to separate himself from the fatal crash, the events of September 30, 1955, had become part of Wütherich's persona. Although he was apparently treated well at Honda, he was a tormented, argumentative presence, the way he had been at Competition Motors. And working on Hondas was too much of a compromise for a person who'd developed some of the most intricate cars in the sport of auto racing. At a certain point, he decided that he needed to be around Porsches again. While maintaining the attic apartment and the personal car he'd acquired while working at Honda, he took a job in Neuenstein, assembling turbo engines for Porsche.

He had also begun talking with a publisher about releasing his memoirs—or, more specifically, his recollection of the accident and its aftermath. On July 15, 1981, Rolf signed a contract for 10,000 deutsch marks—$4,100 in US dollars at the time—to write a book tentatively entitled *The Death of an Idol Became My Curse*. The agreement stipulated that Wütherich participate in a vigorous media campaign to publicize the book. Before that, he was planning to travel back to Los Angeles and other locations associated with James Dean to relive old experiences and add atmosphere to the story.

On Wednesday, July 21, 1981, he was invited for a midweek game of skittles at a bar in the village of Haag, near Kupferzell. As usual, he became drunk very quickly. At the end of the night, he bid good-bye to his friends and stumbled to his red Honda Civic. Without bothering to attach the seat belt, he placed the key in the ignition and contemplated the raindrops hitting the windshield. He turned on the wipers and sped off.

At around ten-fifty that night, Rolf was rounding curves near the town center of Kupferzell at about sixty-five mph, as he'd done on countless occasions. The roadway was wet, but Wütherich had intimately acquainted himself with the treacherous turns at Nürburgring, Rheims, and Monte Carlo. He certainly wasn't concerned now. On Market Street, near People's Bank, he tried taking a long curve. But the alcohol, coupled with the other confusing data in his mind, had dulled his reflexes. The car skidded, cut through a chain-link fence, and smashed into the front of a private home, jolting the residents inside. Items toppled and lights flickered on. But no one in the house was hurt.

Outside, the situation was different. Like James Dean, Rolf was pinned behind the steering wheel. As in Cholame, local rescuers were quickly alerted. When the fire department arrived, the emergency team realized that the situation was grave. At age fifty-three, Rolf Wütherich was dead.

"I heard a terrible boom," a witness told *Bild*. "I couldn't help the driver. He couldn't speak anymore, and I saw blood coming from his ear."

It was one of many stories published in Germany, comparing the deaths of James Dean to that of his passenger. Unlike Dean, though, Rolf Wütherich's small slice of fame largely died with him.

41

NOT FORGOTTEN

Winton Dean passed away in February 1995, just short of the fortieth anniversary of the crash that claimed his only child.

By that point, the James Dean estate had some five hundred authorized licensees. "Worldwide," Mark Roesler, the Indianapolis attorney who traveled the globe in pursuit of trademark violations, told the *Chicago Tribune*, "no one can touch James Dean."

With Winton gone, Markie—the little boy whom the actor wanted to set up in Hollywood one day—became the caretaker of his cousin's legacy. He managed the estate and approved every licensed item from an office behind the garage where he kept his extensive classic car collection. On the wall behind the desk, Jimmy peered across the room in shades, from the driver's seat of a race car.

"A friend of his . . . said, 'Jimmy wasn't a rebel,'" Markie told CNN, a glimmer of boastfulness penetrating his Hoosier facade. "'He was just an outstanding actor that, through his character in *Rebel Without a Cause*, he was able to bring a little bit of the rebel out of all of us.'"

Even when Jimmy's image isn't hovering over his cousin, the other sights on the property are reminders of the years that they spent together. The moment he steps outside the garage, Markie's eyes immediately fix upon the farm where Dean ice-skated, played basketball, and fixed farm machinery while his daydreams were occupied with thoughts of appearing on the movie screen.

During his loneliest periods in New York and Los Angeles, Jimmy missed Markie and his parents the most. Now, in a sense, the cousins are inseparable.

The novelty of spotting Jimmy's face on a film poster or in a magazine wore out the moment that *East of Eden* was released. Not only is Markie accustomed to seeing James Dean memorabilia everywhere, but he also lives in a town that has become an altar to the late actor.

"I've never really thought too much about it," he says. "When I see a piece of merchandise, I guess my first thought is always looking at the quality of it to see if it's a well-made product. And I also check to make sure it depicts him in a positive way."

• • • •

In a Marion nursing home, Adeline Nall spent her final months in a bedroom adorned with plaques, busts, posters, and newspaper clippings of her former student, sitting in her wheelchair and regaling medical staff and visitors with stories about her trip with Jimmy to the National Forensic League championships in Colorado and trivia she'd picked up from Deaners over the years.

"Jimmy, he's my life," the eighty-nine-year-old retired educator boasted in 1995, a year before she was buried at the Estates of Serenity cemetery, in the city where her favorite pupil was born.

Among Dean fans, Adeline would always hold a special place, even after it was revealed that the actor himself once disparaged her as a "frustrated actress" attempting to live through his triumphs. But, during an interview with *Chicago Tribune* reporter Jan Ferris, Nall seemed concerned about the way she'd be remembered. One Dean biographer "doesn't give me very much credit," she griped. Another "takes me up to page thirty-nine, then he leaves me."

While she appreciated the unique type of love James Dean's fans exhibited for him, she fretted about her role in his professional development being overlooked "because the people don't even mention me most of the time."

But the people would mention her—at the James Dean Festival, where attendees would affectionately reminisce two decades later about their encounters with Nall, and in the Fairmount Historical Museum, where her photo would hang among the material devoted to Jimmy.

It was Fairmount, after all, where the past still lived, and the people didn't forget their heroes.

• • • •

Even in death, Donald Turnupseed couldn't escape his connection to James Dean. "I just can't believe they don't let him die," Wally Nelson, the president of Turnupseed Electric in Tulare, complained to the San Luis Obispo *Tribune*. "Don was a very private person, and I just want to keep it that way."

Questions about the accident followed Turnupseed everywhere, right until he succumbed to lung cancer in July 1995. "That's something that bothered him his whole life," Nelson said.

Like the Winslows, Turnupseed had had to grow accustomed to uninvited visitors turning up at his home and place of business. The difference was that the people who descended on Fairmount had love in their hearts, while the strangers who came to see Donald were often suspicious and overly aggressive. "There's always somebody . . . coming to the door," Nelson told the Tulare *Register*. "We had to push them out the door."

Turnupseed was sixty-three at the time of his death. Although he had many good years ahead, he lived far longer than Jimmy, Sal Mineo, Natalie Wood, Pier Angeli, and Nick Adams, and died under less sensational circumstances. With the fortieth anniversary of the accident just months away, he found himself fielding questions about the crash, even as he attempted to fight through his illness. The final interview request was a phone call from a reporter from Germany—who might have included a question or two about Rolf Wütherich, had Turnupseed agreed.

• • • •

With each anniversary, Paso Robles mortician Martin Kuehl also received a regular flow of phone calls—even after he left the business in 1971—not only from reporters, but from fans and buffs who seemed more curious about what he termed the "gory details" of the accident than the actual circumstances of the crash. To every caller, he'd relay the same message: from the moment he learned the trade from his father, Martin made it a point not to remember the cadavers that he examined.

"I guess I should, but I don't," he emphasized. "In this business, you have to be your own psychiatrist. When you see things that are real bad . . . what you do is, within the next fifteen minutes, you make your mind forget it."

• • • •

After his promotion to sergeant several months after the accident, Ernie Tripke continued his ascent through the California Highway Patrol, retiring as a captain in 1976. His partner, Ron Nelson, had flourished as well, retiring as a lieutenant two years earlier. The two had been friends before the accident, and the connection to James Dean drew them even closer. Both settled in the San Luis Obispo area, where they socialized with each other's families. Eventually, the two purchased identical RVs, enabling the Tripkes and the Nelsons to travel around the western states together.

In 1988, Tripke took a part-time position with the California Conservation Corps, a government department training young people to work in land maintenance, fire protection, and environmental conservation, as well as emergency response to natural disasters. On his first day on the job, Ernie noticed that his manager seemed extremely knowledgeable about the retired captain's personal history.

"How do you know so much about me?" Tripke asked. "I just met you."

"I'm president of the local James Dean fan club."

For years, the former officers were assured that the time would come when they could liberate themselves from their tie to the fatal crash. "I was told that I could expect to hear about James Dean until 2005, which was the fiftieth anniversary of his death," Tripke said. It didn't quite work out that way. With each virgin viewing of *East of Eden* or *Rebel Without a Cause*, a new fan was born, projecting his or her hopes, values, and insecurities onto the tormented young man on the screen, and an absorption into the reasons why he left the world so early.

Apparently, the spirit of James Dean didn't have a calendar.

42

WHAT REALLY HAPPENED?

I n April 2005, an English documentary team gathered at the site of James Dean's car accident to reconstruct the incident in real time for the National Geographic Channel. Assisting the effort were Mike Kennedy and Mike Greenfield, the CEO and director of forensic mapping respectively for a Canadian company called Crashteams Global, which uses twenty-first-century software to examine the circumstances of auto, aviation, and railroad accidents.

Among the questions that the group intended to explore:

Did an obstruction or a dip in the road prevent Donald Turnupseed from seeing James Dean just before the two cars collided?

Did Jimmy try to drive around the other car—as has been reported—or was his foot on the brake?

How fast was he going?

Was Jimmy behind the wheel—or was Rolf Wütherich?

To solve the conundrum, the producers inspected the photographs taken at the scene, as well as the police reports and a sketch. The conclusion: although the drawing was well done for its era, it was not to scale and was geometrically inaccurate. Because of the lack of modern measurement protocols, the show asserted, investigators in 1955 were unable to determine the precise speed and the positions of the two cars.

Selecting a photograph displaying the skid marks, the company converted the picture to a "scale down top view of the scene"—or, in more colloquial terms, a bird's-eye perspective. Utilizing the software's FX momentum tool, the experts alleged that—despite his reputation for living dangerously—Jimmy was traveling about seventy miles per hour at the moment of impact, about fifteen miles per hour slower than the coroner estimated. As Turnupseed made his left turn, the team added, he was moving at between fifty-five and sixty miles per hour.

Using those speeds as a barometer, Mike Kennedy made a 3-D animation movie that he claimed was akin to traveling back in time and viewing the crash as it transpired. Watching the movie in slow motion, it appeared that the 550 Spyder was struck directly in the left front corner by the Ford Tudor. The moment that occurred, Rolf was apparently shoved laterally out the side door. The route of the skid marks clarified why Wütherich was eventually found on the ground, on the driver's side of the vehicle, the documentary stated, since—after his ejection—the animation showed the Porsche continuing to rotate in the same pattern until it came to a stop.

Meanwhile, the documentary emphasized, Jimmy's body took the full force of the impact and was pushed over to the passenger seat.

It was a position that Ernie Tripke had been taking since he responded to the crash. In the video he made with EJ Stephens for the Santa Clarita Valley Historical Society, he acknowledged the theory that Rolf had been behind the wheel, but completely dismissed it: "This wasn't the case because Dean's feet were tangled up in the clutch and brake pedals, so I knew he had been driving."

Nonetheless, Dan Dooley, who'd been fifteen years old when he witnessed the accident from the window of a car some fifty yards away, told the producers that he was certain that Wütherich, not Dean, was in the driver's seat. Dooley remembered being on the highway with his brother-in-law, who managed to maneuver his truck away from the entwined Spyder and Ford coupe. Like others who'd seen the accident, they pulled over and attempted to help.

"James Dean was sitting on the left side, facing us, on the passenger side," Dooley said in the documentary. "The man in the plaid shirt, the mechanic, was doing the driving."

Dooley was accustomed to having his position ignored. At the inquest after the accident, the teen's version was disregarded by authorities who'd said he'd been misled by an "untrained eye." Still, Rolf Wütherich had had to bear the burden of fans who were certain that he'd been behind the wheel, and battle this charge until he died in his own car accident.

Yet, even when confronted with Tripke's words and computer technology, Dooley remained emphatic. "That is what I saw," he maintained. "The things I say, I say truthfully, out of memory. I have nothing to gain by lying about it."

But what about Turnupseed? What had he actually seen from behind the wheel of his Ford? For the documentary, Crashteams Global created an animation from Donald's point of view and determined that he hadn't been distracted by a dip in the roadway or another obstruction. As others had argued in the past, the team deduced that the color of the Porsche had been too close to that of the pavement to draw attention. And, while Turnupseed was turning left, the experts said, he ceased looking directly ahead—concentrating on California Highway 41 instead of 466—and didn't notice Dean until they collided.

Although the popular wisdom had always been that Jimmy attempted to avoid the accident by using his throttle to get around the college student with an auto racing move, the team contended that Jimmy had just been trying to apply the brake—albeit, a little too late.

In other words, Jimmy was apparently driving safely and exercised restraint when he thought that he might have an accident. Undoubtedly, as technology continued to evolve, there'd be more explorations into the events of September 30, 1955. But the National Geographic show seemed to put Jimmy's defenders at ease.

If anyone was at fault that day, they were even more resolute that it wasn't James Dean.

43

AS IF THE STARS WERE LAUGHING

n 2008—after traveling to the crash site in Cholame and compiling a dossier on whether Jimmy stopped in Tip's—EJ Stephens from the Santa Clarita Valley Historical Society tracked down Ron Nelson and Ernie Tripke to gauge what they might be able to add to the narrative. For years, the former officers had been barraged with interview requests. But, as predicted, the inquiries largely stopped—albeit, temporarily—when the fiftieth anniversary passed in 2005, enabling the pair to step away from the spotlight for a few years.

Stephens encountered a receptive audience.

"I think they found it refreshing again to talk about their experience," Stephens says. "If I had called them ten years earlier, they probably would have said, 'Oh no. Not another one.' But it just so happened that, when I did call, they were thrilled to talk. These guys had amazing careers with the highway patrol for decades. They'd seen so much. But this was, by far, the biggest moment of their careers because it was something that kept them in the public memory. So as bad as they felt about being associated with a negative event, I think they liked that they both shared this story, and it gave them a certain degree of fame."

Tripke's daughter, Julie, remembered the way her father would receive letters from all over the world. "It became a little bit obnoxious for him," she told the *Los Angeles Times*. "However, in the long run, I think . . . it was fine with him. I think he was tickled."

In his previous research, EJ had met other figures like Tripke and Nelson, and even had a name for them: "'History bumpers.' They're people who just bump into history. They're going about their lives when, all of a sudden, they're in a hailstorm of events that they never foresaw when they left for work that day."

The next year, when the two participated in a panel discussion sponsored by the Santa Clarita Valley Historical Society, fans surrounded the pair. Among the sights Julie Tripke recalled was her eighty-seven-year-old father smiling as he signed a James Dean commemorative license plate.

By then, his health was declining and, in 2010, he was placed in a San Luis Obispo skilled nursing facility to address his heart and lung ailments. But even there, Julie said, "the nurses and physical therapists all wanted to know about James Dean."

He died later that year. In 2012, Nelson passed away at age ninety-four, a week after suffering a stroke. Both incidents received national coverage.

• • • •

Marion, Indiana, is known for many things—both positive and negative. Every October, reenactors dress as US Cavalrymen and Native Americans, as they reconstruct the Battle of Mississinewa, a military expedition ordered by Governor—and future president—William Henry Harrison in 1812 against Miami Indian villages, following raids on Fort Wayne and Fort Harrison. Although the Grant County Courthouse was the site of the last confirmed lynching of blacks in the northern United States in 1930, efforts to place a memorial plaque there have been unsuccessful. But if you look hard enough, you can find another dedicatory object: a ceramic miniature of the Seven Gables apartments, where James Dean was born a year after the hangings. It was commissioned by a community organization in 2001, when Jimmy would have turned seventy, and copies can still be obtained at stores around town.

The real building was torn down long ago. "Marion has just kicked theirself for the last twenty years," Markie told the *Chicago Tribune* in

2005, "because they really don't have anything to show people. No one realized the importance at the time, I guess."

It's different in Fairmount, where Dean's aging high school classmates still enjoy a special bond, greeting visitors and socializing with one another. They've even developed a series of jokes about their unique distinction. "What would James Dean look like if he were alive today?" goes one. "He'd look like we do."

The building where Jimmy attended high school closed in 1986 and, in the decades that followed, both alumni and James Dean fans attempted to restore the three-story, brick-and-limestone structure.

"There was a lot of interest," David Loehr of the James Dean Gallery told the *Daily Mail*, "but the money didn't come with it."

At one point, a California developer attempted to raise the funds to fix the 1898 Romanesque revival and neoclassical schoolhouse, but the celebrities approached preferred dedicating their resources to animal cruelty, refugee relief, and global warming. Then, in 2013, a section of the building collapsed, all but obliterating the prospect of salvation.

Fortunately, the stage had been rescued from the auditorium several years earlier. In 2013, the Fairmount Lions Club was keeping it in storage, in the hope that the money would be raised for the platform to be refurbished in another setting—so local kids could continue to perform, quite literally, in the footsteps of James Dean.

Today, the Winslow farm is three hundred acres, far larger than it was in Jimmy's day. Markie is more selective about the livestock than his predecessors, running just a few head of cattle.

"We have some ground here that's not farmable because a creek runs through it—the ground's just too rough to farm," he explains. "So that's where we run the cattle. But it's a real good cattle operation. And, of course, I'll be seventy years old in a couple of months, so I'm not doing it anymore."

His sons have their own lives. When I meet Markie, Charles Winslow is forty-two and his brother, Coy, is forty-eight. But both recognize their history, the principles that farming instilled in the family, and the void created by the unexpected death of the talented cousin who they would have considered an uncle. "From the time they knew anything, they knew about Jimmy," Markie says. "It's just something they've grown up with. It's always been a part of their lives."

But, then, why wouldn't it be? Preserving Jimmy's memory has been Markie's mission for decades. When reporters call, he generally calls back. It's not that he needs to see his name on the printed or digital page another time. But he understands that once he's gone, his words will remain to convey a sense of dignity that he believes many of the news stories lacked. "There's been so many untrue articles written over the years," he says, "that, to be honest with you, I don't trust too many writers."

Because I don't really know Markie, there's no expectation that he'll consider me a different breed than the authors who overemphasized Jimmy's moodiness, bisexuality, fascination with the occult, or misunderstandings on the set, never mind suggestions of a James Dean curse. Yet, Markie continues to give of himself because he loves Jimmy, and relives the ephemeral period that they spent together with each anecdote about Dean's consideration, wit, and family fidelity.

"I sincerely hope that you'll write a good, honest book," he says. "Don't take a bunch of crap out of other books and put it in yours. The fans truly want to hear the truth."

Or maybe the reality is that the fans actually know the truth. Because—regardless of what anybody else says about Jimmy Dean—they appreciate the man whom the Winslows, Lew Bracker, Sammy Davis Jr., Elizabeth Taylor, and so many others loved in a way that was as genuine and timeless as his performance in front of the camera. Despite the lies, the insults, and the fairy tales, James Dean was the dutiful child of Fairmount, the soulful seeker who bore his spirit to the universe, and the beguiling actor whose work has yet to be truly surpassed. Although he really wasn't Cal Trask, Jim Stark, or Jett Rink, he was a combination all of them, a supernova that—in one, epigrammatic moment—outshone the entire galaxy.

Just as the pious look to the Bible to put the world in perspective,

Jimmy's fans can find the message of his life story in his favorite book. "In one of those stars, I shall be living," reads *The Little Prince*. "In one of them, I shall be laughing. And so, it will be, as if the stars were laughing, when you look at the sky at night. And when your sorrow is comforted (time soothes all sorrows), you will be content that you have known me. You will always be my friend. I shall not leave you."

Selected Bibliography

In order to gain a sense of James Dean and his impact on both his fans and Western culture, I culled through hundreds of sources, in addition to conducting firsthand interviews. While not a complete record of the reference material used in this book, the following sources provide a window into the diverse variety of data that add to the legend of James Dean.

BOOKS

Alexander, Paul. *Boulevard of Broken Dreams: The Life, Times and Legend of James Dean*. New York: Plume, 1997.

Bast, William. *Surviving James Dean*. Fort Lee, NJ: Barricade Books, 2006.

Beath, Warren Newton. *The Death of James Dean*. New York: Grove Press, 1986.

Bracker, Lew. *Jimmy & Me*. Fulcorte Press, 2013.

Dalton, David. *James Dean: The Mutant King: A Biography*. Chicago: Chicago Review Press, 2001.

Holley, Val. *James Dean: The Autobiography*. New York: St. Martin's Press, 1995.

Hyams, Joe. *James Dean: Little Boy Lost*. New York: Warner Books (now Grand Central Publishing), 1992.

Spoto, Donald. *Rebel: The Life and Legend of James Dean*. New York: HarperCollins, 1996.

NEWSPAPERS AND MAGAZINES

The Deanzine, published by the James Dean Remembered Fan Club, Volume 13, Issue 43, March, 2013. Driscoll, Sean F. "A Shy, Quiet Dean Made Childhood Friends with Ease." Marion *Chronicle-Tribune*, June 3, 2005.

Hartlaub, Peter. "A Lasting Tribute." *San Francisco Chronicle,* September 30, 2005.

Hutchings, Harold. "The Woman Behind James Dean." *Chicago Tribune,* March 3, 1957.

Hyams, Joe. "James Dean: His Brief Life Reflected the Doubts and Dreams of His Generation." *Redbook,* September 1956.

Kashner, Sam. "Dangerous Talents." *Vanity Fair,* March 2005.

Kinser, Jeremy. "James Dean: A New Film Tells the Sexual Truth." *The Advocate,* July 16, 2012.

Kipp, Rachel. "The Heart of a Racer Found Friends Nearby." Marion *Chronicle-Tribune*, June 3, 2005.

McCartney, Anthony. "Natalie Wood Death Reopened: Robert Wagner Refuses Interview in New Inquiry." Associated Press, January 17, 2013.

Middlecamp, David. "James Dean's Death Casts a Long Shadow." San Luis Obispo *Tribune,* October 2, 2005.

Riccius, Gerd. "Early Death for Injured James Dean Passenger" (translated from German). *Bild,* July 7, 1981.

Smith, Patrick. "James Dean's Legend Lives On—But What About His Films?" *The Telegraph,* October 3, 2014.

Smith, Ron. "The Car, the Star and the Curse that Linked Them." *The Robb Report,* August 1990.

Wiensowski, Ingeborg. "Behind the Mask: The Singular Life of James Dean's Analyst." *Der Spiegel,* October 1, 2013.

WEBSITES

Biography.com

Carscoops.com

CNN.com

Filmsite.org

JamesDeanArtifacts.com

JamesDeanGallery.com

LATimes.com

MailOnline.com

MTV.com

Popeater.com

TIME.com

Index